"Catholic literat a great deal to Mother Mary Loyola. There is a certain wholesomeness, naturalness, geniality about her spirituality that at once wins a place in the Catholic heart for whatever she writes." —The Ecclesiastical Review, volume 58, January 1918

About Mother Mary Loyola:

Most Catholics today who have heard the name Mother Mary Loyola know her as the author of *The King of the Golden City*, which has enjoyed a resurgence in popularity in recent years. But few know that she wrote over two dozen works, and that she was once a household name among Catholics of her era. What made her unique among Catholic authors was her ability to draw in her listeners with story after story—and not just any stories, but ones that incorporated current events and brand new inventions of the time. Despite the fact that those events are no longer current, and those inventions no longer brand new, her books scintillate with the appeal of an active mind that could find a moral in the most unusual places. And while the printed word lacks the animated facial expressions and vocal inflections which reveal a gifted storyteller, hers convey her enthusiasm so capably that the reader can easily imagine sitting at the feet of this wise old nun.

About *With the Church*:

Mother Loyola remained vigorous into her later years, until in 1923, at the age of 78, she suffered a fall that resulted in a serious hip fracture. Without the benefit of hip surgery to relieve the pain, she was confined to her bed for the remaining years of her life. Undaunted, she continued to receive visitors and to write prolifically, penning *With the Church*, a two-volume set of meditations for the liturgical year, as well as numerous pamphlets for the Catholic Truth Society. In these her last works, we are privy to the meditations of one who felt the need to be ready at any moment for the call to eternity. Her urgency reminds us that we too must watch and be ready, for we "know not the day nor the hour." (*Mt. 25:13.*)

To learn more about Mother Mary Loyola, visit our website at
www.staugustineacademypress.com.

ADDITIONAL WORKS BY MOTHER MARY LOYOLA

How to Help the Sick and Dying (1890?)
First Communion (1896)
Questions On First Communion (1896)
Mass For First Communion (1896)
Confession and Communion
for Religious and Those who Communicate Frequently (1898)
The Child of God *or* What Comes of Our Baptism (1899)
The Soldier of Christ: Talks Before Confirmation (1900)
Coram Sanctissimo: Before the Most Holy (1901)
Forgive Us Our Trespasses: Talks Before Confession (1901)
First Confession (1901)
Hail, Full of Grace: Simple Thoughts on the Rosary (1902)
Welcome! Holy Communion: Before and After (1904)
Credo: A Simple Explanation of Catholic Doctrine (1905)
Jesus of Nazareth: The Story of His Life Written for Children (1906)
Home For Good (1907)
Holy Mass (1907)
Heavenwards (1910)
The Children's Charter: Talks with Parents and Teachers
on the Preparation of the Young for Holy Communion (1911)
The Little Children's Prayer Book (1911)
Why Must I Suffer: "A talk with the toilers" (1911)
Abba, Father (1912)
Ita, Pater (1912)
On His Majesty's Service: "A talk with our wounded" (1916)
Blessed Are They That Mourn (1917)
The King of the Golden City: an Allegory for Children (1921)
With the Church, Volume I: Advent to the Ascension (1924)
With the Church, Volume II: The Ascension to Advent (1928)
Trust (1928)

With the Church

Volume I: Advent to the Ascension

by

Mother Mary Loyola

with a Preface by
Rev. Herbert Thurston, S.J.

2015
ST. AUGUSTINE ACADEMY PRESS
HOMER GLEN, ILLINOIS

This book is newly typeset based on the edition published in 1924 by Burns, Oates & Washbourne. All editing strictly limited to the correction of errors in the original text and minor clarifications in punctuation or phrasing. Any remaining oddities of spelling or phrasing are as found in the original.

Nihil Obstat
INNOCENTIUS APAP, O.P.
Censor Deputatus

Imprimatur
EDM. CAN. SURMONT
Vicarius Generalis

Westmonasterii, die 2a Junii 1924.

This book was originally published in 1924
by Burns, Oates & Washbourne.
This edition ©2015 by St. Augustine Academy Press.
All editing by Lisa Bergman.

ISBN: 978-1-936639-76-2
Library of Congress Control Number: 2015958358

Unless otherwise noted, all illustrations in this book are public domain images.
Cover image: Genève, Bibliothèque de Genève, Comites Latentes 54, f. 13r.
(www.e-codices.unifr.ch)

CONTENTS

PREFACE — VII
FOREWORD — IX

THE SACRED INFANCY AND THE HIDDEN LIFE

I. ADVENT 2
II. ADVENT 6
III. ADVENT 10
IV. ADVENT 17
V. THE IMMACULATE CONCEPTION 21
VI. CHRISTMAS EVE 28
VII. BETHLEHEM—I 33
VIII. BETHLEHEM—II 34
IX. BETHLEHEM—III 37
X. SEAT OF WISDOM 43
XI. THE VIRGIN MOTHER 45
XII. FELLOWSHIP 49
XIII. "A CHILD IS BORN TO US" 53
XIV. THE MOUTHS OF BABES 57
XV. "HE LOVED ME" 59
XVI. NEW YEAR'S DAY 62
XVII. THE NEW YEAR 66
XVIII. JESU DULCIS MEMORIA 70
XIX. LOVE 72
XX. THE EPIPHANY—I 74
XXI. THE EPIPHANY—II 79
XXII. THE EPIPHANY—III 82
XXIII. THE EPIPHANY—IV 85
XXIV. HUMILITY 89
XXV. THE PURIFICATION AND THE PRESENTATION 91
XXVI. THE PRESENTATION IN THE TEMPLE 96
XXVII. HOLY ANNA 101
XXVIII. ST. JOSEPH 105
XXIX. THE ANNUNCIATION 110
XXX. THE HIDDEN LIFE—I 114
XXXI. THE HIDDEN LIFE—II 123

THE PUBLIC LIFE

XXXII.	THE PUBLIC LIFE	128
XXXIII.	FELLOWSHIP—I	135
XXXIV.	FELLOWSHIP—II	146
XXXV.	FELLOWSHIP—III	153
XXXVI.	LENT	160
XXXVII.	ASH WEDNESDAY	165
XXXVIII.	THE "VICTORY" WAR LOAN OF 1917	172
XXXIX.	THE CALL TO PENANCE	175
XL.	"ATTENTION!"	178
XLI.	ENCOURAGEMENT	185
XLII.	"NOT BEATING THE AIR"	188
XLIII.	SEEKING	193
XLIV.	"BEHOLD, I STAND AT THE DOOR AND KNOCK!"	197
XLV.	TREASURE	200
XLVI.	"REJOICE!"	203

THE SACRED PASSION

XLVII.	PASSION WEEK	210
XLVIII.	FRIDAY IN PASSION WEEK	215
XLIX.	THE CHURCH'S WAYS	219
L.	HOLY WEEK—I	220
LI.	HOLY WEEK—II	226
LII.	PALM SUNDAY—I	229
LIII.	PALM SUNDAY—II	231
LIV.	"ONE OF THE TWELVE"	235
LV.	THE "UNSPEAKABLE GIFT"	240
LVI.	"A PRIEST FOR EVER"	246
LVII.	"THE FATHER"	251
LVIII.	GETHSEMANI—I	254
LIX.	GETHSEMANI—II	261
LX.	"HESITATED NOT"	266
LXI.	"O CRUX, AVE, SPES UNICA!"	268
LXII.	"OBEDIENT UNTO DEATH"	272
LXIII.	"FATHER, FORGIVE THEM, FOR THEY KNOW NOT WHAT THEY DO"	274
LXIV.	"THIS DAY THOU SHALT BE WITH ME IN PARADISE"	277
LXV.	"BEHOLD THY MOTHER!"	281
LXVI.	"MY GOD, MY GOD, WHY HAST THOU FORSAKEN ME?"	286
LXVII.	"I THIRST!"	289

LXVIII. "IT IS FINISHED!" 293
LXIX. "FATHER, INTO THY HANDS I COMMEND
         MY SPIRIT" 295
LXX. "EVEN THE DEATH OF THE CROSS" 298
LXXI. THE NIGHT AFTER THE BATTLE 300
LXXII. "HIS SEPULCHRE SHALL BE GLORIOUS" 302

THE RISEN LIFE

LXXIII. "RESURREXI!"—I 308
LXXIV. "RESURREXI!"—II. 311
LXXV. "HAEC DIES QUAM FECIT DOMINUS!"
         ALLELUIA!. 314
LXXVI. "REGINA COELI, LAETARE!" ALLELUIA! 316
LXXVII. "MARY!" "RABBONI!" 320
LXXVIII. "AND JESUS MET THEM" 322
LXXIX. "AND PETER" 328
LXXX. DISCOURAGEMENT. 332
LXXXI. "PEACE BE TO YOU". 334
LXXXII. "SEE, THAT IT IS I MYSELF!" 339
LXXXIII. THE SECRET OF PEACE 343
LXXXIV. THE ASCENSION—I 346
LXXXV. THE ASCENSION—II 350
LXXXVI. THE ASCENSION—III 354
LXXXVII. "OUR ADVOCATE WITH THE FATHER". 357
LXXXVIII. "POST HOC EXILIUM". 360

PREFACE

THOSE of Mother Mary Loyola's friends who may know something of the conditions of acute physical suffering, or at best of uninterrupted malaise, under which this latest book of hers has been written, will find no difficulty in believing that the many valuable spiritual lessons which its pages convey are likely to carry with them a very special blessing.

As a few moments' examination of the volume will show, it does not pretend to offer a systematic commentary upon the offices, lessons and prayers of the liturgical year. It is a collection of thoughts suggested by the different phases of the Church's mind, as her sacred seasons recur in due order, but the chapters are disconnected and reflect something of the writer's mood, as well as the spirit of the devotional formulas to which she so frequently appeals. It is this, in fact, which constitutes the charm of the book, for we all of us find it both pleasant and helpful to be taken into the confidence of those who think highly of high things. There is also a reality about many of these musings, casual as they may appear, which is often lacking in more formal treatises. The kindly earnest word spoken in private or written in an intimate letter is more likely to effect a permanent change of heart than the eloquent periods of a rhetorical sermon.

Although, as must inevitably be the case in a book of this kind, the chapters do not all reach the same high level of inspiration, there are nevertheless many beautiful thoughts in the pages which follow—notably, for example, in the sections devoted to our Lord's Sacred Passion—while readers who are familiar with the author's earlier works will marvel that her characteristic gift of simple and graceful expression remains with her still in spite of infirmities which would daunt a less courageous spirit.

It is now almost thirty years since it was my privilege to write a few words by way of preface to Mother Loyola's earliest book, that on *First Communion*, which, as it was then published anonymously, she thought would be helped by some sort of ecclesiastical endorsement. If any need of so feeble an advocacy ever existed, it ceased from the moment that that volume came into the hands of the reviewers. I can only express here my deep sense of gratitude for the honour of having been associated, however humbly, with the good which her books have effected among readers of every class and in every part of the world. Lastly, I venture to add the hope that the reception accorded to the present volume will be such that the author may be encouraged to realise that her special apostolate of devotional literature has not even yet reached its final term.

HERBERT THURSTON, S.J.
31 Farm Street
May 10, 1924.

FOREWORD

TWO little children had heard for the first time the history of the Passion and been taken to kiss the Cross on Good Friday. They were talking about it later:

"Well," said one, "it's all over now."

"For a little while," replied the other. "He'll have to have it all over again next year."

They were distressed, when Easter came, at the unbelief of the Apostles in the story told by the holy women:

"Do you think they'll believe it next year?" they asked.

These babes were nearer the truth and more in touch with the Church than some of us. She tries to bring us to the realisation of our privileges by setting before us in her Liturgy, as actually taking place, mysteries of long ago, but meant for all time and for each one of us in particular. Venerable, yet ever young, oblivious of time, eager like the young to anticipate and to prolong seasons of joy, she would have us bring to her festivals this freshness of expectation, this readiness to identify ourselves with her spirit. On Holy Saturday she tells us: "This is the night when our forefathers passed through the Red Sea with dry feet." And all through Easter week she is singing: "*Haec Dies*—this is the Day which the Lord hath made." We have to fall in with her ways and methods. Children can and do. And we are reminded that unless we become as little children we shall not enter into the Kingdom of Heaven.

Few of the Gospel scenes enable us to enter more fully into the feelings of our Lord's disciples than those which set before us the stupendous mysteries of the Resurrection. We see the running to and fro as the various reports of those who had come from the Sepulchre spread, and reach headquarters. We hear the eager questionings and objections. We note the glad acquiescence of the women incessantly besieged for the repetition of their story, the gradual yielding of unbelief to confidence and joy.

The Church seeks to inspire us with the spirit of those who gathered about our Lord in the Supper Room, "wondering for joy." She would have us watch the awestruck faces, hear the whispered words, see the disciples troubled when they think they behold a spirit, and reassured when our Lord says to them: "Peace be to you. It is I, fear not."

The Church was there, receiving the glad tidings from that "glorious Sepulchre" of which Isaias spoke. She was in the Upper Room, and by the Lake, and on the mountain of Galilee whither, by the appointment of the Lord Himself, His followers hastened to see Him. For these were her first disciples, and so much is she at home among them, that her questioning of them in our own day sounds across the centuries like an echo of the words that must have been heard from many lips that Easter morning long ago: "*Dic nobis, Maria, quid vidisti in via?*" "Tell us, O Mary, what you saw by the way."

We complain, perhaps, that her festivals go by year after year, leaving us much as they found us — cold, irresponsive, uninfluenced. Might we not more profitably question ourselves as to the reason of this? What do we do to catch her spirit? Thomas kept aloof from his brethren and was cold and irresponsive. But there was remedy at hand. He remained with them, and when our Lord came again, He came *for him*. Later, when Peter said, "I go a-fishing," and the six who were with him answered loyally, "We also come with thee," Thomas is named first among them. We are never safer, never happier and holier, than when we see and feel *with the Church*.

The aim in these pages is merely to follow with the rest of her children where the Church leads, gleaning here and there in a field open to all.

THE SACRED INFANCY

AND

THE HIDDEN LIFE

I
ADVENT

FIRST SUNDAY

"Be prepared to meet thy God."—Amos 4:12.

ITH the first Sunday of Advent we begin the ecclesiastical year. The Church is our guide throughout its course, and we can do nothing better for the quickening of our faith and hope and charity than enter with her into the spirit of her various seasons and feasts as they come round. They touch life at all points. They have coloured the thoughts, and fed the hopes, and hallowed the lives of men and women for nigh two thousand years. Ever the same, ever changing, as they adapt themselves to the character and needs of each generation, they provide our spiritual life with the variety it requires for its vigour and development.

Our forefathers understood this. They had fewer devotions than we have, but who shall say that the simplicity and heartiness with which they threw themselves into the mysteries, whether of joy or of sorrow, that the Church put before them, did not build up a solid piety which later ages might envy! Were we, like them, to take the Church as our guide and try to steep our thoughts and our religious exercises in the spirit of her seasons and feasts, we might gain much, and find the mysteries of our Faith exercising a new influence on our lives.

For this is what we need: to make our devotion *practical*, to bear in mind that it does not consist in sentiment, in a vague appreciation of what is noble or beautiful. God looks more to what is done than to what is felt. Happy those who begin this year and every year with a fresh start in His service, and set out on their journey like a child holding its mother's hand, going where the Church goes, seeing with her eyes, feeling with her heart; learning the ways of Christ from her lips; and preparing those ways in their own souls by the means she points out—prayer, more frequent and fervent; fasting, or some penitential practice that may satisfy for sin and share in the sufferings of Christ; almsdeeds—*i.e.*, charity to Christ's needy members—by the corporal or spiritual works of mercy done for His sake.

Advent: "The Coming." What a mainstay to the world was this word of hope and joy during the four thousand years of expectation! For it spoke of One who was to put right all that had gone so wrong, reopen for us the long shut gates of Heaven, and lead us back to the innocence, peace, and happiness we had lost.

It was the word ever on the lips of the prophets, ever in the hearts of those who, weary with sin and sorrow, invoked, as the one remedy for the world's misery, the coming of Him who was to be sent. Kings and prophets, our Lord tells us, desired to see the things we see and did not see them. Oh, why do we not make more of our privilege! Why do we not fix our eyes with rapture upon Him as soon as He appears! How is it that, during these weeks of preparation, we do not make our own the ardent aspirations of the Church for the Advent of the Desired of all Nations? "O Emmanuel, our King and Lawgiver, the expectation of the Gentiles and their Saviour, come to save us, O Lord our God!"

The Church would have us consider during Advent three comings of Christ—the first, His visible appearance upon earth in our flesh, to work out our redemption; the second, His invisible coming to us by His grace, and by His real Presence in the Eucharist whereby He brings to our souls the fruits of His Redemption; the third, His Coming at the Last Day to award to each member of the human race reward or punishment according as there has been acceptance or rejection of these fruits. So that the result of the third Coming to each of us individually will depend on the way we have treated our Lord in His dealings with us during life. If we have made Him a welcome Guest, in this His second coming, we need be in no fear for the third. "There are three Comings of the Lord," says Peter of Blois—"the first in the flesh, the second in the soul, the third at the Judgement—in His first, a Lamb; in His last, a Lion; in the one between the two, the tenderest of friends."

When we think of the long ages before Christ came, how grateful we must be that we did not live in those heathen times, when wickedness was so general and so appalling, when the difficulties of salvation were so much greater than now, and the number of those who sought to know and serve God was so few! Would not those few have envied us? Would they not say that the way to Heaven is easy now, that the man who in these happier days fails to save his soul is inexcusable? Yet we need constant reminders and renewals.

Therefore the Church begins her year as she ended it, on the note of that holy fear which is the beginning of wisdom.

Again she sets before us the terrific picture of the Last Judgement: "There shall be signs in the sun and in the moon and in the stars; and upon the earth distress of nations, by reason of the confusion of the roaring of the sea and of the waves, men withering away for fear and expectation of what shall come upon them. For the powers of heaven shall be moved; and then they shall see the Son of Man coming in a cloud with great power and majesty."

All, we are reminded, shall pass away, all we see and hear and lay our hands to—our occupations, pleasures, joys and troubles—everything. All things made for our use will be destroyed, for their work will be done. And we ourselves shall pass. But whither? Into "the house of our eternity," into whatever house we have built here. Our Catholic faith, the Sacraments, our circumstances, our daily duties, and pleasures, and trials, are the materials with which we are to build ourselves a mansion in our Father's House. What would not help but hinder this building, we must keep clear of. What will help if used in moderation, we must use with the prudence that keeps the end steadily in view. These are first lessons that we all know. But how apt we are to forget them in practice! To awaken a salutary fear in the minds of those who may be sleeping; to rouse us all to the alertness our eternal interests demand, is the aim of the Church to-day. Her voice startles like a trumpet call:

"Brethren, it is now the hour for us to rise from sleep... the night is passed, the day is at hand."

"Stir up Thy might, O Lord, and come, that by Thy protection we may deserve to be delivered from the threatening dangers of our sins, and by Thy deliverance be saved." (Collect, First Sunday, Advent,)

II
ADVENT

SECOND SUNDAY

"Show me Thy ways, O Lord, and teach me Thy paths."—Ps. 24.

HOW hampered the saints must be when they come to speak of Divine and heavenly things in speech equal only to the puny needs of earth! We make use of images supplied by our senses, and describe by means of comparisons. But these have no place in the things of eternity. "Eye hath not seen nor ear heard, neither hath it entered into the heart of man to conceive" the realities of the life to come. "For My thoughts are not your thoughts, nor My ways your ways, saith the Lord. For as the heavens are exalted above the earth, so are My ways exalted above your ways, and My thoughts above your thoughts."

God's estimates of good and evil, His dealings with us, His valuation of failure and success, are for ever running counter to our expectation. And because we do not set ourselves in earnest to adjust our standards to His, we are continually thrown out in our calculations and taken aback by surprises when we have no business to be surprised at all.

It is wonderful that He condescends to work with us, that He can leave His eternal designs at the mercy of our narrow views and our blundering co-operation. But He so prizes the glorious service of freewill, that He puts up with our clumsy efforts, rectifies our mistakes, and makes all things work together for the good of those who love Him.

Still, for His glory, and for the furtherance of our own best interests, we must strive to re-form our judgements. We must pray to see things from His standpoint. He has come into the world to introduce new ways, new means of grace, a new and more perfect service of God, a new familiarity with Him, new love of Him, a union with Him even here such as had never entered into the heart of man to conceive. "Behold, I make all things new." What is needed to meet His advances with the concurrence He desires? That we should understand and value them. Therefore we pray: "Show me Thy ways, O Lord, and teach me Thy paths."

Had the world's ancient sages been told that God was coming upon earth to teach a new philosophy leading to eternal happiness, with what eagerness would they have flocked to the school where He was to appear, there to take their place as learners, to study, and to follow in His ways. He is coming to Bethlehem. We must be there, and prepared. God looks for preparation when He is about to work. "Be prepared to meet thy God, O Israel."

And we must be eager. It is the eager only who learn by what they hear and see. "Let us go over to Bethlehem," said the shepherds, "and let us see this word that is come to pass which the Lord hath shown to us. And they came with haste.... And seeing they understood..." We will go also and with the same freshness of expectation, as if we knew nothing of the mystery and were come to watch and see how God would come upon earth. With wonder and admiration we will try to take in the ways of God made man, His first object lessons, welcoming them, perhaps, with the shyness of surprise—all is so unexpected—but trying to fall into line with them, and by patient study and prayer to fit our own ways into the new mould.

To our first parents, had they known more, God's ways would have been more unexpected still. Had it been revealed to Adam after his fall that there had been an earlier and more glorious creation; that a vast number of angelic spirits had fallen likewise, and that it was the intention of God to glorify His Justice in one of these creations and His Mercy in the other, with what trembling would he have waited to learn the fate of each! So much would incline him to suppose the angels would be preferred to man. Countless in number, more magnificently dowered, more like to God, they had sinned in thought only. But God spared not His angels. For that one sin of rebellion in thought, "they were delivered...to the lower hell unto torments"; while for us, who would prove sinners so often, "He spared not His own Son, but delivered Him up for us all." "God so loved the world as to give His only-begotten Son, that whosoever believeth in Him may not perish, but may have life everlasting." What undreamt-of mercy! What "plentiful redemption"! For pardon was not to be gratuitous. If Mercy claimed us, Divine Justice was not to be defrauded of its rights. There was to be an adequate satisfaction. And because no creature, nor all creation united, could make this, God would Himself provide it. In the human nature which had sinned, a Divine Person would pay the debt it owed: "Who for us men and for our salvation came down from heaven, and was incarnate by the Holy Ghost of the Virgin Mary, and was made Man. Was crucified also for us, suffered under Pontius Pilate, and was buried." Why that long course of three and thirty years when a moment would have sufficed? Why at such cost to Himself when a prayer, a sigh would have been enough? How unaccountable it all is! We can only lift up our hearts to God in humble thankfulness that He is the God He is, and strive as best we may to rise to the surprises and unexpected ways the Incarnation opens out to us.

Humility alone has the key to Divine mysteries. Think what a surprise awaited the Magi at Bethlehem—the star resting *there*, over that poor cottage! The Desired of all nations, the King of kings so housed; an artisan the sole attendant of the Royal Mother and her Child! Yet how quickly they adjusted themselves to it all—"and falling down they adored Him." Only by divesting ourselves of our preconceived notions and creeping up to Christ with the open mind of one who knows nothing of His ways but is prepared to be a docile student, do we come to feel—first wonder, then admiration, love, gratitude, and at last, God helping, *the desire to follow.*

"Stir up our hearts, O Lord, to prepare the ways of Thine only-begotten Son; that through His advent we may be worthy to serve Thee with purified minds. Amen." (Collect, Second Sunday, Advent.)

III
ADVENT

THIRD SUNDAY

"Rejoice in the Lord always, again I say rejoice."—Philip 4:4.

THE first word of the Church to us to-day. Advent is a season of mingled penance and joy—penance for the sin which needed a Redemption so full of pain to the Redeemer, joy for the love which brought Him down to us "rejoicing as a giant to run His way." On the third Sunday of Advent it is this joy that fills the mind of the Church. It breaks forth in bright vestments, and organ, and song—all those skilled ways of hers for helping the spirit by means of sensible things to rise above the things of sense.

She is herself a lovely combination of the natural and the spiritual. Her ordinary garb, like Nature's, is green. Her feasts with varied hues colour the year all the way down, and when she has no feast she robes herself in the brightness of hope, thus linking her festivals together in a circle of perennial gladness. She is so possessed by the Holy Spirit, the Comforter, the Spirit of Joy, that even when she sets herself to mourn and to do penance, we have but to wait awhile to find her breaking forth in words of hope and joyous expectation. The six weeks of Lent might call for a *Laetare* Sunday. But why, after only two of Advent, must she check her sighs to sing "*Gaudete*"? Only because, like her who is the Cause of our joy, she is the "Mother of fair love, and of fear, and of knowledge, and of holy hope."

Third Sunday of Advent

The second Sunday of Advent might be called the Sunday of joyful hope. The Introit strikes a note of joy: "People of Sion, behold the Lord shall come to save the nations, and the Lord shall make the glory of His voice to be heard in the joy of your heart." And the Gradual: "Out of Sion the loveliness of His beauty...Gather ye together His saints to Him. I rejoiced at the things that were said to me, We shall go into the house of the Lord." In the Epistle St. Paul tells us that "what things soever were written, were written for our instruction, that through patience and the comfort of the Scriptures we might have hope. Now the God of patience and of comfort...the God of hope, fill you with all joy and peace in believing that you may abound in hope." And see the Offertory, "O God, Thou wilt turn and bring us life, and Thy people shall rejoice in Thee." The Secret finds a childlike plea for mercy in the acknowledgement that we have done nothing to deserve it: "Be appeased, we beseech Thee, O Lord, by the prayers and sacrifices of our humility, and since we cannot plead any merits of our own, grant us the succour of Thy protection." Lastly, in the Communion we have the triumphant assurance of joy to come: "Arise, O Jerusalem, and stand on high, and behold the joy that cometh to thee from God."

After this preface comes *Gaudete* Sunday, when the Church calls upon us to rejoice like good children as a matter of duty.

There are those who say: "I find it hard to rejoice in the things of faith. I believe them of course. But I cannot rejoice in them as in the possession of such goods as I naturally love and prize. I understand the immense good to the soul of rejoicing in God and in the things that lead to Him and unite us with Him. But it would be foolish to pretend that I feel such joy myself—that I find the practice of my religion a real joy to me."

Granting the gain to the soul of such joy, it is worth our while to see if there is any way of attaining to it. That is a most valuable question and answer in the Catechism which runs: "How may we obtain a hearty sorrow for our sins?" "We may obtain a hearty sorrow for our sins by earnestly praying for it, and by making use of such considerations as may lead us to it." The sure way to obtain whatever we need for our soul's good is here pointed out to us. Our Lord Himself shows us the same road: "Ask," He says, "*and seek.*" Pray to God, and take some trouble yourselves. Everywhere throughout God's dealings with man, we find the working of the same law—salvation and the means to it, to be the joint product of Divine grace and man's concurrence. It is not enough to beg of God to enlighten our intellect and move our will. We must use to this end the powers He has given us: the intellect to examine the matter in question, the will to embrace what the intellect presents to it as true. If we are ruled by our convictions, we must see to it that these are sound and determined by faith. In short, we must take the trouble to think if we want our faith to bear its proper fruits, and among them—joy. "With desolation is all the land made desolate because there is none that considereth in the heart."

We have the most solid grounds for joy. We are the servants of God, and it is due to such a God that He should be served with joy. A joyous service is a glory to Him. It is the service He desires of us. "Serve ye the Lord with gladness." "Let the just rejoice before God and be delighted in gladness." Joy is useful to us, giving courage and strength: "The Lord ruleth me and I shall want nothing." The innumerable proofs of God's goodness to us call for joyful praise: "I will sing to the Lord who giveth me good things," here in this life as an earnest of those He reserves for me in eternity.

Our souls desire nothing so much as joy, obeying thus a law of our being, for we are made to His image and likeness who is absolute Joy. Joy overflows from Him upon all creation. It is laid upon Nature as a command: "Let the heavens rejoice and let the earth be glad, let the sea be moved and the fulness thereof; the fields and all things that are in them shall be joyful. All the trees of the woods shall rejoice." "Sing joyfully to God, all the earth; make melody, rejoice and sing." "The rivers shall clap their hands, the mountains shall rejoice together at the presence of the Lord." "The mountains skipped like rams, and the hills like lambs of the flock." "The stars have given light in their watches and rejoiced; they were called and they said: Here we are; and with cheerfulness they have shined forth to Him that made them."

In the supernatural order it is the same. Christianity overflows with joy. The angels singing over Bethlehem announced joy to the shepherds. The Church on earth perpetuates and sheds abroad that joy. She goes down the centuries singing on her way. Song is an integral part of her worship. Her teaching is full of hopefulness and joy. The graces she dispenses, the rewards she holds out to us, the peace she restores to us, the aspirations she satisfies, all have joy giving as their end. There is exultation in her morning Sacrifice, peace in her evening Benediction, praise, thanksgiving, and trust in her every rite, and blessing, and prayer. Whether she carries the glad tidings of salvation to the heathen, or forgives sin, or releases from punishment; whether she pours the strength and consolation of her sacraments into hearts that sorrow, opens the door of Heaven to us in Baptism, or lifts up her suffrages for us beyond the grave, she is everywhere and always a fount of everlasting gladness whose source is the Holy Spirit of Joy.

Joy, then, like all good things in the supernatural order, has its root in faith, and the stronger the faith the deeper the joy. Where was faith stronger than in those who had learned it from the lips of Christ Himself, who had companied with the Twelve "all the time that the Lord Jesus came in and went out amongst us"? These had the first-fruits of the Spirit, therefore joy pervades all their words. The Acts of the Apostles and their Epistles overflow with joy. It was the spirit of their Master. "These things I have spoken to you," He says, "that My joy may be in you and your joy may be filled." It was not to be found in the possession of any purely natural good. "Rejoice in this," He says, "that your names are written in Heaven." Nor was it to fail them under the severest trials. "Having joy set before Him He endured the cross, despising the shame." And they, following in His steps, "went from the presence of the council rejoicing that they were accounted worthy to suffer reproach for the name of Jesus." One after another they give us the injunction, not only to preserve our joy in the midst of affliction, but to make affliction itself the matter of rejoicing. St. Paul writes: "I am filled with comfort, I exceedingly abound with joy in all our tribulation." "Let us run by patience," he says, "to the fight proposed to us, looking on Jesus, the author and finisher of faith, who having joy set before Him endured the cross, despising the shame, and now sitteth at the right hand of the throne of God." St. Peter says: "If you partake of the suffering of Christ, rejoice that when His glory shall be revealed you may also be glad with exceeding joy." And St. James: "My brethren, count it all joy when you shall fall into divers temptations." The words of St. John are an echo of his Master's: "These things we write to you that you may rejoice and your joy may be full." Our Lord Himself had spoken of the joy in Heaven upon one sinner doing penance. The Beloved Disciple tells of the joy there when the time for penance has passed, when "the Lord God shall wipe away all tears from their eyes...nor mourning, nor crying, nor sorrow shall be any more." "And a voice came out from the throne saying: Give praise to our God all ye His servants and you that fear Him little and great. And I heard as it were the voice of a great multitude and as the voice of many waters and as the voice of great thunders, saying, Alleluia; for the Lord our God the Almighty hath reigned. Let us be glad and rejoice and give glory to Him, for the marriage of the Lamb is come."

Here is the fulfilment of our Lord's promise: "You shall lament and weep, but the world shall rejoice, and you shall be made sorrowful, but your sorrow shall be turned into joy. I will see you again and your heart shall rejoice, and your joy no man shall take from you."

It remains for us to prepare ourselves for this; to rehearse now the Alleluia that is to be our eternal song; to chase from us whatever is a hindrance to this "rejoicing in the Lord." Sin, self-seeking, want of confidence in God and of generosity in trials, a morbid dwelling upon trouble in the past or difficulties in the future—all these are hindrances to the joy which comes of trust in God. "Be nothing solicitous," says St. Paul in to-day's Epistle, "but by prayer and supplication let your petitions be made known to God."

IV

ADVENT

FOURTH SUNDAY

"The Lord is nigh."—Philip 4:5.

HERE are those among our educationists who tell us that in dealing with the child mind we have gone from one extreme to another. From the days when one's father was addressed as "Sir"; when school discipline was stern, and demand upon the feeble brain of the child exacting; when holidays were few and far between; when story-books were ill-disguised homilies, and even prayer was formal and stilted, we have passed to a time when the infant mind is so abundantly catered for as to create a danger in the opposite direction, that of throwing the whole burden of its education upon the teacher.

One is tempted to ask: Is there not some such parallel between the conditions that obtained under the Old Covenant and those that prevail in the New? Are we not now spoilt children? Are we not considered and met at every turn by the sweet provisions of the Gospel and the indulgent, tactful ways of Mother Church? Do we run no risk of forgetting the law that holds good under both dispensations—that our correspondence must meet the advances of grace? Is there no danger of our spiritual faculties becoming atrophied for want of healthy exercise? Look at the Sacraments, on which spiritual life mainly depends. For validity, if not for plentiful fruit, how little is required on our part—a hearty act of sorrow, and our sins are forgiven; the state of grace with a right intention, and we are welcomed to daily Communion, if we will. Every good work we do, grace inspires, accompanies, and crowns with perseverance; in every effort we make, it meets us more than halfway.

The Church knows us and our easy-going propensities. Her canonical penances of the first fervent ages she had to forego when charity grew cold. In their stead she gave us Indulgences, hoping that over and above their own proper effect they might encourage some little effort in the direction of self-denial. Has her desire been justified? What proportion of her children ever give a thought to these treasures? To the greater number, five *Paters* and *Aves* for the Pope's intentions, after Communion, are too heavy a price to pay for the extinguishing of purgatory's fires!

What can the Church do for us, seeing that she cannot dispense us from all effort, that we must lay hold on her means of grace if we are to profit by them? She can only pray that God would Himself move our sluggish wills. Hence those vehement supplications of the Advent Sundays. Not only: "Stir up Thy might, O Lord, and come! ...Stir up Thy might and succour us with great power." But: "Stir up our hearts, O Lord, to prepare the ways of Thy only-begotten Son. Incline Thine ear unto our prayers and enlighten the darkness of our mind by the light of Thy visitation." On the third Sunday of Advent she cries to us: "Strengthen the feeble hands and confirm the weak knees. Prepare ye the way of the Lord, make straight His paths. Every valley shall be filled, and every mountain and hill shall be brought low; the crooked ways shall be made straight and the rough ways plain, and all flesh shall see the salvation of God."

We notice that the first thing required by way of preparation is straightness: "Make straight in the wilderness the paths of our God." Valleys have to be filled, and rough ways made plain. But this is not enough. A second time comes the injunction about the straightening of the ways, as if crookedness were specially repulsive to Him who comes. That it certainly is, we gather from the delight with which our Lord welcomed Nathaniel at the first interview:"Behold an Israelite indeed in whom there is no guile!" We see this repulsion for double-dealing again and again in His attitude towards those who were to show themselves His chief opponents on earth, the main hindrance to His preaching and mission. Our Lord's words of severity as recorded in the Gospel are few and reserved almost exclusively for one form of sin—hypocrisy. "Woe to you, scribes and Pharisees, hypocrites!" His denunciations of these men are terrible; they are "whited sepulchres," "serpents," "a generation of vipers," "blind guides," "children of hell," "full of rapine and uncleanness," "on whom is to come all the just blood that hath been shed upon the earth."

How different this from the tenderness with which His Heart was wont to welcome sinners! "Be of good heart, son, thy sins are forgiven thee." "They that are in health need not the physician, but they that are sick." "I am not come to call the just, but sinners." "The Son of Man is come to seek and to save that which was lost." "There shall be joy before the angels of God upon one sinner doing penance." "Bring forth quickly the first robe and put it on him, and put a ring on his hand and shoes on his feet ...and let us eat and be merry." "This day thou shalt be with Me in Paradise." "Hath no man condemned thee?... Neither will I condemn thee, go now and sin no more."

The hatred our Lord shows of hypocrisy in every form may well lead to some heart-searching, and prompt the question: "Is it I, Lord?" But hypocrisy can hardly exist with goodwill, and this is within the reach of every one of us, however poor our spiritual attainments. Self-deception is common enough, but it is not this precisely that our Lord reprobates. He expects to find shortcomings "in the wilderness," but its crookedness must be set right beforehand. This done, He is ready to deal with the tangle or the desolation on every side, and say like St. Paul: The rest I will set in order when I come."

Still, the more painstaking our efforts to clear the ground, the greater will be our reward. It is the way of a little Child that we are smoothing. It is for the little Feet the valleys should be filled, and the mountains made low, and the rough ways plain. Let us look to our omissions. Are they in our spiritual concerns? Or in our duties to those dependent on us? Do those of our household find us harsh or inconsiderate? Is it the heights of pride that bar the road? Or our rough ways? Our Lord's design of coming to us at Christmas, His desire for a more intimate union with each one of us, dates from eternity and has had a preparation on this earth of four thousand years. Does He ask too much when He bids us remove the stumbling-blocks from His path? Advent is nearly over, let us be sorry for all neglect and strive to make up for lost time.

"Stir up, O Lord, we pray Thee, Thy power, and come, and with great might succour us; that by the help of Thy grace that which our sins impede may be hastened by Thy merciful forgiveness." (Collect, Fourth Sunday.)

V

THE IMMACULATE CONCEPTION

"The Lord possessed me in the beginning of His ways, before He made anything from the beginning."—Prov. 8.

THE Church takes us on a long journey to-day. We have to go back through the ages, as far as thought can travel; to the eternal years "before the mountains with their huge bulk had been established, or the earth, or the rivers, or the poles of the world": back to "the beginning" as Holy Scripture calls it: "In the beginning was the Word."[1]

And because the Word was there, His predestined Mother was there with Him in the designs of God: "I was set up from eternity, and of old, before the earth was made."[2] He might have come to us without her. He might have been created like Adam in the fulness of manhood. But, once it was decreed that the Word Incarnate should have a mother, then the Mother we know, the "full of grace," the "blessed among women," was in the Divine counsels a necessity. For she was called to the most sublime dignity of which a creature is capable, and it is God's way to furnish those whom He chooses for a special work with what is requisite for the honourable discharge of the duties it imposes. Even the material things used in His service must have a certain fitness to qualify them for it. God required this in the Tabernacle of the wilderness and in the Temple of Solomon. The qualities He exacted were chiefly three: purity and richness in the material,

---

1 John 1:1. 2 Prov. 8:23.

and beauty in the construction. "They shall make Me a sanctuary and I will dwell in the midst of them. The house which King Solomon built to the Lord...was covered with roofs of cedar...and within with cedar. And there was nothing in the Temple that was not covered with gold...the altar he covered with gold. And the floor of the house he also overlaid with gold within and without.... And the oracle he overlaid with most pure gold."[1] "And men were filled with the spirit of God, with wisdom and understanding to devise whatever may be made of gold and silver, of marble and of precious stones."[2] A holy vesture, too, was to be made for Aaron, "for glory and for beauty," and there were minute prescriptions, not only as to the purity and richness of the material, but as to the care with which every detail was to be elaborated and adorned.

All this for the sheltering and enshrining—of what? The Ark of the Covenant, a chest containing the tables of the Law. Or was it not, rather, to give us some idea of the care with which God Himself would fashion the House of Gold, the living Ark of the Covenant wherein the Giver of the Law was to dwell! If He gave to men wisdom and understanding for beautifying a mere material temple, what would He not Himself do for her who was to be united to Him in the almost inconceivably close relationship of mother! The works of His Hand in Nature are beautiful, but Grace far surpasses the rough drafts that Nature provides. The Temple was beautiful, but what was it compared with the soul of Mary! Here, as in that House of God, we notice the same Divine predilections—purity and incorruption, richness and beauty, and all on a scale

---

[1] 3 Kings 6.   [2] Exod. 31:3-4.

of magnificence of which we can only say that it was a Divine design carried out in every detail by the Divine Hand Itself.

Of the dazzling purity of our Saviour's vesture on the Mount of Transfiguration, St. Mark says: "His garments became shining and exceeding white as snow, so as no fuller upon earth can make white." To what then shall we liken the spotlessness of His Mother, of that sacred flesh with which He deigned to robe Himself! All created purity is outshone by hers:

> Mother most Pure! The Himalayan snows,
> That since the morning of the world have lain
> White as when God created them, would stain
> Thy whiter feet...[1]

Eve came spotless into the world she was the first to defile by sin. Could the Woman who was to crush the serpent's head be less favoured than the victim he ensnared? A Protestant child hearing that Our Lady never had the least stain of sin upon her soul, said in her quaint Lancashire dialect: "Eh, nay, that would never ha' done." Would Mary have been full of grace if she had ever been infected by his poison? Beyond all conception must have been her innocence who was to be united with God with an intimacy only short of the Hypostatic Union. The lifework of the saints is to undo the work of sin in their souls—to regain, as far as may be, the original justice in which our first parents were created. But it was here that Mary started. She came into the world sinless, one of the redeemed, indeed, but by prevention, not by cure. "Redeemed with such a choice redemption," that the

---

[1] *Mater Purissima*, "Theta."

original stain was never in her. "Who is this?" the angels asked in admiration, as they beheld in this child of earth a purity more dazzling than their own. "Who is this that cometh forth fair as the moon, bright as the sun, as the morning rising?" "Her foundations are upon the holy mountains," which others, after a life of climbing, hardly attain.

Think what it must mean to start from such a height! For Mary's Immaculate Conception was not a solitary grace. It brought all others in its train. Thanks to her freedom from the consequences of original sin, there was no darkness in her intelligence, no weakness in her will. Every power of her soul was open to the influx of grace. Its gaze was ever fixed on God. Her heart was wholly consumed with His love. Her every action was directed to His glory. Body and soul worked together in harmony and peace, the lower faculties in perfect obedience to reason, and reason to God. What must that body have been which was the fitting companion and instrument of so glorious a soul? "Spiritual Vessel, Vessel of Honour, Tower of Ivory, House of Gold," we love to call her. And still how far below the glowing words of Scripture are our poor words of praise. "Clothed with the sun, crowned with stars, the moon beneath her feet"—so St. John saw her. "Full of grace," Gabriel found her as a child.

At the outset of life she was enriched with graces which exceeded, in kind as well as in degree, those given to any of the saints and to all of them together. They were provided as servants for the work entrusted to them. She whose office stands without peer or rival, was dowered as such a dignity demanded.

With the first use of reason this child of benediction began to turn to account the treasure confided to her. She was able then to give to her Creator the most perfect service He had yet received. But it was capable of ever-increasing perfection. Like us, Mary was a wayfarer and a steward, entrusted with talents to be put out to interest, with the obligation of trading with her enormous capital, and of meriting the praise: "Well done!" And grace in Mary was never idle. If her first grace was altogether independent of her, it was not so with every other. Because of her perfect and unswerving fidelity to every grace, it multiplied at a rate of increase that defies all calculation. To what a height of sanctity it must have brought her when she had finished her course! If she was beautiful when she came forth from the hands of her Creator, what must she have been when she returned to Him at her Assumption to be crowned Queen of Angels and Apostles and Martyrs and All Saints—Queen of Heaven!

God alone knows what is due to Himself. Therefore He alone knows what was due to the Mother whom from eternity He had chosen as His own. "To the Lord was His own work known from the beginning,"[1] that work of preparation for the Incarnation of His Son upon which He was to lavish all the treasures of His Wisdom and His Power. It was His own work by excellence, dearer to Him than any other, His own work because wholly His, the only work in which His action was not only unhampered, but was aided in fullest measure from first to last. It is the one work in which His ideal has been realised with

---
1 Acts 15:18.

absolute perfection, the one perfect triumph of His grace: "My perfect one is but one."[1] Let us rejoice with Him in this His perfect one, in the fulness of content He has in Mary. Let us beg that we may share as far as is possible to us His esteem of her, by an intelligent appreciation of her greatness and admiration of her holiness. And let us remind her that, sun-clothed and star-crowned as she is, we sinners may call her Mother.

He that is mighty hath done great things for thee, O Mary Immaculate. So great that all generations shall call thee blessed. But in thy sinlessness, thy happiness and thy glory, remember us, remember thou art one of us. Lift up thy pure hands to God for us. Pray for us sinners. "Remember, O Virgin Mother of God, as thou standest in the presence of God, to speak good things to Him for us and to turn away His anger from us."[2]

> O Earth-born Mother, undefiled by Earth,
> Despise us not who kneel and reach to thee
> Earth-spotted hands...[3]

Because thou art so near to God, thou art like Him in thy tenderness and compassion. Speak for us, plead for us, O clement, O kind, O sweet Virgin Mary.

> He made her fair, she was to be
>   Above all mortal maidens blessed,
> The snowy shrine of purity,
>   And hide all Heaven within her breast
> He made her stainless, to endure
>   The calm eyes of her Baby Son;
> She must be as the lilies pure,
>   Whom His dear vision fed upon.

---

1 Cant. 6:8.   2 Offertory, B.V.M. of Mount Carmel.
3 "Theta."

The Immaculate Conception

> But oh, this Virgin was to be
> Refuge of all humanity!
> All men's true Mother—this in mind
> He made her kind![1]

---

[1] E. Knight.

VI

CHRISTMAS EVE

WHY does not our English name for the Feast of our Lord's Nativity speak to every man, woman, and child of the Midnight Mass which it commemorates?

We welcome to-night the Desired of all nations who comes, not only to redeem us by His Blood, but to serve us by example. He comes amongst us that we may study Him in the various stages of the life that is to be lived for us, and draw into our souls by contemplation and prayer the special virtues characterising each. Whilst waiting for the midnight hour which is to give Him to the world, let us try to share the thoughts and the affections of Mary and Joseph as they awaited His Coming.

Must not all have been summed up in His own words later: "God so loved the world as to give His only begotten Son"? Love alone can be the explanation of this mystery, not any love such as we have seen on earth, or heard or dreamt of, but such as God alone can know and give. "For the love of God is broader than the measure of man's mind." And because He loves He must give. And His Gift is Infinite—is Himself: "God so loved the world as to give His only begotten Son." "And the Word was made flesh and dwelt among us."

Familiar words, thrice a day repeated in the Angelus by many of us, pondered, perhaps, by hardly any! Their very familiarity dulls the awe and gratitude that ought to stir the heart the oftener they are heard. What can we do to present the truth they signify with the freshness of a new revelation?

Let us suppose an impossible case—in some remote island which no ray of revelation has reached—a man enlightened by reason only, giving some such account of himself as this:

"I find myself encompassed by a creation so vast, so complex, so grand, that my intellect bows down in reverence before the power and the wisdom that have devised it. Moreover, the beauty of this wondrous universe, and the beneficence to which it bears witness, call forth my admiration and begin to stir my heart to love. But it is a beginning only. For love, as I understand it, needs a more powerful stimulus, and some proportion between itself and its object. If He who created me and all I see around me demands from me, His intelligent creature, not only the homage of my intellect by adoration, but of my heart by love, there must be something more intimate than this. His Immensity and His Almightiness compel my worship, but are almost a barrier to love. A God without form or feature, who cannot be reached by any of my senses, who transcends all my ideals and knows nothing of my experiences and emotions—how can I love such a One as this?

"My God must come nearer to me if I am to clasp Him in my embrace. He must know my nature, not by His Omniscience only, but by devising some means of entering into the closest personal relations with it. If He would have my love, He must love me first and prove His love, not by benefits alone, but by sympathy and by sacrifice, the test all men accept and exact....I hardly dare to say it—He must prove it by sharing my nature, by leading a human life at my side. Nay more. All that my nature would give Him, He must be ready to sacrifice for me. All that is hardest in human life He must be willing to endure for my sake—toil, and hunger, and cold, pain of body, anguish of mind. There is an almost unthinkable depth to which I can scarcely conceive even infinite love could go. What if my happiness and my life were at stake, and His life were the only price at which these could be secured! What, again, if the insatiable thirst of the soul that no created thing can fill should demand that for the sustaining of its life, the Divine Life should be poured into it!...To such follies as these my mind surrenders itself at times as the conditions which would constrain my love—all my love in return."

Against these extravagances the instincts of those around the speaker would surely rise in rebuke. "Why," they would say, "should the Infinite, the All-sufficing God, buy at such a price a thing so worthless as thy love? Why must He come down from His throne and not only assume thy nature, but all its miseries, death not excepted? And how should He, having given His life for thee, still sustain thy life with His own? Man, in the heroism of self-sacrifice, will offer the stream from his own veins to stay the ebbing tide of another's life, but is this a sacrifice to expect from a God?"

But we have acknowledged the impossibility of such desires. The human mind could never conceive of love gone to such lengths that Scripture can only call it "excess." It hath not entered into the heart of man to conceive what God has prepared to show His love to man—*to me*. He took up and laid down, and assumed again the life by which we set such store. He has carried it into the heavens. He brings it down and distributes it from ten thousand altars. He infuses it daily and hourly into the souls that hunger and thirst for it, that they may live by Him. Beyond the audacity of any mind to imagine, the Divine Goodness has stooped to gain our love. More than we could have believed possible to Omnipotent Love, It has achieved. And with what result?

> As I in hoary winter's night
>   Stood shivering in the snow,
> Surprised I was with sudden heat,
>   Which made my heart to glow;
> And lifting up a fearful eye
>   To view what fire was near,
> A pretty babe, all burning bright,
>   Did in the air appear;
> Who, scorchèd with excessive heat,
>   Such floods of tears did shed,
> As though His floods should quench His flames
>   Which with His tears were bred:
> "Alas!" quoth He, "but newly born,
>   In fiery heats I fry,
> Yet none approach to warm their hearts
>   Or feel My fire, but I!
> My faultless breast the furnace is,
>   The fuel wounding thorns;
> Love is the fire, and sighs the smoke,
>   The ashes shame and scorn;
> The fuel Justice layeth on,
>   And Mercy blows the coals,
> The metal in this furnace wrought
>   Are men's defilèd souls,
> For which, as now on fire I am,
>   To work them to their good,
> So will I melt into a bath
>   To wash them in My blood!"

With this He vanished out of sight,
 And swiftly shrank away;
And straight I callèd unto mind
 That it was Christmas-day.

>R. Southwell, S.J. (1560-1595): *The Burning Babe.*

VII

BETHLEHEM—I

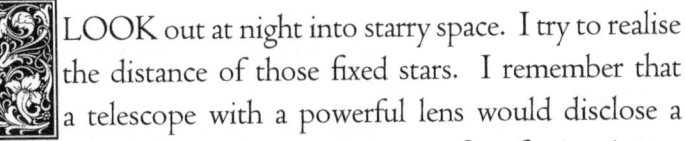

I LOOK out at night into starry space. I try to realise the distance of those fixed stars. I remember that a telescope with a powerful lens would disclose a new universe, and that with every increase of perfection in my instrument fresh fields of illimitable space would open out before me. I transport myself in thought beyond, indefinitely beyond, all that would be thus revealed. I reach the confines of space and look back. Lost to view long ago was my tiny world. Immensity is on every side. God is here, upholding me as when I stood on that speck in creation called earth. But I am lonely, overwhelmed, lost. Oh for some nook wherein to hide, some limit to draw round me and shelter me, some lowliness whereon to rest, some human hand to touch my own!

What relief to speed back to earth, my home, to enter a cave in a hillside; to see the Infinite God circumscribed, trembling, tender, tearful; to lay reverently in my palm that tiny hand, and feel and know that very God as He is, stretching beyond all space, He is my Brother with a human heart like my own!

> Given, not lent,
> And not withdrawn—once sent,
> This Infant of mankind, this One,
> Is still the little welcome Son.
>
> Sudden as sweet
> Come the expected feet.
> All joy is young, and new all art,
> And He, too, whom we have by heart.

ALICE MEYNELL: *Unto us a Son is Given.*

VIII

BETHLEHEM—II

"To the Lord was His own work known from the beginning of the world."—Acts 15.

BETHLEHEM teaches us that God's ways are not our ways, nor His thoughts ours. Once it was decreed that He should be seen on earth and converse with men, we should have said that all the resources of matter and mind, of nature and of art, would be exhausted on the work of preparation. We should have piled up our poor little splendours at His feet, and deemed it essential to safeguard His dignity with all manner of stately formalities and restrictions. We might have figured to ourselves a temple of dazzling beauty coming down from heaven like the new Jerusalem and set in the midst of earth's fairest scene. We might have peopled it with angels, and placed the cherubim with flaming swords beside its gates. Through these gates we should have seen approaching at distant intervals men and women of mature years who after long purification are to be admitted to the one interview with the God-Man that is the event of life for all who believe in Him.

This intercourse with us would have implied a wondrous condescension on the part of the eternal God. It would have been a marvellous evidence of love and means of grace. But where would have been the close application to our need, the brotherliness, the craving for participation in all that enters into our human life, which the Cave of Bethlehem brings home to us?

Truly our thoughts are not His thoughts nor our ways His. He would take our nature and our miseries. What we call our goods were beneath His notice. A little milk, a little straw; just enough of warmth to keep the blood from freezing in His veins; just enough shelter to prevent the frail lamp from being extinguished as soon as it was lit: that was all He would accept, enough, just enough to keep His foothold on the earth. Our wisdom, of the earth earthly, would have been destructive at the outset of the end for which He came. To the Lord was His own work known from the beginning of the world, and the result was the cold and the damp, the darkness, the dreariness, the desertion of the first Christmas night.

What was this end of His? To take from our mistrustful hearts all fear of Him. To force us to own that here is love indeed. That we might be drawn to give Him in return for His divine affection the love of our poor hearts.

A good teacher believes in illustration. He has constant recourse to object lessons. God is a good teacher. Coming into our midst He does not convert us by the persuasion of even Divine words. He does not develop the principles of His Kingdom, nor the lines on which the plan of Redemption is to be worked out. But He finds a deserted stable and holds out His hands to us from the straw.

Unaided by revelation men could never have guessed that scene on Christmas night. As vindictive and cruel, as flinging thunderbolts, as exacting a loathsome worship and horrible sacrifices—thus they could figure to themselves the God who made them. But it never entered into the heart of man to conceive what God had prepared that we might love Him—a little wailing Child, waiting in His crib for our welcome and our pity, for the shelter of our arms, for the kiss of our lips, for the love of hearts human like His own.

CHRISTMAS NIGHT

Ah! Garnish thy house and sweep thy floor,
And build a fire for warmth and light;
And stand thou close to the open door,
And watch till they come in sight:
Watch down the road from Bethlehem,
Watch and wait through the dark for Them—
For Her and for Another,
For the Child with Mary His Mother,
Who are seeking a Home to-night.

Stretch out thine arms to the black and white:
To the snow-bound earth and the gloom above.
For down the Road of the Years to-night,
Far-spent will our Ladye move;
And there seemeth no place for Her and Him.
When the wind blows chill and the day grows dim—
No room for Her and one Other,
Oh! To-night the Child with His Mother
Will be searching the world for Love.

Hold thou the lantern to light their way!
Hang thou the Star in its sable dome!
Spread thou the manger with fragrant hay,
For the little Guest to come!
Offer, thyself, to Him and Her
The gold and the frankincense and myrrh,
For this night, from one to another,
The Child with Mary His Mother,
Will go seeking for Love and Home.

RUTH LINDSAY.

IX
BETHLEHEM—III
LEARNING GOD'S WAYS

AS we look out upon the world that first Christmas night, the world unmindful of God, and the small spiritual world of His faithful expectant ones, we keep saying to ourselves: How different it all is from what we should have looked for, what we should have believed must be, because congruous and befitting the dignity of Him who was to come!

God's preparation for this Coming dates from eternity. There was never a moment, if we can speak of moments in eternity, when it was not going forward. It was magnificent, but in an order that is not of this world. The promise to our first parents in Paradise was that One should be sent to undo what their miserable folly had done. Who He was and when He was to be expected was unfolded gradually by type and by prophecy. The nation, the tribe, the family, the place, the time became known. His character, His office, His sufferings were described that men might not be taken by surprise. The varying fortunes of the chosen race bore Him on their tide to His appointed hour. It was a grand heralding of four thousand years, God moving behind the scenes of the world's history, leading all things by mysterious ways to the furtherance of His designs.

Yet, when Messiah came, how unready, except for its utter misery and need, the world was! Jerusalem, Bethlehem, His own people, His chosen priesthood, how heedless they were one and all! To even the most enlightened under the Old Law, God's ways were inscrutable. The prophets, indeed, had described the Promised One, but their words were impenetrable, and to many must have seemed conflicting. David proclaimed Him "King over Sion," "He shall rule from sea to sea…all kings of the earth shall adore Him, all nations shall serve Him." Yet He was to be "a worm and no man, the reproach of men and the outcast of the people." How could these things be reconciled? What could men do but wonder and wait?

And this was the resource of the two who were to be nearest to Him, who were the only watchers by Him that first Christmas night. The ways of God are so unlike ours, that the Scripture says they are "past finding out." Yet not to faith and love, and study that is humble and persevering, are they wholly impenetrable. The Babe's blessed Mother and His foster-father were the first learners in His school and the models for all who were to follow. Confidants of His secrets as they were, we find them moving always with reverence and circumspection, waiting for Divine plans to disclose themselves. From her earliest years Mary had offered herself to God, to be wholly His by the vow of virginity. Yet when His Providence so ordered it, she accepted Joseph as her spouse. The perplexity into which he was cast before the mystery of the Incarnation was made known to him was keenest agony to her. She knew that a word of hers would change his trouble into joyful thanksgiving. But she was silent, preferring to "wait on God with patience, to join herself to God and endure." And Joseph, accustomed to follow her lead in the things of God, committed to Him in silence what he could not understand, till the season of trial passed, and the angel came with good tidings, saying, "Joseph, son of David, fear not."

Actors in tremendous mysteries, Mary and Joseph were conscious that at every step they were treading holy ground. It was for God to go before them and disclose His designs, when and as He would; their part was to follow humbly where He led. We can see them, when the angel had turned their sorrow into joy, studying the Scripture together, a new light cast now upon type and prophecy by the revelation made to them. Time wore on, and even the dull world was becoming conscious that the Desired of all nations must be at hand. The sceptre had passed from Juda; Daniel's seventy weeks of years had run; the eyes of men were turned to Judea in expectation. Christ was to be born in Bethlehem, as Mary and Joseph knew. Their home was Nazareth and there was nothing to take them south. But they were not solicitous. In tranquillity and in trust they waited for God's Providence to declare His Will and prepare their way. Joseph came home one evening saying that Nazareth was all astir. A decree had gone out from Caesar Augustus that the whole world was to be enrolled, every one in his own city. The enrolment was not to be an altogether Roman, nor a strictly Jewish census, which, making no account of women, would have taken Joseph alone to Bethlehem. It was to be a combination of the two. Mary listened, looked up, and smiled. By the mouth of Caesar God had spoken.

One of their earliest lessons was to see the Will of God thus in all the events of life, the commonplace no less than the marvellous. Angels came to both, with explicit orders from God. And then they were left to themselves to carry out these orders as best they might, through all manner of untoward circumstances and trials. If God had set the whole world in motion to bring them to Bethlehem, might they not suppose He would provide them there with necessaries at least? But no. They set out poorly provided for a journey of nearly a hundred miles. The well-to-do members of their tribe, travelling in comparative comfort, passed them on the road, to secure such accommodation as the caravanserais afforded, while *they* were left to trudge on wearily, and find at the journey's end that "there was no room *for them.*"

They were learning God's ways in all this, learning by experience as we do, but oh, how much faster! They were "learning Christ," as St. Paul says. Here was the solution of those apparently conflicting prophecies. And here were the chosen ones who saw all verified. The angel had said to Mary: "Thou shalt call His name Jesus. He shall be great and shall be called the Son of the Most High, and the Lord God shall give unto Him the throne of David His father, and He shall reign in the house of Jacob for ever, and of His kingdom there shall be no end." To Joseph the angel showed the other side of the Saviour's lot: "Thou shalt call His name Jesus, for He shall save His people from their sins."

We may be sure that Mary and Joseph had this twofold destiny continually before their eyes. The marvellous interventions of Providence on the one hand, and the ordinary troubles of life which brought such a contrast, were no perplexity to them. They were constantly realising what His Name was to cost the Saviour and those whose lives were so closely bound up with His. Consolation and pain were equally the messengers of God. They pondered all. They learned Christ in all. He was to save His people from their sins by taking on Himself the punishment of sin. And He was to begin early, losing no time. Even before His birth He was to be an outcast and a beggar, to ask for a lodging in His own royal city—and to ask in vain. Joseph's quest on the first Christmas Eve was fruitless. No one could take them in. But Mary's peaceful face showed her contentment to share the lot of her Babe from the first. And Joseph bowed his head and followed her as closely as he could in her simple, unfaltering acceptance of the ways of God.

So it was when shepherds came at midnight to the cave and told of the sky filled with angels and heavenly music. When Eastern kings laid costly offerings at the Child's Feet. When the angel brought the order for swift flight from Herod's wrath, and the Three hastened over the desert to seek safety in a foreign and idolatrous land. So it was when at the bidding of the angel they returned to their own country, and Joseph toiled at his carpenter's trade with the Boy-God for his apprentice. So it was when Mary and Joseph saw Him whom they knew to be very God of very God, sweeping and mending, carrying work home on His shoulders and bringing back His modest pay. The Divine and the human were for ever blending, and they saw the action of God equally in both. How readily they learned Christ! How easily they reconciled the various portrayals of Him by the prophets! How quick were they to see the working out of Divine plans in the events and vicissitudes of their lives!

Must we not do the like? "These things," St. Paul tells us, "were written for our instruction." And perhaps there are few things in which we need instruction more than in this—the art and the habit of seeing God moving behind the scenes of everyday life, manifesting Himself, but under veils; working through ordinary channels as well as in the crises that call for all our faith and all our trust. Like John on the Sea of Tiberias, we must be ready to cry out in all that befalls us: "It is the Lord!" Those who have learned this lesson have found rest to their souls, the peace of God which surpasseth all understanding, which the world can neither give nor take away.

X

SEAT OF WISDOM

THE need that oppresses us all as we kneel before the Crib, the Cross, or the Tabernacle, is to *realise* what we believe. I hold with firmest faith that He who lies or hangs there is God—and there my power of penetration stops. The truth does not let me down into its depths. I am willing to learn, but the lesson is too full of mystery for me to fathom. I pray, "Lord, that I may see," but light comes slowly and dimly.

St. Francis of Assisi, to whom we owe the Crib, felt as we do the desire to realise. He has brought the scene at Bethlehem vividly before us—the straw, the swathing bands, the shepherds, that through these externals we may come little by little to discern what lies hid beneath. A dull student can often learn better from a companion than from the master. The lessons of Him who teaches at Bethlehem and on Calvary are so sublime, the depths of His condescension, the secrets of His Wisdom, the devices of His Love, are so astounding, that our minds are bewildered and overwhelmed. We may help ourselves by thinking what these scenes meant to that pupil of His, the most apt Christ ever had—His own most blessed Mother. What must it have been to see and hear and handle the Word of God Incarnate, as was Mary's privilege for thirty years when she had Him all to herself, when her sanctification was the task with which He contented Himself before the work of Redemption came to claim His last three years of life!

He had here a perfectly free hand; there was nothing to check the action of His grace, the Divine influence which flowed out to her from His every look and word and gesture. "Virtue has gone out from Me," He said later when a sufferer was healed by the touch of His garment. What must have been the result of His Divine action on His one perfect one, who needed no healing, but only to be led on by rapid steps to dizzy heights of holiness!

How different in His work upon our souls! How many of His invitations are wasted altogether on us, how meagre is our response to all! Yet at a distance we can follow Mary. She kept all His sayings, pondering them in her heart. Even to her they did not give out their full meaning all at once. "They understood not the word that He spoke unto them," was said of her and of St. Joseph. She was always learning Christ and reproducing Him more and more fully in her life and actions. If we ask her she will teach us how to study Him, how to watch beside the Crib, the Cross, the Tabernacle, in the humble, docile spirit that ponders Divine lessons and brings forth fruit in patience.

XI

THE VIRGIN MOTHER

"Show me Thy Face!"—Cant. 2:14.

WHO shall tell her longing to see that Face! Angels, kings, and prophets desired to look upon it, but not as Mary. And when it looked up to hers from the stable floor, who shall say what it revealed to her! A mother's eyes see deeper and truer than any others. But no mother ever read her babe as Mary hers. For beyond that little Face stretched an eternal history. Deep down, farther than her daring adoration dived, lay the abysses of the Godhead, disclosed to her as to no other by a faith to which all other faith is dim indeed. She is a creature only. She is one of us. Yet when we come to the operations of her soul, we have to cast aside our measurements, and take standards which have no counterpart on earth. Her Immaculate Conception placed her at once on a level apart, at an infinite distance, indeed, from the Creator, yet immeasurably nearer to Him than any other creature.

> Most ancient of all mysteries,
> Most Holy Trinity,
> On Mary's throne we climb to get
> A far-off sight of Thee.[1]

The desire of God to communicate Himself found no obstacle in Mary. We have so little affinity to spiritual things that only very slowly do they penetrate and influence

---

1 Faber.

us. To her they were the breath of her native land. Her soul responded fully to the lightest touch of grace, assimilated all, grew upon all, and at a rate of increase that baffles all calculation. When she looked upon the infant form before her, she saw what the Immaculate alone could see, what it was the Mother's privilege alone to enjoy.

And Mary looked to learn. Where there was no darkness nor dulness to intercept them, how must the rays of the Sun of Justice have streamed into her soul! With what rapidity must she have learned Christ and been always learning! In what new light did she see Humility when God in the likeness of flesh, and of sinful flesh, lay before her on the ground! What treasures did she discover in the Poverty that has made us rich, that has found so many joyful followers and been the strength and consolation of multitudes whose lot in life is hard from the cradle to the grave! And Sacrifice. Could it be carried higher than here, where He who, being in the form of God, thought it no robbery to be equal with God, "empties Himself, taking the form of a servant, being made in the likeness of man, and in habit found as a man"?

Here, at the Crib, all the saints have learnt what they have transferred to their own hearts and shown forth in their lives. Here they have been won by that special excellence which has become their characteristic. But Mary's pondering heart read better than any other the Heart of her Son, and drew its virtue into her own with a plenitude and a splendour that has surpassed and outshone all others.

After telling us that "His parents understood not the words He spoke to them" in the Temple, St. Luke goes on to say: "And His Mother kept all these words in her heart." Even she did not seize all at once their mysterious meaning. But she kept them in her heart, pondering them, using her intelligence and her will to fathom them and to see their bearing on her own life and conduct. She is our model here. If, as the year goes on, and the Church brings before us, one by one, the mysteries of our Lord's life, we try to see them by Mary's side, with Mary's eyes, with Mary's eager heart, we shall profit greatly by the lessons they teach. Let us make a beginning as we kneel beside her here at Bethlehem, and take for our first lesson from the Crib a very cheering one—the fellowship with us which the Babe comes to claim and to establish.

"Grant, O God, that we who joyfully receive Thy only-begotten Son as a Redeemer, may behold without fear the same Lord Jesus Christ coming as Judge."[1] "O God, who hast made this most sacred night to shine forth with the brightness of the true light, grant, we beseech Thee, that we may enjoy His happiness in heaven, the mystery of whose light we have known upon earth."[2] "Grant through this sacred intercourse that we may be found like unto Him in whom is our substance united with Thee."[3] "Grant that by a worthy conduct we may deserve to arrive at a fellowship with Him."[4] "Grant that as the Saviour of the world born this day is the author of divine generation to us, so He may also be Himself the giver of immortality."[5]

---
1 Collect for the Vigil of the Nativity.
2 Collect for Midnight or First Mass of Christmas.
3 Secret for the First Mass of Christmas.
4 Postcommunion prayer, First Mass of Christmas.
5 Postcommunion prayer, Third Mass of Christmas.

Yet if His Majesty, our sovereign Lord,
Should of His own accord
Friendly Himself invite,
And say: "I'll be your Guest to-morrow night,"
How should we stir ourselves, call and command
All hands to work: "Let no man idle stand!
Look to the presence: are the carpets spread,
The dazie o'er the head,
The cushions in the chairs,
And all the candles lighted on the stairs?
Perfume the chamber, and in any case
Let each man give attendance in his place!"

Thus, if a king were coming, would we do;
And 'twere good reason too;
For 'tis a duteous thing
To show all honour to an earthly king,
And after all our travail and our cost,
So he be pleased, to think no labour lost.
But at the coming of the King of Heaven
All's set at six and seven;
We wallow in our sin,
Christ cannot find a chamber in the inn,
We entertain Him always like a stranger,
And, as at first, still lodge Him in a manger.

Preparations (CHRIST CHURCH MS., OXFORD).

XII

FELLOWSHIP

"You are called unto the fellowship of His Son, Jesus Christ."
—1 Cor 1:9.

IF this were not a word of the inspired Word itself, should we have presumed to use it? But with this sanction the Church employs it boldly as soon as Christ appears amongst us. She prays that "we who rejoice in celebrating by these mysteries the Nativity of our Lord Jesus Christ, may deserve by a worthy conduct to arrive at a fellowship with Him."

The word opens out to us a whole world of Divine condescension and incomprehensible love. He has come, the only-begotten Son of God, who has been in the Bosom of the Father from eternity, coequal with Him, self-sufficing like Him, with no need of anything created to satisfy Him or increase His joy. We see Him. We may gather round Him. We may gaze into the little Face as into that of any other babe, and try to read what those infantine features, those smiles and tears conceal and yet reveal.

To whom has He come? To those fallen in Adam, and fallen time after time by their own free act. Fallen from that high estate, only a little lower than the angels, into depths in some respects lower than the very demons who sinned but once. St. Paul reminds us that we, so sinful, so ungrateful, were foreknown by God from eternity. It was for us, known one by one, just as we are, with the return we should make Him for His goodness, that "He spared not even His own Son, but delivered Him up for us all," sending Him down amongst us to live as one of us before dying for us, that with His life and example before our eyes, we might be won to that imitation of Him which all the elect must have. "For whom He foreknew He also predestined to be made conformable to the image of His Son, that He might be the first-born among many brethren....For see your vocation, brethren, you are called unto the fellowship of His Son, Jesus Christ our Lord." It is not to be redemption only, but "plentiful redemption," more, much more than reinstatement—fellowship with the only-begotten Son. All He can share with us, He will share. We are to be by adoption what He is by nature: "You have received the spirit of adoption of sons whereby we cry: Abba, Father...And if sons, heirs also, joint heirs with Christ. Yet so"—mark the condition—"if we suffer with Him, that we may be also glorified with Him."

Does this seem hard, or is it not rather implied in fellowship? What else do we understand by the term? We must suffer with Him now if we are to rejoice for ever with Him by and by. The very effort of the members to conform themselves to their Head means suffering. Therefore He comes amongst us to lighten that effort and to lessen that suffering by His example and by His grace.

"Sons," "joint-heirs," "brethren,"—is not this fellowship indeed! Has not St. Paul a right to ask triumphantly: "He that spared not even His own Son, how hath He not also with Him given us all things?"

This and much more than this the little Face says to me as He looks up to me from the straw. I agree. I come to accept the terms on which we are to live together during this year and throughout my life—fellowship. He has come to be a wayfarer like me. He claims no exemption by reason of the dignity of His Person. He will take as a matter of course the ordinary privations and sufferings of a human lot, whilst reserving to Himself the terrific sufferings decreed for Him alone. "Ought not Christ to have suffered these things?" He will say quite simply when His work is done.

The servant is not greater than his lord. He has done His share. It is now my turn. Ought not I to bear cheerfully the difficulties and troubles of my daily life, as well as the agony of its crucial hours—the losses, the partings, the sacrifices that, sooner or later, life must bring? These things are not only the sad consequences of sin, they are also the conditions and the cost of fellowship with Christ here and hereafter. I must be faithful to my engagements as a child of God and a soldier of Christ if I expect Him to own me as such hereafter. I must take courage, "looking upon Jesus," as St. Paul bids us: "Look diligently on Him that you be not wearied, fainting in your minds."

Let me begin this Christmas to look diligently, coming at the call of the Church to the contemplation of the mysteries of His Sacred Infancy, and Public Life, and Passion; coming with the eagerness of a learner, saying: "What will He teach me here?" coming with the weariness of a traveller for promised refreshment and rest; coming with the trust of a fellow-worker for the counsel my Divine Friend and Ally has to give me, and to find my strength in fellowship with Him.

O why on earth should man be sad,
When Christ is here to make him glad;
From out the darkness came a light
Which makes all angels sing this night:
Glory to God and peace to men;
May it be evermore. Amen.

OLD ENGLISH CAROL.

XIII

"A CHILD IS BORN TO US"

Isa. 9:6.

TO us and for us—to bring joy to us one and all, young and old, rich and poor, simple and learned; to bring us hope, salvation, peace.

And first, hope. To the Innocents who gave their lives for Him, it was more than hope. They were made secure of their eternal happiness without knowing the strife with self, the weariness of exile, the agony of suspense that come with years. Our Lord comes as a child, that He may know by experience the joys and sorrows of child-life; to win the love of children; to learn like them on His Mother's knee; that their earliest recollections may be interwoven with the sweet memories of Bethlehem and Nazareth.

To the aged also, the Babe brought hope as His first gift. With Zachary and Elizabeth, the desire of earlier days had long given place to patient resignation. And Gabriel brought them word, not only that the Promised One was at hand, but that their own child was to be His forerunner, the Prophet of the Highest, to prepare His way.

To the aged of all time Christ brings hope. Long years of barrenness may yet be fruitful, for nothing is impossible to God. It is never too late for a generous service of God. It is not the hours of service but fervent service that He rewards, as we learn from the labourers in the vineyard. At the eleventh hour our labour will be, not accepted only, but requited beyond all expectation or desire. Oh, what a good Master we have to deal with—how is it we mistrust Him as we do!

Simeon and Anna, grown old in service, how richly they were recompensed by the Babe of Bethlehem! Simeon's desires had brought a promise from God; Anna had no promise, but counted on God as if she had; to both He showed Himself, as is His wont, not faithful only, but liberal. Not only did He satisfy their longing, but He made them the first to welcome to His Temple the Lord of the Temple, to present Him to His people and speak of Him to all who looked for the redemption of Israel. This done, they were ready to sing their *Nunc Dimittis* and carry the message of hope beyond the grave. What joy they must have brought to Limbo! If the Innocents were welcomed as heralds of the glad tidings that Messiah had come, still greater would be the rejoicing in the prison-house on the arrival of the two who had held Him in their arms.

To the poor above all the Babe in swaddling bands brought hope. They had waited for it long, four thousand years. What were the poor to the pagan world? But that trembling Infant brought a new force into the world—the power of love, of unselfishness, of disregard of self for the sake of others. That force will be the mightiest this earth has ever known. It will thrill it through from pole to pole and transform it. It goes from Him now as He lies shivering with cold upon the straw. He has come to share the lot of the poor, but at what a cost! To the well-to-do poverty is little more than a name. It needs the change from affluence to real want to realise the suffering the word implies. As a rule, it means exclusion from the privileges, the pleasures, the opportunities of life; from the sphere in which talent or taste may find development and exercise; from independence, influence, honour, advancement, ease and rest. It involves inability to relieve the lot of those more hardly pressed than oneself. It stands for humiliation, discomfort, anxiety, disappointment, the cramping of well-nigh all legitimate aspiration, not for oneself alone, but for those one loves.

Could this ever be the portion of God made Man? His lot in His own world? Yet this was His deliberate choice that He might bring hope to the poor. He would show them how from such materials are fashioned the most glorious crowns of the life to come, the riches, the compensations for soul and body beyond anything the mind can conceive, the joys, the satisfaction containing all the heart can desire, for whatever the patient poor have wanted here below.

To the sufferers of every age and class the Little Child brought hope by taking to Himself the extremity of pain both of body and mind. It might seem befitting the majesty of God that His contact with the things of earth should be of the lightest compatible with the work He came to do. Riches, pleasures, worldly honour He might put from Him as unworthy of Him. And this He did. But because He was truly man, He felt the privation thus entailed. The slightest discomfort and pain had for Him a keenness of edge unknown to any of us. Because of the dignity of His Person and His office of Victim, His human nature was endowed with a perfection of organism, a sensitiveness, and capacity for physical and mental pain which belonged to Him alone, and His desire to bring us plentiful redemption, to show Himself one of the human family in very deed, made Him will to be like His brethren in all things except that, as our Elder Brother, He would take for His share all that was most painful in our lot. From the first moment of His life He would suffer all that the Divine Nature could enable that frail infant form to endure. He would pass through the years of boyhood and youth and be treated by neighbours, kinsfolk, and employers as one of no account. There is no appearance of condescension. He is too glad for that. One would suppose that our society and ways make up to Him for the Heaven He has left, for He frankly owns to the charm He finds in our company: "My delights are to be with the children of men." From eternity He has looked forward to this hour of coming into our midst.

Let us at least run out to meet Him; take Him reverently from Mary's hands; feel His little arms about our necks; welcome Him with kisses and with tears:

> Without the welkin may be wild,
>   Without, may rage the wintry storm:
> When Christmas comes our thoughts are mild,
>   When Christ is born our hearts are warm.
>
> All men are children once again
>   Because of Mary's little Son:
> For love of Him we all are fain
>   Unto His manger-crib to run.
>
> Christmas makes children of us all;
>   Ah, childlike may we ever be,
> That when shall come Thy final call
>   We may be Thine eternally!

R. H. Benson.

XIV

THE MOUTHS OF BABES

WE are fairly accustomed by this time to the aberrations and the audacities of the human intellect. The most extravagant theories, the most appalling blasphemies fail to surprise us. Yet now and again an act of revolt that rises above, or rather sinks below, the usual level, does stagger us and we wonder how the long-suffering Patience of God can restrain His Justice.

"God is patient," it has been said, "because He is eternal." But he has His own ways of vindicating His rights. He chooses His champions where He wills and with a Divine fitness which enchants us. From the beginning He has chosen "the foolish things of the world that He may confound the wise, and the weak things of the world that He may confound the strong." And in these days of ours when the pride of intellect is receiving its just reward by being delivered over to follies that a simpler age would have scorned, we find the Wisdom of God descending lower than ever among "the things that are contemptible and the things that are not, that He may bring to naught the things that are." He suffers this conceit and that to come before the footlights and have its little day of notoriety, and then, by some simple means, it is shown up and discredited, and passes away with its fellows, to be forgotten or despised. And meanwhile He reveals unseen realities by lips that owe little to the teaching of this world. Beside a girl in her teens who tells you with a simper that her intellect is too much developed to make it possible for her to believe in God, we hear a dying child murmuring in her delirium:"To know Him, love Him, and serve Him in this world..." In the misery around them men find an argument against the Providence of God. And a babe of four, told to commend to Him some pressing need of friends, answers gravely: "Holy God knows it, an dat's enough."[1] A class of boys being asked what miracles occurred at the death of our Lord, one answered: "The graves were opened and the dead arose." Another, "The earth rocked." A little fellow of nine said: "The Mother lived."

Truly the Most High is stooping low to find His witnesses! "Out of the mouths of babes and sucklings Thou hast perfected praise—*because of Thy enemies.*"[2]

---

[1] Nellie Aherne of Cork, "Little Nellie of Holy God," born August 24, 1903, died February 2, 1908.
[2] Ps. 8:3.

XV

"HE LOVED ME"

Gal. 2:20.

PROSTRATE before Thy manger with my face in the straw and my heart at Thy feet, I adore Thee, eternal Son of God, O Word made Flesh, O Babe of Bethlehem! I rejoice with Thee that Thou art Son of God from everlasting, the Only-begotten of the Father, coequal with Him. I thank Thee for that Divine decree by which Thou wert eternally predestined to be likewise the Son of Man.

I thank Thee for that incomprehensible love for Thy human brethren which drew Thee down from Heaven to work out their salvation upon earth. I thank Thee for the generosity of that love which made Thee crowd into Thy human life pain of body and distress of soul, in a measure unshared by any other, that in all our troubles we might find in Thee a fellow-sufferer, able to compassionate us with human sympathy, to encourage us with human words, to lead us by the constraining force of example, and the confidence we give so readily to the experience of a human heart.

O Lord, I thank Thee that my span of life was not set by Thy Providence in the four thousand years before Thy coming. If with Thy life on earth before me I am what I am, what should I have been had I lived in that dark, far-off past, with only Thy dim outline as sketched by the prophets to sustain my efforts and my hope!

But if this thankfulness is genuine, where are its fruits? What return have I made to this "God with us," for His Life on earth *for me?* Have I even taken the trouble to know it in any detail, to bring myself under its influence, to study its lessons, to suffer myself to be won by His generosity so as to return Him love for love?

This is what the saints have done and are doing on earth to-day. To them Christmas is not simply a season of merriment that happily closes the year. The Crib is not a mere accessory of the time, to be visited by the elders out of condescension to the children or for the satisfaction of curiosity should it happen to offer any attraction to artistic taste. The Crib of St. Francis was a study, a model for imitation. How many of us go to it for this?

Our Lord may say to us as to His disciples: "To you it is given to know the mysteries of the kingdom of Heaven, but to them it is not given...for, amen I say to you, many prophets and just men have desired to see the things you see and have not seen them." Could David have knelt for one hour in the stable or before the Tabernacle, could Isaias or Jeremias have known the details of the Three and Thirty Years, how overflowing would have been their love of Christ, how earnest their endeavour to walk in His footsteps!

When our Lord spoke those words, was He thinking not only of the Jewish prophets, but of those ancient seers who, in the midst of pagan darkness, had caught some glimpse of Israel's light, and, like the chosen people, were waiting for the Desired of all nations to appear? Had Plato or Socrates been told that first Christmas night that He had come, how they would have hastened to Bethlehem!

And then? Would they in pagan pride have turned away from the destitution and suffering of the outcast Child, or have opened their minds humbly to the lessons of the new Teacher, and been numbered with the simple shepherds among His first disciples?

"To you it is given to know the mysteries of the kingdom of Heaven, but to them it is not given." Oh, the dulness and hardness of my heart that can look upon the manger and the Cross and the Tabernacle without finding itself constrained to any personal return of love and service, any real recognition of the individual love of Christ *for me*, in all He did and suffered! I have to own with St. Paul: "He loved me and delivered Himself *for me*." Can I be content with the acknowledgement He has had from me up to now?

XVI

NEW YEAR'S DAY

"Behold, I make all things new!"—Apoc. 21:5.

A GLADDENING thought for the New Year! And who so fit to bring it as the Divine Child on His Name Day, when He was called Jesus, because He came to save His people from their sins? The world was old when He came—old, and hardened in wickedness, so sodden in corruption that it was hard to see how it could be cleansed unless by fire. Renovation seemed too late. But desire had not died out in the world, and where desire is, renovation may always follow.

"*Behold*, I make all things new," He said when the fulness of time had come.

"Behold!"—that bugle note of Scripture, calling to "Attention"; that word which has ushered in God's greatest mysteries: "Behold the handmaid of the Lord!" "Behold the place where the Lord was laid!" "Behold, I am with you all days!" "Behold, He cometh and every eye shall see Him!"

"*I make all things new*"—I to whom all things are possible, who can restore the first robe, and make that which was scarlet white as snow.

"*All things*"—a new heaven and a new earth; heaven at peace again with the earth renewed in Christ; angels and men united in one brotherhood, under one and the same Head; a new Gospel brought to the world, a new fire to cleanse, inflame, and expand the hearts of men.

How cold and hard was the old world before He came—society divided between tyrants and slaves; on one side an appalling selfishness, luxury, and cruelty, on the other a misery without limit and without hope. No protection for the weak, no justice for the oppressed, no mercy for the poor. Not a hospital for the sick, not a refuge for the homeless, the needy, the aged, the orphan, the failures of life. "Men, lovers of themselves, covetous, haughty, disobedient to parents, ungrateful, wicked, without affection...without kindness," says St. Paul. As to humility, for a virtue unknown to it, the world had not even a name.

He came. "When all things were in quiet silence and night was in the midst of her course, Thy Almighty Word came down from Heaven," and His Spirit renewed the face of the earth. The heathen world was renewed to the very core. Wherever the influence of the Gospel prevailed, and in the measure in which it prevailed, pagan ideals, institutions, laws, society—all were transformed. A new Covenant succeeded to the old, a new Church to the Synagogue that had proved unfaithful to its trust, a Church with new authority, new privileges, new means of grace, a new Tabernacle of God with men, whence all good flows to man. To the members of this Church He says to-day, says to them one by one: "Behold, I make all things new. I am ready to forgive and forget the past, to bind up what was broken, to strengthen what was weak, and what was sound and strong to preserve."

Jesus, dear Lord, in whose sacred Name we begin each year of our pilgrimage, fulfil in me Thy promise. Come to me to-day to make all things new within me. Do more than cleanse: *Cor mundum crea in me, Deus.* Create a new heart in me, O God." A workman seeks new material to display his skill. In default of this, he will accept what is deteriorated or repaired, but his choice is for the new. Create a new heart in me, O God! I appeal for this to Thy Almightiness, Thy Wisdom, Thy Goodness. All things are possible to Thee. All ways are known to Thee and are open to Thee. And Thy Will to do this for me I cannot doubt, seeing that Thou bringest me as Thy New Year's Gift—Thyself!

Say to me, then, on the threshold of this New Year: "Behold, I make all things new!" Give me a new interest in the things of God, in all that leads to Thee, in all that belongs to Thy service, in all work for Thee that may come to my hand this year. Give me an increase of faith and hope and charity, a new strength against myself and all that bars my way to Thee or hinders our closer union. Be more and more to me as the year goes on.

O Lord, increase my Faith. Let Thy Real Presence on the altar be an ever-growing reality to me. Draw me oftener to kneel before Thee, O great High Priest, as Thou offerest Thy Morning Sacrifice; as Thou spreadest Thy hands to us in the evening Benediction; as Thou callest us to the Communion rails for our daily Bread. Let me face courageously the difficulties and trials the year may bring, and behave in them as the spirit of faith dictates.

And strengthen my Hope. Let my trust in Thee grow day by day till it comes to be the instinct of my soul that no chance nor trouble can disturb.

Above all, increase my love by a frequent lifting of my heart to Thee through the busy hours of the day; by the offering to Thy glory and service of all I think, and do, and suffer; by a more docile following of Thy guidance, a greater readiness for self-sacrifice, a gradual lessening of the self-seeking that taints all my work for Thee. I offer to Thee by a new oblation all I have and am, as a possession to be Thine more and more fully as the months go by. This is my New Year's gift to Thee. Thine to me, dear Lord, is Thyself. More than this is not in Thy power to give. More I do not ask till in the New Year of Eternity Thou showest Thyself to me face to face.

XVII

THE NEW YEAR

"Let us so live that in Heaven we may rejoice to have lived so."

A WISE resolve at the beginning of a New Year. But to make it efficacious we must consider how to give it practical effect.

Life is made up of Past, Present, and Future, and the making is, under God, in our own hands. Hour by hour we are shaping our character and our life by the trend of our habitual thoughts. They need to be watched and guided.

Some people live in the Past:

> . . . the stately ships go on
>   To their haven under the hill;
> But O for the touch of a vanish'd hand,
>   And the sound of a voice that is still!
>
> Break, break, break,
>   On thy cold, gray stones, O Sea!
> But the tender grace of a day that is dead
>   Will never come back to me.

We may have seen the picture of a girl lost in a dreamland entitled "What might have been." If we are wise we shall forbid ourselves thoughts that unbrace us, that make us self-centred and morbid, irritable, disgusted with life such as Providence has arranged it for us. Even our past sins must not have a dispiriting effect upon us. "Sadness," we are told, "is sorrow with self in it." "Discouragement is the devil's humility; true humility is the holding out of our hands to God in the sense of our nothingness and our need."

St. Peter is a perfect model of contrition. For him the past was a subject for continual sorrow, but not for any abatement of that joyous trust in his Master which characterised him. Twice he flung himself into the sea to reach that dear Master—once before, once after his denial. Before, his protest was: "Lord, I am ready to go with Thee both to prison and to death....Why cannot I follow Thee now? I will lay down my life for Thee. Although all shall be scandalised in Thee, yet not I." After his fall, to the question: "Lovest thou Me more than these?" came the answer:"Lord, Thou knowest all things, Thou knowest that I love Thee." His frailty had but strengthened his trust, and rendered more persistent and vehement the affirmation of his love. So should it be with all true penitents.

Some people live in the Future, creating scenes and exploits wherein they figure as heroes or heroines. Such castle-building makes those who indulge in it unreal. They grow selfish and restless, unfit for actual life and duties.

To live in the Past or in the Future is to spoil the entire life, so far as the higher Christian aspirations are concerned. And as both are beyond our control, it is waste of time to occupy ourselves with either.

To live in the Present is to turn our whole life to the best account. For the Present which we have secured will be Past directly, and the Future will be Present.

A widely advertised system of training has been started of late years for the scientific development of the powers of the mind. Its aim, we are told, is to quicken the faculties and extend mental energy in order to bring efficient minds to bear upon the various problems and difficulties which have to be overcome in daily life. Its appeal is to all. In the world of business and in the world of art we find judges, generals and admirals, clergymen and mechanics, peers and clerks, women workers and labour leaders, go through the training this system provides. Enthusiasts declare that it makes them observe, think, realise their powers, discover in themselves capabilities unrecognised hitherto. This may or may not be true, but we can draw a lesson from it for our own efforts in the pursuit of virtue.

Our Lord told the men of His day that they knew how to read the signs of the times. Why should not we read them and learn a lesson from the eagerness we see around us to intensify life by increasing the efficiency of one's mental powers? Who that is worthy of life would not be fired with the resolve to make the most of such a gift!

The means is within the reach of every one of us. If we will but concentrate our energy, if we will but live in the Present, we shall find Opportunity always knocking at our door, golden treasure around us on every side. To focus the activities of the soul on the Will of God as manifested in the actual duty of the moment, secures for them that concentration which, according to Napoleon, is the secret of success. It calms restlessness and fears, procures peace of mind, union with God, and rapid advance in holiness. Sanctified by purity of intention, the most humdrum work, the lowliest household duties, have supernatural value entitling them to an everlasting reward, supposing, of course, the state of grace and work honestly done as for God, that is conscientiously and thoroughly offered for the Divine acceptance. Success is not the mainspring of such action, yet it is often more surely attained by this means than if it were. To say nothing of inspiration in the conception, and help in the execution, work done in the consciousness of a Divine Witness has a singleness of purpose, a cheerfulness and calm confidence about it, which may well augur a successful issue. And if material success is not always achieved, a loftier reward never fails. These are the works of which our Lord says: "He that doth truth cometh to the light, that his works may be made manifest because they are done in God."

Lastly, the habit of living in the Present removes the fear of death. It is a matter of wide experience that those who were once terrified at the thought of this awful moment have, as it drew nearer, beheld its approach without alarm: living in the Present has kept it at bay, for it has made the whole of life a preparation.

Seeing, then, that we can only live our lives once, let us so live that in Heaven we may rejoice to have lived so. Let us take hold of to-day with both hands that it may yield a bright to-morrow.

> Tarry no longer: toward thyn heritage
> Haste on thy way, and be of right good chere,
> Go ech day onward on thy pilgrimage
> Thynk how short time thou shalt abyde here.
>
> JOHN LYDGATE.

XVIII

JESU DULCIS MEMORIA

WHAT a rush of feeling the name of a friend calls forth! His name stands for himself. It epitomises him and brings to mind all that has made him what he is to us. I ask myself: Has the Name of Jesus this effect upon me? If not, why not? It is sweet in the ear, on the lips, in the heart of one that loves. It holds in itself all that we worship, all that we crave. Like a creed it is the compendium of our faith, the motive of our hope, the incentive to love. Through all ages that Name has been the strength of Martyrs, the light of Confessors, the joy of Virgins, the trust of sinners, because one and all have sounded its depth and come to realise what we have in Jesus.

That it should appeal to us as it has appealed to millions, we must be able to say with them: "I know in whom I have believed." Unless I get to know Jesus, neither His Crib, nor His Cross, nor His Name will stir me to love or gratitude, still less to sacrifice for His sake. His Name is light and heat. Let me choose as my favourite aspirations those in which this blessed Name is found, and my heart will begin to glow. I may use it as a familiar ejaculation that will take its tone from the season or the feast, or from my actual mood or want. In temptation, in trouble, in perplexity, the cry: "Jesus, Jesus!" (25 days) will be all I need: "Jesus, Mighty God; Jesus our Refuge; Jesus, meek and humble of heart, have mercy on me!" (300 days). I may use it as a prayer, in thanksgiving for a favour received, or a danger averted. If I use it after Communion, it will be in turn adoration, thanksgiving, love, praise, petition, contrition, trust. In this way Jesus will come to be that Friend at the sound of whose Name my heart will leap: "By Him, with Him, in Him," I shall find all I desire.

Now, at the beginning of a New Year, I will resolve to use this Holy Name oftener, and with ever-growing reverence, confidence, and love.

"Jesus, my God, I love Thee above all things." (50 days' Indulgence.)

"Jesus, Son of David, have mercy on me!" (100 days.)

"My Jesus, mercy." (100 days.)

"Heart of Jesus, in Thee I trust." (300 days.)

"Sweetest Jesus, be not Thou my Judge but my Saviour." (50 days.)

"Divine Heart of Jesus, convert sinners, save the dying, deliver the holy souls in purgatory." (300 days.)

XIX
LOVE

"Jésus, je voudrais l'aimer comme il n'a jamais été aimé."
"I want to love Jesus as He has never yet been loved."

Saint Thérèse of Lisieux.

AT first sight this might seem an extravagance. To say nothing of the ardours of divine love by which some of our poor human race have emulated the glowing seraphim, there is the love of Mary, the love of the Father, and of the Holy Spirit of Love, for Him whom we call, and who is in very deed, our Brother.

And yet in a very true sense we may each of us say: *"Je voudrais l'aimer comme il n'a jamais été aimé."* For it is precisely this individual love of each human heart that He covets, by which He desires to be repaid for the individual and quite special love of His Sacred Heart for each one of us. It is for this that He made us. There is something in the love of my heart which He cannot find elsewhere, which, if I refuse Him, He will never have. He has made it capable of some form and expression of love which singularly delights Him. That I might give it Him, He made me. And so my desire is that He should not be defrauded of the fruit of an eternal desire, that He should have for His own what is poor, no doubt, and unworthy of Him, yet because He is pleased to prize it and to ask it, what I desire with all my power of desire to give Him.

Non est inventus similis illi, the Church says in turn of each of her canonised bishops. And the praise is literally true. There are no two of them alike. Hence the love of each for Jesus is stamped with his own individuality, and in the eyes of his Beloved has a charm which gives it a special acceptance.

Could there be anything depressing in those marvellously stimulating records, the Lives of the Saints, it would be the thought that I acknowledge the same Master as they, have the same personal indebtedness to Him, hear His teaching, approach the same means of grace, have the same inducements held out to me—*and am what I am!*

Yet against this thought I may set another, and one that has a peculiar helpfulness. Though my love be poor and scant, it is a love that from eternity has attracted Him, and to such an extent that He thought it worth His while to leave His Kingdom to win it. For this "joy set before Him He endured the cross, despising the shame."[1]

"He loved me and delivered Himself for me," that so He might invite a return of love. Can that be altogether worthless which He values? Must I not prize what has captivated Him, prize it and hoard it lest its treasures be squandered on the things of this world—that is, on self—and there be none left for Him? The remembrance that He has bought it at the price of His Blood, that it is His by right, that He covets it and makes much of every little expression of it, will lead a long way on the road of sacrifice—the road of love. "Give me thy heart," is a wonderful prayer on the lips of the Son of God. How can my heart respond except by an immense desire to give Him at least all that I have to give!

Jésus, je voudrais l'aimer comme il n'a jamais été aimé.

---

[1] Heb. 12:2.

XX

THE EPIPHANY—I

"A Child is born to us."—Isa.9:6.
"And they offered Him gifts."—Matt. 2:11.

HERE, on His Mother's lap, lies the God of Heaven, God made Man: the God of Sinai, but with no environment of fire or thunder; no burning mountain, nor wind, nor cloud. A helpless babe, He lies there, dependent for all things on the two to whose care He is confided, the two whose poverty and labours He comes to share. How can we welcome suitably a God who comes amongst us like this?

We have to remember that He is a real child, with all that is characteristic of and engaging in a child. Children who know what it is to have a birthday expect a present of their own. Everyone connected with them, friends and relations above all, must bring something. This little One looks for a gift from us. What are we going to give Him? We cannot bear to disappoint a child. We must not disappoint Him. As a child He is easily satisfied. His little outstretched Hands will not hold much, a small thing will content Him. Look at Him. He is attractive and lovable. If we are afraid of Him as Man, let us go to Him as a babe in His Mother's arms. However guilty or miserable, we need not fear to draw near to Him there.

We all know by happy experience how a mere nothing, skilfully offered, will please or appease a child. With the sure appreciation of instinct, it obeys the injunction of à Kempis to consider "not so much the gift of the lover as the love of the giver." It is the smile, the tone, the soothing words that work the charm.

And all this is true of the Child on Mary's knee, or playing at Mary's feet. Very God of very God, He was a true child still:

> Yes, dearest Babe, those tiny hands
>   That play with Mary's hair,
> The weight of all the mighty world
>   This very moment bear.
>
> Whilst thou art clasping Mary's neck
>   In timid, tight embrace,
> The boldest seraphs veil themselves
>   Before Thine Infant Face.[1]

The ever-present consciousness of who He was must have been pain to the Blessed Mother many a time. To the rough folks of Nazareth He was but an ordinary child, to be dandled and humoured and talked nonsense to like any other. How this will have jarred upon her sense of reverence! How she will have striven—so soon as the door was closed behind His well-meaning but unsuspecting visitors—to make up to Him by the homage of her faith for their unseemly familiarity.

Her tenderness and embrace and smallest service were always steeped in adoration. That He was what He was—her Babe, her God—was a wonder and a joy which never lost their freshness. And it was in little things that her love was most endearing, her worship most profound.

Little things must be the refuge of our love and worship too. What else have we to offer? Saint Thérèse of the Infant Jesus tells us it was by little things that she won

---
1 Faber.

His Heart. She traded on the knowledge that He was a true child. The Sacred Infancy was the mould in which her own simple character and specially attractive type of holiness was cast. The record of her few and, as the world would say, uneventful years, might lead us to wonder what it was that so endeared her soul to God and made Him so liberal in rewarding. But when we find that from the age of three she refused Him nothing, our wonder ceases. Think what a multitude of little things—little acts of obedience, fidelity, and self-restraint—this babe of three must have offered to the Divine Babe for His acceptance! She gave Him her heart for a ball to use, play with, cast aside as He pleased. She is the apostle of little souls and little things, and assures us with Father Faber that

> Little things on little wings
> Bear little souls to Heaven.

Mother Juliana of Norwich, the English anchoress whose "Revelations of Divine Love" give us so sweet a picture of our Lord amidst His elect in Heaven, says she was particularly struck with His Divine courtesy towards His blessed servants and friends. Courtesy and fidelity are shown in little things—little services, kindnesses, tendernesses, anticipation of desires. It was such marks of love that charmed her. And it is by such means that we may all of us draw to ourselves the love of His Sacred Heart, like to ours in Its appreciation of the little ways and devices in which affection finds expression.

One of God's heroes of our own time[1] made this resolution: "I will strive to perform each action as perfectly as possible, putting my best effort into each duty as it

---

[1] Father William Doyle, S.J. (1873-1917). *Life,* by A. O'Rahilly.

comes round, paying special attention to small duties...I will try to do each as Jesus would have done it, with the same pure intention, exquisite exactness, and fervour; to copy in all my actions—walking, eating, praying—Jesus, my model in the little house at Nazareth. By this means I am to find the chief road to sanctity."

This was the starting point of a life of self-immolation. The crowning sacrifice came on the battlefield at Frezenberg, where, on August 16, 1917, the desire of his life and his continual prayer was granted, and he was found worthy to give to the Master for whom he was working the greatest proof of love a man can give to his friend.

How surely his spiritual instinct as to the value of little things had guided him from the outset of his religious life, is shown as much from the testimony of those who lived and worked with him in the daily intimacy of a religious house and the labours of the Apostolate, as from the tribute to his gallantry by those who saw him day after day among the dead and dying, knowing apparently neither fatigue nor fear. The resolve of long ago to "pay special attention to small duties, *e.g.*, saying grace, odd Hail Marys, etc.," had led him to the heights of heroism before God and man, to face for God and for souls, not without fear but without flinching, perils and horrors without parallel in history. "He was afraid and felt fear deeply, how deeply few can realise," wrote one who saw him daily amid the flying bullets and bursting shells. But devotion to duty at any cost, his intense personal attachment to Christ, and his all but uninterrupted prayer, bore him up through a life of extraordinary strenuousness at every stage, and brought him, as he prayed it might, to sanctity. He was found faithful unto death because trained in the path of self-sacrifice by unswerving fidelity in little things.

> Death came unheralded—but it was well,
>   For so thy Saviour bore
> Kind witness thou wast meet at once to dwell
>   On His eternal shore.
>   All warning spared,
> For none He gives whose hearts are for prompt
>   change prepared.

CARDINAL NEWMAN.

XXI

THE EPIPHANY—II

"We are come to adore Him."

THIS was the object of that long journey of the Magi—not curiosity, not to find favour nor win gifts from Him who was born King of the Jews, but *to adore Him*. Is this our main intent when we fall on our knees before Him, as truly present on the altar to which Faith leads us, as He was in the house at Bethlehem to which they were beckoned by the star?

In Eden, adoration and thanksgiving—the first two among the four duties of creatures to their Creator—were clear as noonday to the unclouded intelligence of our first parents, and dear as life to their unspoilt hearts. After the Fall all was changed. Adoration, thanksgiving, and petition were as incumbent as ever, and a fourth obligation, propitiation for sin, was added to their duties to God. But the spontaneity of their worship was checked by the disorder brought into their faculties by sin. The claims of God had now to be enforced by repeated commands. Outside the people of God, they grew ever dimmer and dimmer in the conscience of man, till the worship of his Maker was practically reduced to the last two points which immediately concerned his own personal and material advantage. That the Deity had been grievously outraged long ago, was a fact transmitted by tradition. But that God had been appeased by the merits of a Redeemer to come, this was ignored. Hence, adoration and thanksgiving, as duties to God, held but a small place in the conscience of men, and worship of Him was confined to appeasing His anger and securing His gifts—in other words, to what directly concerned their own interests.

And is not this still, even among Christians, the main idea of prayer? Is not petition the one form it takes in the minds of most men who give the matter thought at all? Have we not to be continually reminded by our Lord Himself and by the Church of those duties of adoration and praise which come before all others? "Thus, therefore, shall you pray: Our Father who art in Heaven, hallowed be Thy Name; Thy kingdom come; Thy will be done on earth as it is in Heaven." Every Mass, the Church reminds us, is offered first for these ends, and then as propitiation and petition.

How fully this primeval idea of worship possessed the Magi appears from their own account of themselves to the inhabitants of Jerusalem. "We have seen His star in the East, and are come *to adore Him*." It was not to receive but to give on which they were bent. Clear-sighted though simple-minded men, they were under no delusion as to what their resolve was to cost them—not the richest produce of their land only, but risk of every kind, opposition of their nearest and dearest, the loss of credit and position, possibly of life itself, in what would be deemed a foolish quest. They saw sacrifice from first to last, and they were ready for it— "we are come to adore Him."

Our Lord gives us the end and model of all prayer in the words: "Seek first the Kingdom of God and His justice. Hallowed be Thy Name. Thy will be done on earth as it is in Heaven." There we see the ideal of unfallen Paradise restored, the rightful order of our petitions observed. Indeed, the last two, which all but monopolised attention on earth, have to a great extent disappeared from the list of duties, so far as the Blessed themselves are concerned, for their work is done. Adoration, praise, and thanksgiving occupy the whole field of the glad worship of Heaven, and that for eternity!

Shall we not rehearse for it now? When we enter His Presence who in His Sacred Humanity is really present on the altar, shall not our attitude of mind and of body bear us testimony that we are come *to adore Him?* "And falling down, they adored Him."

> Jesu that wast in Bethlehem,
> Three Kings there unto Thee came;
> They offered gold, incense, and myrrh;
> And Thou forsook none of them there,
> But wished them well all the three
> Home again to their own countree.
> Right so our offerings that we offer
> And our prayers that we proffer,
> Thou take, Lord, to Thy praising;
> And be our help in everything.
> That all our perils be done away,
> Our good desires Thou grant alway,
> Of our misdeeds Thou us amend,
> In all our need Thou succour send.[1]

---

[1] This rhymed prayer used to be recited at the Offertory of the Mass, especially on "high feasts," by our Catholic forefathers.

XXII
THE EPIPHANY—III

A Lesson of Sacrifice.

THAT sacrifice is the law of success in any enterprise involving effort, is a truth vouched for by the deepest instincts of the human heart; by every life that has had a noble aim; by every love story, human and divine; by the history of every soul. God, the supreme need of every soul, is to be reached by no other, no lower road. The Eastern Magi on the way to Bethlehem show the working out of this law. Do I think myself exempted from it, or do I recognise and accept it? A widely circulated story by a popular American author was sent as a gift to a children's library with these words from the giver:

> A book full of smiles and empty of God!
> The pity of it!

The description is true enough and justified the sigh. And yet, were there in these letters any direct reference to the Providence that had watched over the orphan girl, there would have been less interest in viewing them as an allegory.

One of the trustees of a "Home" happens to read a description of it written by one of the orphan inmates, and is so struck by the literary promise it shows, that he resolves to send the girl to College and make a writer of her. The matron informs her of his intention and of the conditions he lays down. She is to write regularly and frequently to her patron, telling him of all that concerns her studies and of whatever interests her. But she is to expect no answer from him except through his secretary, and she is never to see him. The book consists of her letters, natural, bright, and spirited, now expressing gratitude for the generosity and delicacy which provide for every need and enable her to hold her own among her fellow-students, now chafing under the restrictions he imposes as to her intercourse with himself, or to the greater freedom she would desire in the matter of friendships and visits. In a wayward mood she even breaks out into remonstrance, but this is quickly followed by self-reproach and penitence. At last comes a letter from her telling him of an acquaintance which is growing into a friendship. At the home of a college friend she has met one who is winning her affection, though not without some misgiving on her part lest the gift of her love in this direction should be robbery in another where the claim to it is higher and stronger. A violent struggle ensues, but the instinct of loyalty to her first friend and benefactor prevails, and when at length the proposal of marriage comes, she refuses the young man. But the cost of the sacrifice is more than she can endure alone, and with the childlike confidence which marks her correspondence throughout, she pours out her heart to him for whose sake she has made it. Her letter to him brings no answer, and after weeks of painful suspense, she hears he has been seriously ill and wishes to see her. With mingled joy and fear she crosses the threshold of his home for the first time, and—not without many injunctions on the part of his attendant—enters the darkened room. There, on a couch, pale and weak from recent illness, she beholds with amazement, in one and the same person, her rejected lover and the benefactor of her early years. The sequel to the story needs no telling.

A habit of seeing analogies between the material things that strike the senses and spiritual realities is well worth cultivating. This story can easily be read as an allegory. Recognising the claim of the Creator, from whom it has received everything, to its undivided love, a generous soul may renounce the creature which seems to dispute this claim. By such fidelity it will find eventually in God, its eternal Benefactor and Lover, not only more than it had sacrificed, but the very happiness it had renounced for His sake.

This is the law we shall see exemplified in every case when the secrets of all hearts shall be revealed. It will be the story of the Magi over and over again.

> He or she that hopes to gain
> Love's best sweet without some pain
> Hopes in vain.
>
> Cupid's livery no one wears
> But must put on hopes and fears,
> Smiles and tears.
>
> And, like to April weather,
> Rain and shine, both together,
> Both or neither.
>
> ANON., HARLEIAN MS.

The partings, the opposition of friends, the perils and fatigues of the journey which they were content to pay as the price of their fidelity to the call of God, were these not repaid a hundredfold when the weary travellers from the East fell down before the Child in Bethlehem!

XXIII

THE EPIPHANY—IV

"He that dwelleth in heaven shall laugh at them,
and the Lord shall deride them."—Ps. 2:4.

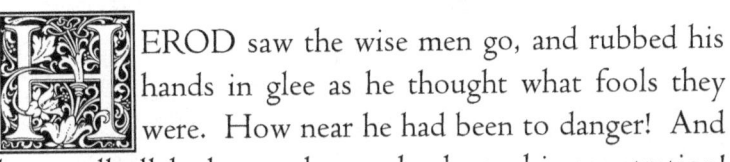

HEROD saw the wise men go, and rubbed his hands in glee as he thought what fools they were. How near he had been to danger! And how well all had turned out, thanks to his penetration! Here, only a few miles away, was this "Desired of all nations," whom the whole world was expecting. There could be no doubt about it. These stargazers had been led from the East by Heaven itself. They were evidently acting under strong conviction, and will have talked freely of their errand as they came along. Even in his own capital they had dared to speak of another king. It was all very disturbing—or might have been but for the luck that brought the mischief-makers his way. But they were doing him good service now, and when they returned to him the world would have seen and heard the last of them. "Ha! Ha!" And he rubbed his hands again.

"He that dwelleth in heaven shall laugh at them." And not only He that dwelleth in heaven, but He that lieth a helpless Babe in His Mother's lap shall catch the crafty in their own conceits. Is it not surprising that Herod never thought of sending a messenger with the strangers to make sure they were not playing him false? He must have known they could not have been an hour in Jerusalem without hearing from every quarter of his terror of being supplanted by a rival monarch, and of the lives even of his nearest and dearest that had been sacrificed to his fears. They might well have had their suspicions. His own people, too, might have been moved to compassion for these noble-looking, fearless men who had come so far and run such risk to find the new-born King. Had none of the priests who had sent them on their way to Bethlehem seen through his fair words and warned the Magi, and thus saved both their lives and the innocent life that was at stake? But no. The most suspicious of tyrants was blinded and had nothing but congratulations for himself for the cleverness with which his plans had been laid.

The Holy Family and its friends were in deadly peril. So it seemed. But God was watching. All these lives were in His keeping, and safe. When His time was come He interfered. A word to the Magi sent them home another way. Herod was balked of his prey. Not only was his cunning defeated, but Providence used it to give these Gentiles the Scriptural authority they needed as to the birthplace of the Messiah. No one can take credit to himself for being made the mouthpiece of God. Caesar served God's purpose when his edict set the whole world in motion and brought about the Birth in the City of David. Caiphas served it when he declared it was necessary that one man should die for the nation. Pilate served it when he bore testimony again and again that he found no cause in this Man. He who made use of Balaam's ass can select His instruments where He wills; His choice is no guarantee for their final acceptance by Him. All must work out their salvation with fear and trembling. All who minister to others in the things of God must pray that they may not themselves become castaways.

How quick are some to see God moving behind the transparent veils of this life—how slow are others! An unknown star appears in the Eastern sky. To the population generally it is an object of curiosity only. To the habitual students of the heavens it is interesting certainly, a problem for scientific research; to three only is it more, much more. It is the Star of prophecy, "His star," His forerunner for whom the whole world is, or ought to be, in expectation. "We have seen His star in the East...and are come to adore Him"—a matter of course. Was not the heavenly visitor an invitation from Heaven? To what other purpose was it sent?

They are quick not to recognise only but to follow and to trust. How did they know the star would go before and guide them? They did not know, but they trusted. The God of whom they knew so little they trusted more than do most of us with our fuller knowledge and our developed faith. They asked for nothing further than He was pleased to give, for no assurance of guidance or protection, still less for any reward. He, the Desired of all nations, was their Desire and they would seek Him at any cost.

> Oh, glory be to God on high for these Arabian kings,
> These miracles of royal faith, with eastern offerings:
> For Gaspar and for Melchior and Balthazar, who from far
> Found Mary out and Jesus by the shining of a Star![1]

From the journey of the wise men we may learn that if, in obedience to the Voice of God, we follow where He leads, He will watch over us and turn all things to our good. We learn, too, that we must not look at every turn for Divine interventions in our behalf. The commingling of the natural and the supernatural in the early life of His Incarnate Son is very striking. A new

---
1 Faber.

star appears in the heavens and starts the Magi on their way. Before they reach Jerusalem it leaves them, and they have to betake themselves to human means for knowing their route. When they need further guidance, the star reappears. A message from above directs them as to their return home and saves the Holy Family from immediate peril. Then, just when we should expect some marvellous interposition of Divine power on behalf of the Child, we see His life saved indeed, but by the weakest of human means—by flight, flight by night! All through it is the same—supernatural interference, and then, the working out of natural laws and everyday occurrences. Why is this, if not to show us that in all events we must see God's leading and abandon ourselves trustfully to Him? The same Providence that watched over the Holy Family and directed every circumstance of their lives, cares for the smallest detail of mine. I am as safe in Its keeping as were Jesus, Mary, and Joseph.

Even "His parents," we are told, "understood not" all the ways by which they were led, because faith, not sight, is to guide us "till the shadows retire." But the lifting of the veil here and there from the lives of others is a guarantee for our own. A little while, and we shall see in the changes and troubles through which we are now passing, what we can already see of the years past—that God has been with us throughout, guiding and guarding and blessing, keeping us from harm here, remedying our mistakes there. A little while, and we shall be saying in fervent gratitude: "He hath done all things well." Till then, our daily prayer shall be in childlike trust:

"Lead Thou me on!"

XXIV

HUMILITY

"He is honoured by the humble."—Ecclus. 3:21.

WHAT was the supreme trial of the Magi in that long series which followed on the appearance of the Star in the East? Not the strife between all that Nature holds dear and all that Grace might demand. Not the breaking with home and country, not the uncertainty of finding Him for whom they were risking all. The reproaches of some and the bitter tears of others, the weariness and dangers of the way, the disappointment that awaited them when as they neared Jerusalem the star disappeared, the apathy of priests and people, the sense of loneliness as they passed out of the Jaffa gate on their way to Bethlehem—it was none of these things. For the King whose star they had seen in the East lured them on. His attraction overmastered every obstacle and tempered every trial. But when the King himself seemed to have failed them, when there was no palace, nor royal state, nor rejoicing throng, but poverty, and neglect—then came the test of their loyalty and their faith. When the star, descending low, rested over the tiny house; when, entering, they found a helpless, apparently unconscious babe, an outcast pauper child, devoid of the barest necessaries of life—this was trial indeed. Their angels must have trembled for all that hung in the balance. Would these men with their Oriental notions be able to rise to the sublimity of the mystery, or would they turn away in disgust and with crushed hearts slink back to their homes?

No, they were ready even for this. Their childlike hearts sought the King alone, and not any earthly pomp that might surround Him. With the humility of little children they bowed before a manifestation of majesty that took them completely by surprise; they opened their minds to a lesson that upset all they had learned hitherto. Humility opened to them the treasures of that lowly home. It led them straight to the Heart of the Babe. They saw; they understood. What was hidden from the wise and prudent was revealed to them. Before their docility all prejudices of race and rank vanished, all marvels were explained, obstacles became stepping-stones and darkness light. "We shall be like to Him because we shall see Him as He is," says St. John. The Babe was humble and meek. They were like Him—how should they not see and understand!

XXV

FEAST OF THE PURIFICATION, AND OF THE PRESENTATION OF OUR LORD IN THE TEMPLE

"A Light to enlighten the Gentiles and the glory of Thy people Israel."

WHAT a day this is for Light! The Liturgy is aglow with it. The churches, like firmaments, tell the glory of the Lord who comes to His Temple. At the words of the aged Simeon star after star shines forth to welcome Him. With lights we stand at the Gospel to meet the Bridegroom. With light again we make ready to greet Him at the Consecration, and there in our hands it remains, testifying to our faith and hope and love, till He disappears from the altar to enter our hearts in Holy Communion.

Can we do better to-day than pray for the light of the knowledge and love of Jesus to be spread over the whole earth? How much still remains in darkness—vast regions which the Gospel has not yet reached, dark corners whence the light is wilfully shut out even in Christian lands! Nay, darkness everywhere, it must seem to them in Heaven as they look down on us from their unclouded brightness. We are all groping our way home. At times the sun comes out, and we see with gladness that we are on the right track. And then—all is dark or dim again, and the brightness awhile ago appears an illusion or a dream. "*Veni Lumen cordium,*" the Church puts on the lips of us all, and we might well make it a daily prayer.

But our own wants must not engross us wholly, to the exclusion of other needs. Rather should they stimulate us to active charity. "Let your light shine before men," is our Lord's injunction to us every one. Such light as we can give out may not, we think, go far. No matter; if it cheers the pathway of one trudging on at our side, it is well worth while. And we should bear in mind that it is just those nearest to us who have the first claim upon us. It is a mistake to sigh after the slums and the heathen and to neglect the crying needs at home. We must give with both hands. Time, money if we have it, personal service if we can; it may not be much, but God will use it if we have done our best, and *if we pray*, trusting more, much more to prayer than to action. By prayer, the poorest and the busiest amongst us can help to spread around us the light and the warmth of Catholic faith that will attract to the true Fold. We forget at times how warmth attracts and cheers. Friendliness, real sympathy, tenderness, do a wonderful work for God and for souls. It is hidden for the most part, but now and again the veil is lifted. We find some sufferer, in a lowly sphere perhaps, shut out, it would seem, from opportunities of doing good, exercising a marvellous influence far and near. It is the sympathy and kindness of the Heart of Jesus, overflowing from a heart that He has won, upon others, and winning them in turn. Here is the result, but the secret is prayer. "Soak your work in prayer, specially your work for others, and you will see what a difference it will make."

This Feast of the Presentation, which shows us the fruit of persevering prayer, is surely a day for the prayer of intercession.

And first, for the revelation of the Light of the World to the millions of the heathen; for the missionaries, priests and nuns, gone out from among us to spread that light by their toils and sacrifices. Too often we lose sight of the cost at which souls are won. We complain of the incessant calls upon our purse, and forget the lives of hardship, isolation, and disappointment—sufferings of every kind, which those must bear who have cut themselves off from all that makes life joyous. Could we not help them more than we do? By a little sacrifice on our part might we not bring a joyful surprise now and then to those—because human—often weary and dispirited hearts?

Look around on every side and note what need cries out to us, what prayer can win:

Light for the multitudes in Christian lands, who, for the darkness of sin or of ignorance in which they are plunged, might almost be reckoned among the heathen;

Light for those who see but, unlike the wise Magi, dare not follow. We may—nay, we must—get them that stronger light which is heat as well as illumination, which will kindle their hearts and bring them safely into the shelter, peace, and rest of the one Fold;

Light for all bound in the toils of sin that they may see their danger and, while there is yet time, be restored to the friendship of God;

Light for the rulers and statesmen of so-called Christian States, that they may be guided, not by narrow, sordid, and selfish views, but by Christian principles which will uplift and save the world from the materialism and infidelity into which it is drifting;

Light for all, that "we may discern those things which are pleasing to Thee and conducive to our salvation; so that after the dark perils of this world, we may deserve to arrive at never-failing light." (At the blessing of the candles.)

Nor let us forget on this day those to whom "the promised Salvation" was first offered. "Father, forgive them, for they know not what they do," is the daily prayer for them that rises from many sanctuaries immediately after the Consecration, when the Lamb offered once on Calvary for all, and still offered in every Mass for all, pleads for the light and grace so sorely needed. As we think in wistful sorrow of this favoured race, St. Paul's words come to mind with a force that stimulates our zeal:

"I say then: Hath God cast away His people? God forbid. God hath not cast away His people which He foreknew....But by their offence, salvation is come to the Gentiles. Now if the diminution of them be the riches of the Gentiles, how much more the fulness of them....If the loss of them be the reconciliation of the world, what shall the receiving of them be, but life from the dead?

"And if some of the branches be broken, and thou, being a wild olive, art ingrafted in them...be not highminded but fear."

Whilst, then, we pray to-day that the fulness of the Gentiles may come into the Fold of Christ, let us not forget the words of the aged prophet who held Him in his arms, that He should be "a light for the revelation of the Gentiles, *and* the glory of Thy people Israel," and let us pray, as the whole Church will pray on Good Friday, "that acknowledging the light of Thy truth, which is Christ, they may be delivered from their darkness."

Yes, the Presentation is the Feast of Light, the Mass, ending as usual, yet with special fitness, with St. John's Gospel of Light, and the last of the Church's Hours, as usual, with her ever-faithful remembrance of her children in the dark prison-house. "Eternal rest give to them, O Lord, and let perpetual light shine upon them."

XXVI
THE PRESENTATION IN THE TEMPLE

"This Child is set for the rise and fall of many in Israel, and Thine own soul a sword shall pierce."—Luke 2:34, 35.

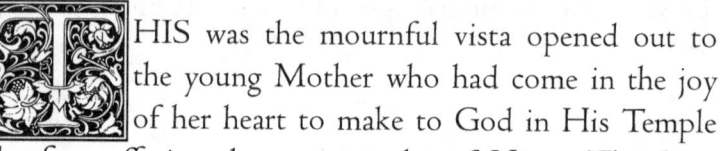

THIS was the mournful vista opened out to the young Mother who had come in the joy of her heart to make to God in His Temple the first offering that was worthy of Him. The forty days of seclusion prescribed by the Law had been a time of mingled sorrow and consolation. If there had been Bethlehem's rejection of her Babe, there was the worship of the shepherds, and the song of the angels proclaiming the peace between Heaven and earth which He had brought. If six weeks must go by before the Lord of the Temple could enter His Temple, He was all the more hers and Joseph's because He was theirs alone. Still, Mary must have longed for the Presentation, knowing it was to be the fulfilment of prophecy, the offering of the Lamb whom fifteen centuries of morning and evening sacrifice had dimly foreshadowed.

The aged priest took the Child from the arms of His Mother, and, in return for that gift of infinite worth, spoke the words which pierced her heart with the first of its seven swords. It is when the tests of God come suddenly and probe a soul to its depths that its true worth is disclosed. If they find it unprepared by daily self-renunciation, the result will in all probability be the failure of an eternal design. The heart of Mary was never unprepared, and the plunging of the sword into its joyful depths found it as ready to welcome the unexpected sorrow as if she had spent the forty days in prayerful anticipation. Joseph watched her face. Anguish was there, but no diminution of its heavenly peace.

As they took their way home again, and day followed day, what sort of reference would there be to that Presentation morning which thenceforth could never be long absent from their minds? Did Joseph think to solace Mary by any suggestion that Simeon's words were ill-timed? That it was cruel thus to turn her rapture into desolation? That such knowledge might have been delayed or at least softened to her? Or did he, as was his wont, follow her lead and try to emulate, as far as might be, her heroic acceptance of the will of God through an appointed channel? Deep as was his tenderness for Mary, and keenly as he felt every hardship and affliction that befell her, he saw in her always the Mother of the suffering Redeemer, with a destiny and a grace he could never fathom; therefore he humbly awaited each manifestation of the Divine will in her regard, seeking only to fall in with them as the privileged sharer in her woes as in her joys.

And we ourselves—how do we act when sorrow sharp and sudden comes to one we love? What shape does our sympathy take? Is it downdragging or uplifting? Do we content ourselves with bare lamentation, or indignant condemnation of those we hold responsible for the blow, thinking to alleviate the grief by aggravating the grievance? Or do we gently lead up to higher and supernatural sources of comfort, looking upon the trial, not in itself, but in the designs of God? It was thus our Lord comforted His own. If He invited the sad sisters of Lazarus and the disciples on the road to Emmaus to open their hearts to Him, it was to take the sting out of their present anguish by the prospect of consolation to come. "Thy brother shall rise again." "Ought not Christ to suffer these things and so to enter into His glory?" He did not always console by removing the cause of suffering. He raised Lazarus from the dead, He revealed Himself to the disconsolate disciples. But He left Dismas on his cross, because in his case solace far more profitable than release from bodily torture was to be given him—contrition for his sins, full pardon, and remission of all punishment after death, canonisation while living, the promise of Paradise before that day's sun had set.

If we will but pour out our troubled hearts to our Father who is in Heaven, we may always trust Him to help us in the way we shall one day see to have been best. It may be relief from pain, it may be strength to bear it as we should. "Father, if it be possible, let this chalice pass from Me!" His beloved Son cried out in His agony. And there appeared to Him an angel from Heaven *strengthening* Him.

"Learn of Me," our Master says to us by word and example. Let us learn of Him how to comfort one another. Not like Job's heartless and foolish friends, who suggested his sins as the cause of his misfortunes. Nor like his more foolish and wicked wife, who, instead of sustaining his faith and fortitude, would have had him resent the action of God and die in despair.

If we offer sympathy at all, for God's sake let it be genuine, not the mere formal discharge of a duty never expected to be of the slightest use to the poor sufferer, who has yet to receive it with gratitude. We want it to be true and helpful compassion, not a mockery. Then we must enter into the suffering and try to deal with it as our Lord's tender and pitying Heart would do. True sympathy can hardly be simulated. An actor is easily detected, and by none so quickly as by the poor.

We must enter into the designs of God regarding our friends if we want to give real comfort. If we cannot remove the pain, let us try to show it in its true light, as a Divine purpose, wisely and kindly framed from eternity in view of their lasting happiness. Children do not understand the painful discipline through which they have to pass in order to fit them for the position their father designs for them. But we can get a fairly reasonable child of a certain age to see that as the father loves it and is kind as well as wise, it must trust him to do what is best for it. If he sets it hard tasks, or takes away what would hurt, this is because he knows what is for its good. Some day the child will *know* too; now it must *trust*. This faith in Him our Heavenly Father expects of all His children: "What I do thou knowest not now, but thou shalt know hereafter." Let us learn a lesson from our little ones and wait in trust—*to see.*

But to urge these thoughts profitably on others, they must first have taken possession of ourselves. It is only from our own overflow that we can give. The troubled heart opens to the words of comfort that spring from a deep-rooted faith, and it is cruel as well as useless to expect merely natural considerations to reach wounds for which God and His grace and His rewards are the only healing.

It may be objected that for the greater number of those who call for our sympathy, supernatural considerations would have no force. Nay, more, they would be accounted an impertinence and do more harm than good. There is some truth in this, and there is no denying the need of tact and prayer. This was no doubt the experience and the resource of St. Monica. She might surely have despaired of helping her heathen neighbours who brought into her overshadowed home the troubles of their own. Yet her charity, her discretion, and, above all, her prayer must have had their effect, for she was the refuge of all in need. Whilst listening with sympathy, she never joined in the condemnation of the absent, never betrayed a confidence, never repeated damaging words to the object of them. Only what could soothe and encourage passed her lips. Her Christian heart must have acquired a secret it might perhaps teach to ours!

XXVII

HOLY ANNA

"A widow until fourscore and four years, who departed not from the Temple, by fasting and prayers serving night and day,"—Luke 2:37.

WE wonder what this aged saint found in the Temple to sustain this long course of mortification and devotion.

It was the Second Temple, which Herod's policy had so richly adorned as to make it a rival of Solomon's. Yet it lacked those manifestations of God's presence and favour which were the glory of the First Temple. The Ark of the Covenant was not there, nor the *Shechinah*, that mysterious radiance which streamed up from the Mercy-seat. A black stone marked the place where the Ark and the Tables of the Law, the pot of manna, and Aaron's rod had in the former Temple testified to the Providence of God over His people. The gorgeous buildings, the stately ritual, the morning and evening sacrifices, the concourse from every nation under heaven at the times of the great Feasts—these, indeed, still made Jerusalem "the joy of all the earth."

But Anna had grown old amid these sights and sounds, and we know but too well the deadening influence of familiarity on what at first captivated the imagination and stirred devotion. At best these outward signs appeal mainly to the senses. What was there to inspire the steadfastness of that service to which all Jerusalem was witness? She was old for fasting, and as for prayer, we find it difficult to conceive on what a life of close intimacy with God could rest and feed before the Incarnation. Yet Scripture testifies to her continual worship in the House of God—"who departed not from the Temple."

"By fasting and prayer"—the two most arduous among the three eminent good works in the life of a Christian! And to the age of eighty-four! This was her service. We are not told of active work for others, which in these days almost monopolises the idea of service. That had doubtless found place in its day. But now, self-sacrifice, self-devotion in a severer form supplied for manual labour. "By fasting and prayer serving night and day." Nightly vigils, then, still further taxed the failing strength, and again we ask ourselves: What was there in that old Temple to sustain such devotion, such heroism of perseverance, such faith—stranger still, such love?

One thing only—Faith, Hope and Charity, for these three are one. It was Hope that burned so brightly in that aged heart as to be guarantee for the other two. She was a prophetess, and there may have been given to her as to Simeon to know that the promised "consolation of Israel" was at hand. In any case it is unlikely that souls thus brought into close contact, and akin as to their one object in life, should not have been bound together in a holy friendship and have shared their patient waiting and desire. "Simeon had received an answer from the Holy Ghost that he should not see death before he had seen the Christ of the Lord. And he came by the Spirit into the Temple. And when His parents brought in the Child Jesus ...he also took Him into his arms and blessed God."

Anna may have known of the promise to the old man and have kept near him in the hope of being a sharer in his joy. She had no promise. But God is better than His promises. He counts desires as prayers and answers them. "Now she at the same time coming in confessed to the Lord and spoke of Him to all that looked for the redemption of Israel." Thus was the fasting and prayer, the service day and night of His faithful servant rewarded.

I think of myself and of my privileges, of my helps, and of my actual service of God. To what does it amount? Does it, in this age of fulfilment of the promises, bear any proportion to that of this aged saint through the long weary years of expectation?

"Serving night and day." I think of her night watches in the precincts of that Temple, the mere shadow of what was to come, and then of myself before the Tabernacle. He is there, really and truly present, whom kings and prophets desired to see. He is willing to be with me every day in Communion if I wish. Do I meet Him at the altar rails, at the morning Mass and the evening Benediction? How will that servant of God shame me one day if my service is so inferior to her own; if my faith and hope and love in the presence of God with us bears no comparison with hers!

Let me thank my God that I have still time to make reparation for my neglect of His Real Presence so easily within my reach. Let me beg of Him that faith, hope, and charity, that frequent recourse to Him in the Sacrament of His love which may prove my grateful sense of His goodness in placing my life *now*, rather than in the time before His coming, and *here*, with His spiritual gifts all around me, rather than in those regions which have not yet heard His Name. Let me remember, too, the responsibility my privileges entail, remember that of those to whom much has been given much will be required. An acceptable way of discharging my debt, so far as may be, would be a frequent and fervent use of that chief among His gifts—Himself, and the practical endeavour to bring that Gift to the multitudes in heathen lands whom my alms to the Foreign Missions will profit.

XXVIII
ST. JOSEPH

PATRON OF THE INTERIOR LIFE

HIS office alone would be guarantee for his prerogatives and his holiness, but Scripture also bears testimony to him that he was—"a just man." Lowliness of heart, wonderful union with God, perfect conformity with the Divine will, and an absolute devotion to Jesus and Mary—these are the chief features of his spiritual beauty.

If union with God is holiness and the degree of that union is the measure of holiness, what must have been the sanctity of St. Joseph, the foster-father and daily companion of the Son of God! In his simple, upright soul there was nothing to check the continual inflow of grace from the Boy, the Youth, the Fellow-workman who shared his toil and cares and hardships for the better part of thirty years.

Think of the wonder which filled his soul when the mystery of the Incarnation was revealed to him, the awe with which he heard himself appointed the guardian and lawful superior of the Son of God on earth! With what tender reverence would he hold Him as a Babe; with what compassion have seen Him suffer; with what joy have worked at His side! We think with envy of those whom grace enables to live always in the Presence of God. This was literally St. Joseph's privilege for all those happy years. The Apostle speaks of fellowship with Christ as the acme of Christian privilege—what saint has ever approached St. Joseph here?

Just and perfect in every respect, his distinguishing characteristic, perhaps, is his self-effacement. No word of his is recorded. Angels come to him at night with orders from God. He asks no questions, raises no difficulties, rises in silence and obeys. They bring him light and consolation, or perplexity and hardship. Both are from God; both, therefore, are welcomed with joy and trust.

With Mary he seeks the Holy Child for three days, cheering her with his tender sympathy, but no word has come down to us. And when at length they find Him, Joseph stands aside to let the Mother tell their pain and make their moving remonstrance.

When the trouble was on Mary's account and a word of hers would have turned his anguish into rapturous joy, he followed her lead as usual, and both in silent agony bore their pain till God intervened with His consolation.

This waiting God's time and falling in with God's ways in patient trust, is another special characteristic of St. Joseph's holiness. Or rather, it is but the consequence and the expression of that self-effacement which to many minds is his most singular and attractive grace. He must have pleaded earnestly at Bethlehem from house to house, but there was no word of expostulation as door after door closed in his face, no touch of complaint in his sympathy with Mary. Simeon and Anna break out into praise and speak of the Child to all who are looking for the redemption of Israel. Joseph listens in silence to the aged saints; neither the future glories of the Babe nor the anguish of the Mother can unclose his lips.

Is he not fitly given to us by the Church as the Patron of the interior life, that life of familiar intercourse with God which it should be the endeavour of us all to cultivate and to deepen? He whose days were spent in constant toil for Jesus and Mary, with intervals of intimate converse with them when work was done, will help us to live more and more in their presence, to unite our thoughts and prayers with theirs, to confide to them our plans, and joys, and sorrows, to labour in their company, for the same ends and in the same spirit.

How Mary would watch the two going out to their work together, and think with unselfish joy of Joseph's happiness in the company of Jesus through the long hours of the day! How, when evening brought them home to her, she would watch at the door and bring them in to the welcome she had made ready! And how they in turn would strive to make up to her for the long absence of Him who was All in all to them both!

That sweet evening converse at Nazareth with God made Man, whose Sacred Humanity is the source of all spiritual good to men—what must this have been to those two whose pure and enlightened souls drank in His heavenly teaching, and, in such intimacy as belonged to them alone, drew from Him the secrets of His Heart!

We say it was their happiness alone. Yet we may share it, one and all. In the morning Communion and the evening Benediction we have a participation in that personal contact with Christ which did so much for Mary and Joseph. It raised them to the heights of grace and of glory to which they were predestined. It is raising us little by little to the degrees of grace and of glory to which we are called, enlightening, strengthening, making good our losses, opening out to us new fields of spiritual enterprise.

All this in our Communions Jesus does for us. All that is good for us *now* we have—a Presence as real as that which was the bliss of Nazareth, pledge of that Presence which makes the beatitude of Heaven. We crave indeed for more, and we *may* crave, for St. Teresa says it is not enough for love to know that the Beloved is in the house, if we see Him not:

> O Jesu, Whom by faith I now descry,
> Shrouded from mortal eye,
> When wilt Thou slake the thirsting of my heart
> To see Thee as Thou art,
> Face unto face in all Thy glad array,
> Tranced with the glory of that everlasting day?

We gaze upon the Monstrance singing wistfully: "*Nobis donet in Patria.*" "*Praestet fides supplementum sensuum defectui.*" Faith and Hope have no place in Heaven. Here on earth they must do their work and earn the Beatific Vision which is to come.

It must have been hard for St. Joseph to exchange Nazareth for Limbo. Or, rather, it would have been hard, had the will of God ever seemed hard to him. But he had no desires beyond that blessed will. He did not ask to see the years of the public life, nor to stand by Mary in her desolation that was to come.

Till his strength failed him he worked by the side of his foster Son. Then, when the call came, he quietly laid his tools aside, and with his head on the breast of Jesus, and his hands clasped in Mary's, gave up his soul to God.

And when for us the time for labour is past and the rest of evening comes, how fitly may we who have sought St. Joseph's help in life turn to him in the hour of our death. In all our cares and troubles the Church bids us "Go to Joseph." But more than ever would she have us commend ourselves to him at our last hour, that with Jesus and Mary he may be there to protect and comfort us:

> "Jesus, Mary, and Joseph, I give you my heart and my soul.
> Jesus, Mary, and Joseph, assist me in my last agony.
> Jesus, Mary, and Joseph, may I breathe forth my soul in peace in your blessed company!"

XXIX

THE ANNUNCIATION

"Be still and see that I am God!"—Ps. 45:11.

EVERY workman needs certain conditions for carrying on his task—the writer, quiet; the architect, space; the photographer, a special arrangement of light; an artisan, the tools proper to his trade. The Divine Worker also has His conditions. He, too, works in silence and repose. His designs are from eternity and the steps of their development are slow. Four thousand years between the promise of the Incarnation in Eden, and its realisation that midnight at Nazareth. No haste even to bring a Redeemer to the world! No haste though He was so sorely needed, and patriarchs and prophets were sighing for Him, and kings desired to see His day, and generation after generation lived and died in expectation. Forty centuries of waiting and still no quickening of His step, though every soul of the millions that peopled and re-peopled the earth was yearned over with all the intensity of the Creator's love!

At length, when the whole world was in peace, when all things were in quiet silence and night was in the midst of her course—He came! Softly as the dew falling on the flower, as the bud opening at night—He came!

How unlike are His ways to ours! A new idea flashes upon us, and with feverish haste we fall upon it to give it shape and consistency. Why this vehemence and impatience? Perhaps because we create nothing. The conceptions we dignify by the name of creations are but borrowed plumes, sense impressions in new combinations. In the Divine Mind all types are from eternity; their visible embodiment adds nothing to the Creator's knowledge or power. His will works silently because of its resistless might. There is no disquiet at opposition, no uncertainty as to results. We are finite and therefore restless and precipitate, vehement and fitful, easily disturbed and cast down. The Divine Worker would have us stand by Him and watch—and copy in our finite way. "*Vacate et videte:* Be still and see that I am God" and that I work as God. Noiselessly, wheels within wheels, the complex machinery of Nature moves. In peace are carried forward the operations of Grace. "The Lord is not in the earthquake, the Lord is not in the fire." "When all things were in quiet silence Thy Almighty Word came down from Heaven."

Mary's close union with God maintained her soul in a perpetual peace. An angel's visit does not affect her recollection; his praise troubles but does not disturb her. The serenity and self-possession with which she treats of the Incarnation are so wonderful as to make sceptics pronounce the whole account incredible. That a Jewish maiden, sharing the expectation of her whole nation as to the immediate coming of the Messiah, should have weighed with such calm deliberation the announcement made to her, appears to them impossible.

But she whom an archangel saluted was "full of grace." We are distinctly told that he was sent to her "from God." His reverently worded message, his glorious praise were dictated by God Himself.

"Hail, full of grace!" He does not call her by her name. Not what she is in the eyes of men, but what she is before God, he notes. And God can trust her with the knowledge of what she is in His sight. He who saw Satan fall from heaven, dazzled by the contemplation of his own excellence, could count on Mary. The Most High could trust the humility of His handmaid.

In her reply to the angel there was no faintest breath of elation, no leaping up of gratitude to accept the proffered dignity, but a singleness of purpose that looked to one thing only—the Divine will. At the critical moment of her own and of the world's history, this girl of fourteen showed herself eminently the "Virgin most prudent." With perfect calmness she put the questions that were to determine her answer—loyal questions with one only intent—to discover the will of God. Once satisfied as to this, her reply was ready: "Behold the handmaid of the Lord, be it done to me according to thy word." And the angel departed from her.

"*Et Verbum Caro factum est et habitavit in nobis.* And the Word was made Flesh and dwelt amongst us."

All had passed swiftly, and in peace the Prince of Peace had come. Simple abandonment to the good pleasure of God is the lesson Mary gives us in the Annunciation. We often hear people say: "If I had my way he or she should do this or that." If we would only let God's way be the keynote of our lives, then might some measure of Mary's bliss be ours.

> He came all so still
>   To His Mother's bower,
> As dew in April
>   That falleth on the flower.

The Annunciation

Mother and Maiden
  Was never none but she;
Well might such a Lady
  God's Mother be.

　　　　　ANONYMOUS (*Fifteenth Century Carol*).

XXX

THE HIDDEN LIFE—I

"I am the Way."—John 14:6.

LENT follows quickly upon Christmas time, and we have to content ourselves with little more than the bare mention of the mysteries of the Sacred Infancy before we have to turn to those of the Passion.

Yet the years of the life at Nazareth are in some respects the most wonderful as well as the most helpful subject for study and imitation. We all of us live two lives—one in our own family or environment, before the world, so far as we enter into its activities; the other in the secret sphere of our own souls. This latter, by far the more important, is concerned with our mental and spiritual acts and experiences, our thoughts, aspirations, motives, sympathies and affections, fears and falls, joys and trials—all that subtle crossing and recrossing of influences which make up the warp and woof of our inner life.

The habitual action of our will upon this material forms the impression we call character. It shapes our principles, those springs of action which determine the direction of our choice in the various circumstances of our lives, and in the last issue, the final choice, decide our lot in eternity. Upon our will, then, guided by the understanding which furnishes it with light, all depends. But where is our poor darkened understanding to get the needed light? Surely from Him who is the Way, the Truth, and the Life. His example is our Way; His teaching the Truth we may safely trust; His Life, the Life of our life.

St. Bernard says that as it would have been useless to us to know the way to our country had we been kept in prison, so it would avail us nothing to have been set free had we been left in ignorance of the way thither. Had our Lord been content to redeem us by the sufferings of one day, how should we, without the example of His Life, have been able to find the road to the Kingdom of Heaven and the Home He has prepared for us? It is a long journey and a difficult one, lifelong and hazardous. Sin has spoilt God's plan for us, and sin is a fact, not only at the fountain-head of the race, but in the life of every one of us, with one single exception. It has started us on our homeward journey heavily handicapped. There is the inheritance of original sin—darkness in the intellect, weakness in the will—and later there are the disastrous consequences of our own actual sin. The road is indeed opened to us by the Death of our Lord, but it is beset with dangers from a relentless foe ever lying in wait for us, from our relations with our fellow-travellers, and, most of all, from our own treacherous selves.

But He who comes amongst us to be all in all to us meets our need. "I am the Way." He has given, not only His Death to redeem us, but His Life to teach, and comfort, and strengthen us. He has set before our eyes a divinely perfect Life, yet one we can all in our measure follow. Its every detail was deliberately chosen with a view to our individual welfare. Because a toiler's lot would be that of the greater part of mankind, He chose it for Himself, that He might sanctify labour and the humblest home. Could we have imagined condescension such as this? That the Creator of innumerable worlds should kneel in prayer morning and night as we do; work as a village carpenter; be subject to His parents and His employers, and as a poor man, patiently earn His daily bread, to teach us by His example how to discharge the duties of our state, to God, our neighbour, and ourselves—who could have dreamt that love even Divine could go thus far!

But alas! there is something more wonderful still—that this Divine love and example should be a matter of complete indifference to so many who call themselves His followers. How many of us can honestly say that we set His Life before us as the Model on which to frame our own? "I am the Way," He says: "Put your feet on this track and it shall surely lead you to your Home." From start to finish, His Life and example are to be our instruction, our comfort, our support. And of the three and thirty years by far the larger portion was given to the Hidden Life. This is the mould in which the inner life of all His followers must be cast, to be fruitful for God and for eternity. The busiest statesman, lawyer, or doctor needs it as much as the missioner or the recluse if the daily work, intercourse with and influence on others is to be turned to good account.

We wonder, perhaps, that in view of its importance we are not told more of the Hidden Life. Beyond the words, "He went down to Nazareth and was subject to them," and another word, dropped, as it were, casually, that He followed a carpenter's trade, we know nothing of the secrets of that long period. One reason must surely be that it was decreed in the Divine counsels to be hidden, as best and most helpful for us. Would it have been hidden and be to us all that it is, had all been revealed that we should like to know? Moreover, seeing how little interest the vast majority of His followers show in learning the details of the stirring Public Life, would they have thought it worth their while to study the uneventful years of a joiner's career?

But there is a deeper reason, we may be sure. The Hidden God loves to be sought, and found even in His hiding-place by those who love Him. Through the chinks of the cottage at Nazareth and of Joseph's workshop hard by, His saints of all time have seen what has fired them with admiration and won their hearts irrevocably to Him.

We are meant to use our minds in meditating on the Gospels; to infer from what we know, what must have been. St. John, from his intimate converse with our Lady during so many years, could have written volumes on the Hidden Life, but he is content to leave us for meditation the few words of St. Luke that "Jesus advanced in wisdom and age and grace with God and men."

We know something of the life of the poor, and can give a tolerably good guess at what a village joiner's life of to-day will be. If we subtract from this whatever makes for comfort and convenience, all the devices for minimising toil, for securing aid in times of trouble, for bringing relaxation and some degree of enjoyment into the hardest life, we can arrive at some imperfect idea of the hardships which were the daily lot of the Son of God during thirty years.

Again: "the child is father to the man." If we would know the attitude of our Lord's mind towards that hard life of His; His ways with those among whom He lived and worked; the ponderings of His Heart during His hours of lonely toil; the refreshment He found in the society of those who knew and loved Him, we have only to turn to the incidents in the Public Life which show Him to us in the same circumstances. Oh yes, where there's a will there's a way! The last little house in the despised hamlet He made His home has discovered its mysteries over and over again *to those who cared to know them.*

Take an example from the Public Life.

A Pharisee comes to our Lord at night. He is feeling the stirrings of grace and his will is beginning to be moved. "Here is a man," he says, "who corresponds wonderfully to the description of the Messias drawn by the Prophets. He comes at the right time when all the world is in expectation. He is born at the right place. He is poor and has been in labours from His youth. He speaks as no man before has ever spoken. He is showing signs and wonders; has certainly changed water into wine; has dared to denounce the scandals in the Temple, and driven out the buyers and sellers. No man could do these things unless God were with him. What if He should be the Christ! The people acclaim Him as such, but the people have run after impostors before now. And then, He comes from Nazareth. Some of the doctors are being won over to Him. But this is a matter too important for anything but personal investigation. An interview would be conclusive. I will arrange it, but cautiously. It must not be known that a man of standing in the city has sought counsel from this teacher without credentials. I will go to him by night." And he goes....Our Lord is tired. He has been teaching all day. He knows His visitor is afraid of being seen, that a patient hearing and a long conversation will have no immediate result. Yet He receives him kindly, makes no allusion to the unseasonable hour, follows his lead, answers his difficulties, and leaves time and grace to do the rest.

Or take another scene from the Public Life later on, when the people "flocked to Him from all sides."

In a room packed to the entrance, "Pharisees and doctors of the law sitting by that were come out of every town of Galilee and Judea and Jerusalem," He is teaching. Suddenly a noise on the roof attracts attention. An opening is being forced. The audience, disturbed and indignant as tiles and chips begin to fall, call out to the intruders above to desist. And He? Stops His instruction; looks up, and with a welcoming smile reassures the indiscreet friends and the poor trembling passenger; makes a sign to those around to give place; stands; steadies the bed as it comes down, and straightway, with loving words, absolves the sick man from his sins; and sends him home, laden with his bed, hale and rejoicing before them all.

Now, can anyone say that these scenes throw no light upon the Hidden Life, upon the thoughts and desires, the character and the plans of "Jesus, yesterday and to-day, and the same for ever," as He worked alone at Nazareth those many years? Were not His toil and serious thoughts broken in upon many a time by some rough neighbour, requiring instant attention to a broken cart or stool? Had He not to deal again and again with the selfish, the cruel, who, relying on His need, grudged Him the modest pay He asked for His services? Does not the Public Life supply the chinks in the walls of the cottage and the workshop of Nazareth through which we may study Him and copy into our own lives what we see?

We mark Joseph's apprentice listening to instructions as to the handling of the clumsy tools, learning by experimental knowledge what by His infused knowledge He already knew, the use of the plane and the saw. We note the uplifted eye, the moving lips when Joseph was gone and none were there to see; the sweat wiped from the brow at noon; the slinging of the basket over His shoulder at eventide when the day's work was done; the sweet words to His Mother as He handed to her the few coins which must serve them for the week.

These are not pious fictions but inferences drawn from the very nature of things, things *that must have been.*

How monotonous His daily life must have seemed to Jesus in the workshop of Nazareth! Yet He put His Heart into it—His dear Heart. And loved it because it was lowly. And loved it because it was distasteful. And loved it because it was His Father's will. And loved it—*for the love of us."*

Yes, it was all for us, all *for me.* He loved me and delivered Himself to this year after year for me. How have I repaid Him? How have I profited? How am I going to profit now? In proportion as we strive to conform our own life to His, we shall find our trying circumstances eased, the monotony of our daily toil brightened, the sense of loneliness relieved by the charm of that divinely human companionship. We are tired—so was He. We suffer from the weather, from misunderstandings and disappointments, from the ill-will of those who dislike us, from the selfishness or the mistakes of our friends. All these things were pain to Him. And He bore them meekly, joyously even, because He could thus glorify His Father and help us who were to come after Him and learn of Him. We are told expressly that "for the joy set before Him He endured the Cross." The joy to which He looked forward, the reward He promised Himself, was the help His example was to be, long years later—*to me!* Should I not have worked patiently by His side if, looking up now and again, I had seen the beads of perspiration on His brow? Have supported the weariness of my daily task as I watched Him mending day after day the rude furniture of the village folk? Would not a hasty word have been checked, a little humiliation have been generously borne as I saw Him listening patiently to the complaints of His customers, or holding out His hand for His pay? And could I not have borne my little share of the cross had I met Him laden with His? We are told of one of the saints that our Lord taught her to bear up against trouble great or small by compassionating the same or a like suffering in Him instead of wasting her pity on herself. Let us learn the same lesson; it takes the sting out of a wound.

"I confess to Thee, O Father, Lord of Heaven and earth, because Thou hast hidden these things from the wise and prudent and hast revealed them unto babes. Yea, Father, for so hath it seemed good in Thy sight." It is not to the wise of this world, but to the simple and the childlike, that the Divine Life, and more especially the years of the Hidden Life, yield their treasures. St. Bonaventure, indeed, was a Doctor of the Church, but he had the heart of a child when he went in spirit with the

Holy Family into Egypt and accepted their invitation to return in their company. So in our own days. A millhand writes: "I wash the dishes and pass them on to our Lady to be dried. When I clean the pans or scrub the floor, I do it by her side. And when the day's work is nearly done, and St. Joseph comes in from his shop, I make myself tidy and sit down with the Holy Family to tea!"

A helpful way of quickening the faith, hope, and charity with which we should desire to welcome our Lord each time He comes to us in Holy Communion, is to read overnight some incident of His Life in the Gospel, and approach Him next morning as did the leper, the cripple, the blind man, the heartbroken mother or sisters, with their prayer for help upon our lips. His merciful glance is turned now *on us*. His Almighty Power is to be used in our behalf. He Himself is coming, tender and merciful always, Jesus, yesterday, to-day and the same for ever. This practice, useful, above all, for frequent communicants, saves us from the danger of routine. By getting to know our Lord better and better, we come to love Him more. By noticing how He dealt with the various needs of those about Him, we not only learn His divinely beautiful character, but grow continually in His likeness, and thus realise in ourselves the meaning of His words: "I am the Way."

XXXI

THE HIDDEN LIFE—II

"Your life is hidden with Christ in God"—Col. 3:3.

THIS living in the sense of a Divine companionship supposes a preparation. It does not come naturally to any of us, for it implies study, effort, prayer, co-operation with grace. But its fruit is—Sanctity. We see the preparation in the lives of all the saints, its fruit in the goal they reached. And in few, perhaps, are preparation and fruit more clearly shown than in the life and teaching of Brother Lawrence of the Resurrection,[1] who gives us the comforting assurance that "everyone, some more and some less," may use the means and attain the end.

What chiefly characterised this holy lay brother was his unalterable peace of soul. Places and circumstances, the frets and worries of daily life had no power to disturb its serenity. In church, in the midst of business—he was cook in a large monastery—he was always the same, nothing distracted nor disturbed him. To those who would draw from him the secret of this stability of soul, his answer was always the same: that he had set out upon the spiritual life with the firm resolve to foster in his heart the sense of the Presence of God. Therein he had continued steadfastly, glorifying God and showing his love to Him by all means in his power. In all he undertook he entreated the aid of

---

[1] Nicholas Herman of Lorraine (1611-1691), after being a soldier and a footman, admitted a lay-brother among the barefooted Carmelites at Paris.—*Spiritual Maxims of Brother Lawrence.* Catholic Truth Society.

God, giving Him thanks when he had performed the work, confessing his negligences and trustfully asking pardon.

The benefits of this practice, he maintained, are priceless. Faith grows more lively in all the events of life, particularly when we feel our need, since it obtains for us the help of God's grace in every time of trial. The soul by a simple remembrance of God sees and feels Him present, and calls upon Him freely and with assurance of response. By faith, it would seem, the soul draws very near to the state of the Blessed until at last it can almost say: Faith is swallowed up in sight, *I see and I experience.*

He acknowledged that to arrive at this state is somewhat hard at the outset, for we must act purely in faith, and must mortify the senses, but pursued faithfully, this communion with God, interwoven with one's daily labour, works in the soul most marvellous effects. So far is it from being a hindrance in a busy life, that the good brother testified he did his work with the greater ease and was much aided therein.

For me," he said, "the time of action does not differ from the time of prayer, and in the noise and clatter of my kitchen, while several persons are calling for as many different things, I possess God with as great tranquillity as when upon my knees before the Blessed Sacrament. In the way of God, thoughts count for little, love is everything. Nor is it needful that we should have great things to do; we can do little things for God. I turn the cake that is frying in the pan for the love of God, or pick up a straw from the ground for His love."

When asked by what means one can attain to this habitual sense of the Presence of God, he answered:

"We search for stated methods of learning how to love God and attaining to a sense of His Presence. And yet it is so simple—to raise our mind to Him as our God and Father in the midst of business, meals, etc., taking care as we are *always with God* to do nothing, say nothing and think of nothing, at least wilfully, which may displease Him....Before taking up any task, to look to God, be it only for a moment, as also when you are engaged thereon, and when you have performed the same. And because without time and great patience this practice cannot be attained, be not disheartened at your many falls; truly this habit can only be formed with difficulty, yet when it is formed, how great will be your joy therein!...Those who set out upon this practice of a *gaze* on God, should offer up in secret a few words such as: 'My God and my All.' 'Jesus, my God, I love Thee above all things.' 'O my God; teach me to love Thee.'"

"To be with God there is no need to be in church. He is everywhere, in our heart, asking us to give Him a little remembrance from time to time—a little act of adoration, of thanksgiving for His goodness to us, of sorrow for our sins, of resignation in our troubles, offering our work to Him, our fatigues. By this practice we come to have a holy familiarity with God, ease in conversing with Him, protection in danger, and in temptation, succour in our needs and in our work....If our mind wanders from God, we must quietly bring it back when we remember....

"Think often of God," he would say, "by day, by night, in your business, and even in your diversions. He is always near you, leave Him not alone....We must *know* before we can *love*. In order to know God, we must often think of Him; and when we come to love Him we shall also think of Him often, for our heart will be with our treasure. Ponder over this often, ponder it well. The practice of *the Presence of God is the schooling of the soul to find its joy in His Divine Companionship* at all times, in temptation and tribulation, in dryness of soul and disrelish of God, yes, and even when we fall into unfaithfulness and actual sin.... God seems so to delight in this communion, that on the soul which would fain abide ever with Him He bestows favours past numbering; and as if He dreaded lest the soul should turn again to things of earth, He provides for it abundantly, beyond its utmost thought and desire."

All the virtues of this holy brother sprang from the same source. He was assured that God would never deceive, never fail him, and would send such things only as were for his good, forasmuch as he on his part was resolved never to grieve Him, but to do and suffer all for His love. Instead of watching his dispositions or stopping to test the way in which he walked, he fixed his gaze on God alone, the goal of his race, and sped along towards Him by daily acts of confidence and love. He set himself to *do*, rather than *to reflect* on what to do.

After he had received the Last Sacraments, a brother asked him if he were in peace and what his mind was busied with. This was the reply: "I am doing what I shall do through all eternity—blessing God, praising God, adoring God, giving Him the love of my whole heart. It is our *one business*, my brethren, *to worship Him and love Him*, without thought of anything else."

Can we do better than follow in the footsteps of Brother Lawrence and respond to the invitation of God Himself: "Walk before Me and be perfect"?

THE PUBLIC LIFE

XXXII

THE PUBLIC LIFE

"God resisteth the proud, but giveth grace to the humble."
—James 4:6.

BEARING in mind the wonders our Lord wrought during the three years of His Public Ministry, and the way in which the whole country was stirred, it must have been all but impossible, one would think, to resist the general enthusiasm.

"Multitudes,"..."very great multitudes," are the only words the Evangelists can find to describe the concourse in the midst of which His days were spent. "The whole city went out to meet Him....All the city was gathered together at the door....There came to Him great multitudes, having with them the dumb, the blind, the maimed, and many others...all sick people that were taken with divers diseases and torments, possessed by devils...and lunatics...and they cast them down at His feet and He healed them."

"Running through the whole country, they began to carry about in beds those that were sick where they heard He was. And whithersoever He entered into towns or into villages, they laid the sick in the streets and besought Him that they might touch but the hem of His garment, and as many as touched Him were made whole...the blind seeing, the lame walking, the deaf hearing, the dead rising again....He sat in a boat and all the multitude stood on the shore....Great multitudes stood about Him, so that they trod one upon another....He could not openly go into the city, but was without in desert places, and they flocked to Him from all sides."

How could any remain cold amid such ardour? How could He have enemies, and so many, and so bitter?

The people, we are told, were in admiration, "for He was teaching them as one having power, *and not as their scribes and Pharisees.*" Here is the secret of the opposition He met with from the ruling classes of Jerusalem. They were being thrown into the shade and "they found fault," says St. Mark. Any influence of theirs had a very different basis. Reverence for the teachers of the law was traditional among the Jews, and on this regard, conveniently independent of personal qualities, their rulers traded. But here was a teacher revered and loved for Himself, One who in every respect stood out in marked contrast to the scribes and Pharisees; whose doctrine and parables the poor and simple could understand; who understood *them*, was at home with them, and showed a tender, individual interest in each and all. One, moreover, who not only shared their sorrows by sympathy, but by His touch or His word cured the foulest diseases and brought brightness into the most desolate hearts and homes.

Among Jews and Gentiles, rich and poor, old and young, He was to be found, day after day, teaching unweariedly, laying His hands on the heads of the little ones, the eyes of the blind, the sores of the lepers, wherever their healing touch was needed; in answer to a word of entreaty: "Lord, come down before that my son die!" "Lord, if Thou wilt Thou canst make me clean," and—where there was no prayer—at the bidding of His own merciful Heart: "Wilt thou be made whole?" "Arise and walk." "Young man, I say to thee arise!" "Woman, thou art delivered from thy infirmity."

Nor was He less tender in dealing with the needs of the soul. For the irresolute, the frail, the sinner, there was the same gentle compassion: "Be of good heart, son, thy sins are forgiven thee." "Hath no man condemned thee? Neither will I condemn thee. Go, and now sin no more." "Thy faith hath made thee safe, go in peace." What wonder all hearts went out to Him!

Seated on the brow of a hill, we might have seen Him teaching. By His side, His disciples, some standing, others sitting at His feet. Pressing close around Him, on the slopes, and as far as the eye could reach, a multitude rippling forward like the oncoming tide, one thought in every mind—to get near Him, to see Him, to hear His voice, to rest their souls on Him, every man, woman, and child in that vast throng, from the aged labourer toiling up the steep to the babe crooning contentedly in its mother's arms, notabilities of Jerusalem, the wives of Galilean fishermen, enthusiasts, stoics, the upright, the cavillers, all dimly conscious of an ideal suddenly realised, a Supreme Good found.

What is the secret of this fascination? Not merely the blended majesty and gentleness that characterised His every look and word and gesture. Still less the self-interest of His hearers that hoped to profit by His wonder-working power. It was the attraction of a Divine Personality, "the glory of God in the Face of Christ Jesus."[1] "the glory...of the only-begotten of the Father, full of grace and truth."[2] Here, in their source, were all the forces that subdue and

---

1 2 Cor. 4:6.   2   John 1:14.

win, Nature and Grace at their highest. He is not perfect, but Perfection, the Ideal whence all have borrowed whatever conceptions of beauty or harmony, majesty or tenderness they possess. Created in the image and likeness of God, each soul in that vast throng represents an ideal in the Mind of God. What wonder if in His Presence without whom nothing was made that was made, the souls of all should leap up in instinctive, if unconscious, recognition of a Divine Prototype!

God must ever be the lodestone of the human soul, an attraction which constitutes its eternal happiness—or misery: "Come, blessed of My Father....Depart from Me, you cursed!" For even in everlasting banishment from Him, its initial impulse remains. It blasphemes, and it yearns; blasphemes, and yearns again. By the irresistible gravitation which is the law of its being, every soul in the next life is impelled towards God. How terrible, then, the perversity that during its time of probation diverts a soul from its Divine objective and substitutes itself as its centre and end!

This was the sin of the Pharisees and other enemies of our Lord. Pride and envy led them to resent, as an injury to themselves, the devotion of the people to His sacred Person. At variance on every other point, Pharisees, Sadducees, and Herodians combined to denounce Him as a transgressor of the Law, or to "catch Him in His speech" that they might accuse Him. After a discourse or a cure that had aroused more than the usual admiration, we find them "meeting immediately" to consider how to nullify its effect upon the people by discrediting His teaching or explaining away the miracle. It was this wilful blindness and depravity that drew down upon them His most terrible denunciations: "Woe to you scribes and Pharisees, blind guides, whited sepulchres, serpents, hypocrites." Hypocrisy was of all their crimes the one on which His heaviest indignation fell. Himself the Truth, to whom falsehood and guile are an abomination, He exposed these wolves in sheep's clothing with a ruthlessness that must have astonished and awed the crowds.

Resisting the known truth is one of the six sins against the Holy Ghost. It often includes or prepares the way for the other five, and, hardening the heart, closes the channels by which grace might enter and save. These blind guides asked for signs. How did they profit when signs were given—nay, were thrust upon them? At His first word in the Garden those who came to seize Him fell prostrate at His feet. When darkness at midday covered Calvary, and the earth rocked beneath the Cross, chief priests with scribes and ancients made their way up to it to mock and revile Him who hung thereon. The people whom they had seduced, "all the multitude that were come together to that sight, and saw the things that were done, returned, striking their breasts." The Roman centurion cried: "Indeed this Man was the Son of God!" The veil of the Temple was rent; saints rose from the dead and appeared to many; the guards at the Sepulchre were the first to proclaim the Resurrection. And to the overwhelming evidence of these signs, the rulers remained insensible. Well might St. Stephen, before the high priest and his council, sum up their offences in the charge: "You always resist the Holy Ghost."

God resists the proud but gives His grace to the humble. Sinners were not afraid of our Blessed Lord.

His holiness, so far from scaring, attracted them. And so tenderly did He receive them that He was taunted with being the Friend of publicans and sinners. Where He found humility and goodwill, He was ready to go any lengths to meet and save a soul. The woman He met at Jacob's well was hardly one likely to attract Him, so we might have thought. Yet with what patience He seeks, with what tact He approaches her, turning to account her national prejudices, her wonder and curiosity, till He brings her to confession and repentance.

"Give Me to drink," He says, begging a service of her, the surest way of exciting her interest and astonishment, for it is a Jew who asks a favour of a Samaritan. Then, forgetting the bodily thirst which had served Him as a pretext for addressing her, He goes on to speak of the living water He has to give, and in words so earnest and attractive that she responds at once: "Sir, give me this water that I may not thirst." "Go," He says, "bring thy husband and come hither." The gentle admonition strikes home and draws from her the story of her life, with the recognition of the Prophet who knew all before she told it. He does not hurry her. When, profiting by such an occasion, she opens up the famous controversy between her schismatic nation and the people of God, He follows her lead, and brings her at last to an act of faith and trust in the Messias who is coming "to tell us all things." Her hour of grace has come: He who hides these things from the wise and prudent, reveals Himself to the heart which through all its wanderings has been waiting to learn of Him.

We are not told of her astonishment and joy and adoration. But that she went her way into the city to preach Him, to win souls to Him, to bring her conquests to His feet: "Come and see a man who has told me all things whatsoever I have done. Is not He the Christ?" How swift is the work of grace in an eager soul: He sought a sinner, He has found an apostle!

With Magdalen, His apostle to the Apostles, with Zaccheus, and Peter, and Thomas, and Paul it was the same. He condescended to the need of each, because of the ignorance or the goodwill underlying even resistance to Him. It is only insincerity and self-seeking in our dealings with Him that we have to fear. If, following the impulse given to the soul at its creation, we seek Him honestly during life, we shall find Him, and our happiness in Him, throughout eternity. "But if," says à Kempis, "thou seek thyself, thou wilt indeed find thyself, but to thy own ruin, for a man does himself more harm if he seek not Jesus, than the whole world and all his enemies could do him."

XXXIII
FELLOWSHIP—I

(SEPTUAGESIMA)

"Jesus Christ, yesterday..."

WHETHER Lent is early or late, it always seems to come upon us suddenly, as a season out of season, as if the Church were taking unfair advantage of us, as if we should have been duly warned and allowed time for preparation. But, as usual, it is not the Church that is to blame. "Preparation?" she says. "By all means," and she grants us a fortnight's grace to prepare. The first words in the Introit for Septuagesima Sunday mark sharply enough the transition from the major to the minor key which for nine weeks is to prevail throughout her Office: "The groans of death surrounded me, and in my affliction I called upon the Lord and He heard my voice... the Lord is my firmament, and my refuge, and my deliverer."

Our dear Lord and Master is very frank with us. He tells us plainly on what condition He accepts us as His disciples—that it is to be a fellowship of toil and suffering here and of glory and happiness hereafter. The compact is binding on all who offer themselves for His service. Where He leads they must be ready to follow: "where I am there shall My minister be."

For themselves and for those they loved, the Twelve accepted His terms. St. Thomas spoke the mind of them all when He said: "Let us go and die with Him." And at the Last Supper one and all protested with Peter their readiness to follow Him to prison and to death. A few hours later they learnt their own frailty; courage failed, but not love; and no sooner were they strengthened by the coming of the Holy Spirit, than they preached Him boldly and rejoiced when they were accounted worthy to suffer for His Name.

This stern lesson they impressed on the early Church, but with the promise that sustained it through three centuries of fiery trial: "If you partake of the sufferings of Christ rejoice, that when His glory shall be revealed you may also be glad with exceeding joy."[1] Through all the centuries that have followed, it was this conviction and this promise that secured the steadfastness of missionaries and martyrs, of the multitudes of men and women serving God in busy cities, among barbarous races, in the solitude of the desert or of the cloister; one and all could say with the great Apostle: "that I may know Him...and the fellowship of His sufferings...I fill up those things that are wanting of the sufferings of Christ in my flesh for His body which is the Church."[2]

It was reserved for the reformers of the sixteenth century to break this tradition of fellowship, to discover that the sorrows of the Head dispensed the members from sharing them, that to presume to do so and to allow anything to have been "wanting of the sufferings of Christ" was to deny the all-sufficiency of His merits; therefore confession, fasting and abstinence, the celibacy of the clergy, religious vows—all the penitential discipline of the Church was a superstition for which a purer faith and practice must be substituted.

---

1 Peter 4:13.   2 Philip 3:10; Col. 1:24.

By their fruits you shall know them, said our Master. We need look no farther than our own land at the present day to see these Dead Sea fruits reaching maturity.

One Church alone has preserved in its integrity the original conception of Christ, of His Personality, His doctrine, and the conditions of fellowship with Him. In the saints of the Catholic Church alone, therefore, do we find in its fulness that familiar friendship with Christ which *is* Sanctity. In their lives we come to know our Lord as His Apostles and friends knew Him when He "came in and went out amongst them," as He would have His memory and His teaching handed down to those who through their word were to believe in Him. In the multitudinous sects which have broken away from her communion, there is no such tradition—it is a distorted Christ that they set before men, and an utterly different teaching as to fellowship with Him that they would have accepted. What wonder that such a travesty of the truth should have little power to constrain worship or love, still less to rouse the enthusiasm that buds forth in holiness!

Nothing short of a strong, personal love of Christ, self-immolating, all-absorbing, is able to make a saint. And how is this love created and fostered? By the same means that enlightened and enkindled the first faithful—means supernatural and natural. There was the working of the Holy Spirit in each and all, and there was the knowledge of the Master as transmitted by faith and prayerful study. Hence it was the true Jesus of the Gospel story.

"*This Jesus, as you have seen Him* going up into heaven shall so come," said the angels to the Apostles on Olivet, as with longing eyes they followed Him till a cloud received

Him out of their sight. "As you have seen Him," that is, as He has been known by you in daily intercourse during three years, with the charm of Person, voice, and gesture, with His characteristic words and ways, so shall He come again. When every eye shall see Him, it will be this Jesus, yesterday, to-day, and the same for ever.

Do we envy those who lived in His day and owned Him as Master and Friend? Why should we? He is as attractive now as then. The centuries that separate us from Him are filled with those to whom He has been all in all. Like us they had not seen nor heard Him, but, partly by natural, partly by supernatural means, by the action of grace and by their own endeavour, they had come to know Him, and His love had become the ruling passion of their souls. We know, perhaps by experience, how a casual acquaintance can ripen into a friendship which makes all the difference in our lives. How did it ripen? By the discovery in the stranger of qualities which gradually won our esteem, our affection, and our confidence, and by realising that we in our turn were valued and our society and sympathy prized. Visits and mutual service became more frequent, our reliance on each other stronger, till at last our friend became a part of ourselves, bound up with every joy, sorrow, and experience of our lives.

So have the friends of Jesus been drawn into intimacy with Him, His grace led them on, and they responded to His invitation. They studied Him in the Gospels. They stood by Him at Naim and walked by Him in the cornfields; saw Him fondling the little children, watched Him coming across the waves in the stormy night, followed Him everywhere with the crowd, and into the homes of

His friends. His character and His ways, what attracted and what repelled Him, His dealings with the poor, the afflicted and the outcast, how He would have dealt with themselves and met their timid desires to follow Him—all this they knew, and the knowledge was the foundation of their love. In His saints of all ages, nationalities, and temperaments, we find this intimate acquaintance with our Lord and Master. They "knew Him by heart." And in the revelations of the mystics among them, we note with delight that it is "this Jesus" of the Gospels whom they present to us, with the same characteristics that marked His intercourse with His friends on earth.

Outside the Catholic Church there is no such living memory of Him. Excepting the visions of Stephen before the Council, of Saul on the road to Damascus, and the mysterious glimpses of Him which St. John gives us in the Apocalypse, we lose sight of our Lord after the Ascension. With the Acts of the Apostles His familiarity with His "brethren" here on earth comes to an end. So those would have us believe who admit no continuity of tradition between the early Church, the Church of the Catacombs, of the Middle Ages, and the Church of all ages. But the children of this Church know that He who by His Sacramental Presence is with her all days even to the consummation of the world, has, right through the nineteen centuries of her existence, been in closest touch with them, not only by the Eucharistic union, but by a real though hidden intimacy with chosen souls, brought to light now and again, and never more in evidence than in our own time. In every age our Lord has had His beloved disciples, and His friendships are marked by the same characteristics as those of old.

He who loved to call Himself the Son of Man nowhere shows Himself more human than in His friendships. The Gospels bear continual testimony to the levelling down of distinctions, the share and share alike which was the law of the Apostolic company. They show us the value He set on sympathy; the fellow-feeling with which He entered into the troubles of His friends; His sensitiveness when they were attacked; the trust with which He confided to them His sorrows, and in the labours of His Ministry looked to them for co-operation and sacrifice.

Weary after a day of teaching and healing in Jerusalem, He would seek a shelter as evening fell, and—since none in the city dared to brave the animosity of His enemies by offering Him hospitality—take the road over Olivet to Bethany. Mark the smile on the tired Face as He sees the sisters watching His approach, His appreciation of the characteristic way in which each makes Him welcome.

An attentive reader of the Gospels must be struck—like the writer of a discreet and helpful booklet[1]—with "the very great respect and tenderness with which our Lord treated women when He was on earth. He sought their society, He chose to have them with Him as He moved about from place to place; He often held them up as examples; and there are few things more touching than that He sought, during the last sad week of His life on earth, the comfort of woman's sympathy in the home at Bethany."

Yes, but why no mention here of her whose close association with Him on Calvary can hardly have been

---

[1] *The Wild Sweet-Briery Fence: Some Thoughts for Girls.* Anonymous. S.P.C.K.

overlooked by the student of "our Lord's last sad week on earth"! Of her who stood by His Cross to the last, for whom, even in His death agony, He provided with filial care! O Mother of God, why should Mary of Bethany alone be remembered by so many who love thy Son!

> For what did Jesus love on earth
> One half so tenderly as thee!

On the morning of the Resurrection our Lord's first thoughts were for the women who had been faithful to Him even unto death. His first joy was to turn their sorrow into rapture by making them sharers in His triumph as they had been in His anguish and His shame.

And these predilections of His, these revelations of His Heart are not merely a beautiful history past and gone; they have their counterpart in His dealings with His beloved disciples of every age, thus furnishing what à Kempis might call "a probable argument" for recognising as His the only Church in which such intimacy of intercourse is a regular and constantly recurring fact. Far be it from us to say that an intense personal love of Christ is a monopoly of the Church Catholic. Thank God, it is to be found elsewhere. But in the Catholic Church alone is the heroism of love—i.e., sanctity—implying an interior life of close intimacy with God—so conspicuously a result of her training as to constitute one of the marks by which she may be known, a mark which by its absence from the separated churches is a signal refutation of the Branch Theory.

As guide and guardian of His Vicar in one of the darkest periods of the Church's history; for bringing about reforms that would have taxed the resources of the ablest and most influential; for the propagation of devotions and Feasts to meet the needs of critical times; for lifting the veil beyond the grave and disclosing terrors of Divine Justice before which we quail; for giving us sweet glimpses of His intercourse in Heaven with His elect; for living presentations of His sufferings in their most awful details—still, as heretofore, our Lord selects the poor, the simple, the weak, those of little account in this world. To those who, sitting at the Lord's feet, hear His word, He once more tells the secrets of His Heart. Through these He sends His messages, and the words are like an echo of those heard long ago on the Mount, and by the Lake and up the steep of Calvary—words of warning, words of love, teaching the same lessons, not smoothed down to suit softer times, not less tender than those of old.

It need scarcely be said that there is no obligation to believe private revelations however authentic or approved. They can never become part of the Catholic faith, and may be accepted or rejected as the evidence for them is found conclusive or not. If we will we can simply leave them alone and go our way. But where the mind of the Church concerning them is clearly shown—as, e.g., in her appointment of a Feast of the Sacred Heart, and of our Lady of Lourdes—it would be rash to reject the evidence on which they rest; rather should we be glad to have this further knowledge of truths which concern us nearly, this further illustration of our Lord's words: "Behold, I am with you all days even unto the consummation of the world."

"All days." The lives of the saints in every age are the fulfilment of that promise. They have endeared themselves to Him by taking Him at His word, by entering into a true fellowship with Him of will and affection, of interests, labours, and sufferings, placing at His service all that they have and are, sharing His very life, and, as His co-workers, transmitting it to others. These respond loyally to His every call or invitation, saying with St. Thomas: "Let us also go and die with Him." These not only accept, they choose hard things—*with Him*. Here is the secret of sanctity. In proportion to their sense of comradeship is the intimacy of our Lord's followers with Him and their readiness for self-sacrifice in His cause.

By fellowship, some understand a readiness to accept all He can offer them—except participation in His sufferings. Or they resign themselves after a fashion to certain trials—sickness, ill-health, heat, cold, toil, even failure. But other misfortunes, those especially which come to them through the intermediary of their neighbour, insults, calumnies, humiliations, they either resent with indignation as undeserved and therefore not coming from God, or suffer to cast them into excessive dejection. What is this but practically to disclaim fellowship with Christ and membership with those who went from the presence of the Council rejoicing that they were counted worthy to suffer reproach for the name of Jesus!

What remedy would St. Paul suggest for this half-heartedness in the service of Christ, this shrinking from the logical outcome of our compact with Him? Nothing better, more powerful, sweeter, than the earnest pondering of the word which meant so much to himself—*Fellowship!* If we love, and in proportion to our love, we shall follow Him. "*Per ipsum, et cum ipso, et in ipso.*" "I can do all things in Him who strengtheneth me." We must learn to love, we must pray for a strong personal love of Christ if the varied trials of life are to find us prepared to show ourselves His true disciples.

At one time or other a heavy cross will probably fall to the lot of every one of us, entering into God's designs as a link in the chain of graces which are to ensure our salvation. Much, perhaps everything, may depend on our falling in with these designs and meeting these tests as we should. Why not make the use of them that the saints have done! We are bound to accept these visitations with at least the fortitude of a good Christian, without rebellion, without repining. Why not brace ourselves to the further striving that will place us among those close followers of our Lord who welcome pain, not indeed for itself, but for the nearness to Him which, aided by grace and goodwill, it never fails to bring! What is wanted is Love. Fear of sin is the beginning of wisdom, but Love is the perfection and the goal. Love alone suffices for all things, is equal to any test, undismayed by any sacrifice, steadfast through all anguish, faithful unto death.

Nor must we despair because sadly conscious that it is just this love that we lack; that in Christ's army we are but the rank and file, far from the generous loyalty of the *corps d'elite*. The rank and file may be fired with a noble ambition. They may attain to promotion, if not at a bound, at least by steps. There are those who find the opportunity of their life unexpectedly. A sudden loss—and their hour has come! And with it the grace, sufficient always, and with prayer all-sufficient to bear them beyond dream or desire. But God's ordinary way with His elect is to train them by an ascent not too steep for the daily march, to the height He has in view for them. Few if any of us, says St.

Ignatius, know how far His grace would lead us were we but willing. As a rule it is the daily striving that prepares the way, and that way, from mediocrity to excellence, is one only—the way of Love.

XXXIV
FELLOWSHIP—II
(SEXAGESIMA)

"Jesus Christ...To-day, and the same for ever."— Heb. 8:13.

"I SHOULD like *to have been* a martyr!" sighed a child who had followed with keen interest the story of a martyrdom. In other words she wanted the prize without the price. Many of us do. Like men in the rank and file, the cadets in Christ's army all, probably, at one time or another dream of promotion. But alas! aspiration does not always bring realisation. "Son, I know thy desires, and I have often heard thy sighs. Thou wouldst be glad to be now at present in the liberty of the glory of the children of God. Thou wouldst be pleased to be now at thy eternal home and in thy heavenly country abounding with joy. But that hour is not yet come, for this is yet another time, a time of war, a time of labour and trial....Thou must yet be tried upon earth and exercised in many things."[1]

The fellowship with Christ into which we were admitted by Baptism, our own freewill has ratified. From children of the Christian family we have been advanced by Confirmation to the active service of the Christian army, bound as soldiers of Christ to espouse His cause, to obey His orders, to fight His enemies, and on this condition only to share His victory and His triumph. What this compact with our Leader implies, how we are to attack

---
1 *Imit.* iii 49.

and overcome the devil, the world, and the flesh, it is for us now to realise.

And how are we *to approve ourselves to our Leader?* For surely we are not going to content ourselves with the very unsafe, very unworthy service that has no lofty ideal to inspire its aims. By His own invitations to us, by His own unlimited sacrifice for us, our Lord deserves something better at our hands than this!

It is voluntary service He asks of us, and not to voluntary only, but to signal service that He invites every one of us. On the other hand, the companionship and familiar friendship with Himself which He holds out to us by way of reward is not subject like earthly recompense to the chances of war. As a rule, it is not by a sudden stroke of good fortune that His friends reach His side, but by patient, persevering effort. Even when His call to higher things is exceptional and startling—a miracle of grace, as we term it—they have to make their way to Him step by step. Grace, however powerful, demands co-operation, and this supposes effort and pain. So far, indeed, do marks of singular favour dispense from suffering, that they are actually a call to it. A word: "Saul, Saul!" and a flash from Heaven overthrew the persecutor on his way to Damascus, but to what end? "I will show Him," said the same Voice later, "how great things he must suffer for My Name's sake."[1]

Our own days have furnished more than one striking example of this truth. Early life gave no promise of the heights to which certain chosen souls attained. There came a sudden crisis, an awakening, the flashing upon them

---
1   Acts 9:4, 16.

of a great truth—Death, Judgement, Hell, Heaven—and in its light they saw what wrought a change in their whole outlook upon life, in the whole tenor of their life thenceforth. Yet not without earnest co-operation on their part. The impulse was from Heaven, the choice lay in their own freewill.

In some cases it was the sudden entry of Christ into a life that wrought the transformation, the sight of a crucifix bringing home to the soul with new meaning and force the personal love of Jesus for itself individually, and the obligation thus entailed: "He wants a return of love *from me*. He has died to win it. He shall have it!" exclaims the soul under the influence of such an appeal. And forthwith it surrenders itself to *ce Cœur sur la croix qui se brise dans un suprême effort pour se faire comprendre*.[1]

That our Lord has His predilections the history of nineteen centuries proves. But this debars no one from the familiar friendship with Himself to which He invites every one of us: "Come to Me all!" Were we fair to Him, how many of us would own to a consciousness of such invitation. How many cannot but be sensible of God's singular regard for themselves. They have been chosen by Him for special service and qualified by exceptional graces: "You have not chosen Me, but I have chosen you." Once chosen, however, it is for these favoured ones to justify His choice, to make their election sure.

The first grace in a series is a germ capable of indefinite expansion, but only on the condition of careful cultivation. Like a young plant, it is tender, easily choked or crushed by its surroundings. The road of life is littered with the

---

1 Paul Claudel, *La Messe Là-Bas*.

failures of promising beginnings. On the other hand, what encouragement there is in the thought that whilst our Lord has His predilections, all His followers are dear to Him; all in the ranks are capable of promotion; to all His intimate friendship is offered and only waits acceptance. Truly, those only are wise who realise that to fall in as far as possible with God's designs for them, is not only simple justice to Him, but so entirely their own interest as to be the sole meaning and value of life, literally the one thing necessary. Of all nations and tribes and peoples and tongues, varying in supernatural as in natural characteristics, we find the elect in one family feature all alike—the simplicity with which they take in the primitive Christian idea of fellowship with Christ suffering, the generosity with which they carry it out in practice. A band of young savages, pages of an African king, come before the Catholic missionary to beg for Baptism, and, questioned as to their readiness to be burnt to death in accordance with the king's threat, one and all accept the condition. These we call heroes, but do we realise to what we ourselves are committed by the simple fact of our Baptism? Every follower of Christ must be resolved to sacrifice all rather than violate a commandment of God binding under mortal sin; to forgo any temporal advantage this world can offer rather than purchase it at the price of a grievous offence against God. The fact that for this principle thousands of martyrs have laid down their lives proves how real is the fellowship of suffering with Christ that may be required of any one of us.

Yet there is a higher degree of comradeship, of which He Himself has given an example, which offers anything and everything for the service of the one beloved, not from compulsion of any kind but purely out of love. Some there are who, like our Lord's first friends on earth, put no limit to their tender of service. All they have and prize they place at His disposal—time, talents, fortune, reputation, life itself—so that, where there is no question of sin of any kind, but only the consideration of a worthier service, a closer following in His footsteps, a greater proof of gratitude and love, they choose, where choice is left them, the hard things of life as their portion, because these were His.

Self-sacrifice is not only the law, it is the instinct of love. And when the love of Christ has become the absorbing passion of a soul, this manifestation of it not infrequently takes forms which appear to infringe the ordinary laws of prudence. The measure of love, says St. Augustine, is to be without measure. "Love is often fervent beyond all measure," à Kempis tells us. It has its own laws—imperious, exacting—its own tribunal of appeal—like the Court of Equity—for cases excepted from the general provisions of the law. It is itself this High Court, than which there is none higher. Here all the saints, with St. Paul, must appeal for justification when they are arraigned before the lower tribunals of prudence, self-regard, and the like. How could Peter, how could any of the saints explain their acts when under the inebriating influence of Love, except by an appeal to Love itself! Those who have not shared their experience or mastered the higher laws according to which they act, can only humbly and in silence reverence what they do not understand.

In the Crucifix we find the explanation of the marvels of Divine Love which abound in the lives of the saints. Here abyss calls upon abyss—the charity of God which passeth all understanding inviting, and the abyss of nothingness responding as it may to the Divine appeal.

The wounded Figure on the Cross, detaching Itself from the nails and with outstretched, pleading arms lowering Itself into the embrace of a St. Francis, or Catherine of Siena, is an image of this reciprocity of love. Christ Crucified calls for a like surrender of self, and, thank God, He meets with it here and there, so far as the finite can measure itself with the Infinite! "He will share crucifixion with me," says the soul He has thus drawn to Himself; "if I take Him into my embrace I must be crucified with Him."

Natural instincts remain. The pleasant things of life—ease, comfort, honour—have not lost their hold upon the heart, but they are overruled by a stronger attraction. To cast oneself into a raging sea from no compulsion but that of love, as a manifestation of love that would be prized, is understood at least by the lovers. The desire to be with the Beloved, to be one with Him, conformed to Him as far as may be, is the one constraining impulse of those to whom their Lord is all in all. Distance must be overleaped, obstacles surmounted, fears ignored; love feels it may and can do all things. "Lord, if it be Thou, bid me come to Thee upon the waters." "Tell me where thou hast laid Him and I will take Him away."

Even human love is said to make the lover beside himself. So does the love of Jesus Crucified: "Blood of Christ, inebriate me!" we pray. An overmastering tendency of madness is to self-destruction, and there are false religions which, by a parody of truth, look upon the annihilation of self as the goal of human existence and endeavour. Perfect love of God tends to a spiritual self-immolation as a means of union with Him, not by self-destruction but by the happy absorption in Him for which man was created: "that God may be all in all."

Full fellowship with Christ, then, is the need, the privilege, and the reward of *the generous*. It is reward even here because nearness to Jesus is its own recompense, and hard things become sweet and easy when shared with Him. These, His *corps d'elite*, stand around Him on the height of Calvary. Below, at varying stages of nearness, stretch the rank and file of the army. Whereabouts do *I* stand?

Let us be glad and rejoice that some of us at least are found to give Him all they have to give. Let us congratulate them in the words that once made Peter tremble, that to him now, and to all the saints are the sweetest of memories: "And thou also wast with Jesus of Nazareth."

And let us rejoice, too, for ourselves, for the stimulating force of their example. It is to example that some of the highest among them owe their crown. They ascended by steps. So may we. Fidelity to little things, to the grace of the passing moment, is the secret of sanctity. If we would only let each day, with its opportunities, its graces, its easy sacrifices, lead us on, we should be astonished, says Fr. Faber, at the heights to which they would bring us before many years were passed.

XXXV
FELLOWSHIP—III
(QUINQUAGESIMA)
"Ascending by Steps."

HOLY Scripture speaks of ascending by steps to the place we have chosen. There is no flight to the heights of Divine Love. We must be content to mount by a gradual ascent. One thing is certain: the example of the saints should not discourage us. Does the Victoria Cross on the breast of a brave man dishearten, or fire with enthusiasm one who has his decorations still to gain? There are, no doubt, people so perverse as to see in the successes of others an injury to themselves. But, viewed aright, what is more encouraging than the example of those who have attained the end for which we are striving; what more stimulating than the Feast of All Saints? Many of those now so high in glory were amongst the most erring; many, like some of us, were cast down by the pattern set before them, till the day came when, lifting up their hearts, they exclaimed: "And why cannot I do what these have done?"

Our Lord is so much in love with human love that He came down from Heaven to seek it. There is not one of us with whom He does not desire to be bound by ties of closest friendship. And He does not exact as a condition a satisfactory *quid pro quo*, an array of brilliant or estimable qualities on our part. He who taught us that it is more blessed to give than to receive has enforced His teaching by example. He has made over to us all He can part with—nay, more—He has given us Himself. He is always giving. If at times we crave for more, if we complain that we have not this or that, either we know not what we ask, or we ask amiss. When we ask what would not make for our happiness, He gives us something better instead. Spiritual goods He will always give if we ask as we should. He gives as far as we are able to receive. He does, indeed, look for goodwill on our part, for a readiness to take some pains to cultivate the friendship He offers. If this is asking too much and the friendship does not strengthen, on whose side is the fault?

The marvel is that He, the Lord of Majesty, the King of Heaven and earth, should make advances to us and condescend to lay down conditions; that, knowing us through and through, His love should be proof against coolness, selfishness, deficiencies of every kind. The most repulsive sinner who in sincerity asks forgiveness, receives over and above, invitation to intimate companionship. But a desire that is genuine takes the means, and in the first place avoids carefully whatever may displease. There is here a wide field for effort and sacrifice. A glance over the day in our examination of conscience at night will show that every sin, every resistance to grace, every shabbiness with God has been due to the determination to secure for ourselves some pleasure or to avoid some pain. When our resolution is to avoid wounding Him in the least little things, we are a long way on the road to true friendship.

The most intimate friends of our Lord, His twelve Apostles, were full of imperfections, but they were men of goodwill, ready to acknowledge their defects and to correct them. Close companionship with Him remedied all that was amiss. The study of Him day by day, His attractiveness, His example, won them to Him more and more, and they grew like Him. So will it be with us. No one can expect to enjoy familiar friendship with Christ our Lord without an earnest effort to know Him. We must follow His life in the Gospels, reading thoughtfully, pondering in our hearts as Mary did His words and ways. We must note what pleased and what pained Him; what moved Him to anger or to tears. Like His friends at Bethany we must show Him sympathy, welcome opportunities of serving Him and His, delight Him with little gifts and pleasant surprises. And this at some cost to ourselves. If a church is within our reach, we shall visit Him from time to time, not refusing Him the courtesy we show to other friends. We shall ask Him to return our visit and meet us at the altar-rails, not at distant intervals, but as often as our duties will permit. At such times His pleasure rather than our own will be our chief consideration, and if our Communions are dry and our thanksgivings difficult, we shall persevere in them at all costs, glad at least to prove that we seek in them, not His consolations but Himself.

We want our dearest Lord to be to us what He was to the Twelve. And what was that? Simply everything. He could lead them and treat them, praise, rebuke, console them as He would. If only they heard: "It is I," all was well. When He was with them they feared nothing—not the raging waves nor storm; not the lepers nor the possessed who approached Him; nor the malice and cunning of His persistent enemies, ever on the watch to catch them in some infringement of the Law, that they might accuse *Him*. When subtle questions were put to them, when censured by their lawyers and righteous ones, they left their vindication to Him. He was a resource that never failed them, compensation for the loss of all beside, their ideal, their joy, their all in all. And this He has been ever since and is to-day to those who have earnestly sought His friendship and been ready like His earliest friends on earth to follow Him in true fellowship, through suffering here to His Kingdom hereafter.

Even here and now, with the generous, He is generous always. Who amongst these has ever regretted his choice, or thought he has paid too dearly for what he has secured? There was a little labour, a little suffering, but—*with Him*. Why should we fear to follow Him with the devotedness that is the everlasting joy of His saints?

Those who have scaled the heights by heroic paths tell us that it is not by these solely or even chiefly that sanctity is attained, but rather by fidelity in the little things that lie along the route of daily life.

"But this is just where we fail," some will say. "Love makes all light and easy, but we have not this strong, personal love of Jesus, this fervour of the will which such fidelity supposes."

Even so, we need not despond. Like everything else we need, this love can be gained by prayer. The saints had no more natural liking for pain and discomfort, the disagreeables of life, and perseverance in distasteful duties than we have. But they prayed and difficulties were overcome. Above all, they set to work to gain that personal love of our Lord and Master which has enabled His friends to conquer every difficulty. Notice how you set about cultivating an acquaintance which you desire should ripen into a friendship, and bring something of that method into your relations with our Blessed Lord. Take some pains. Read the Gospels or a Life of Him. Mingle with the crowds that press upon Him. Catch their enthusiasm. He is the Way and the Life. If we keep our eyes fixed on Him and try to tread in His footsteps, we shall find they have been smoothed for our feet. At last, helped by His grace, our affection will become an unselfish devotedness—then we can do all things with ease.

To one who from boyhood had set martyrdom before him as the goal of all his desires,[1] there came one day the practical question: "I desire a martyr's death, but do I live a martyr's life?" There should be preparation, then, conformity between the two. Thenceforth he strove to deserve promotion in his Master's service by small but frequent sacrifices, generosity in bearing trifling inconveniences, fidelity in little things. How he learned devotion to his Eucharistic Lord he tells us himself:

"Real devotion to the Blessed Sacrament is only to be gained by hard grinding work of dry adoration before the Hidden God. But such a treasure cannot be purchased at too great a cost, for once obtained it makes of this life as near an approach to Heaven as we can ever hope for."

Fed on effort and sacrifice, love grew apace, and when the call came to give the proof of love greater than which no man can give, he was ready. In 1914, with no fervour of enthusiasm, but in face of intense natural repugnance and fear, he volunteered for the Front as military chaplain. There, faithful in great things as in small, he died at his post, a martyr to charity and devotion to duty, August 17, 1917.

---

[1] Father William Doyle, S.J.

The efficacy of fidelity in little things for endearing ourselves to our Divine Master and ensuring intimacy with Him, is proved by the teaching and example of all the saints. It is a practice that, aided by grace, is not beyond the strength of any of us, whilst the frequency of occasions provided, the virtues it puts in requisition, and the perseverance it demands, augur well for a loyal compliance with whatever the designs of God may ask at our hands.

The truth is that Love journeys on an uphill road. Even its intercourse with the Beloved is sooner or later marked by trial. Because it is a lesson hard to learn, the saints never weary of telling us that feelings are not the test of love, which may be at its highest without a particle of sensible fervour.

To realise this we have only to see it in the Garden of the Agony or on the Cross. The dereliction in which the Soul of Christ was plunged from the cry in Gethsemani: "Not My will but Thine be done!" to the loving plaint: "My God, My God, why hast Thou forsaken Me?"—was not this the very climax of love?

So in its measure is it with us. Love is never purer nor stronger than when it is anchored on God and His will alone, with no sensible sustaining force from nature or from grace. The will is what God looks to. Its fidelity under deprivation and trial is what He prizes. What our Lord wants of me is a special love, a personal service which has such value in His sight that He desired it from eternity, and died to secure it. He created me that I might offer it to Him as my own free gift. He condescends to ask it as if it were a thing of worth. Will He refuse it when I bring it to Him? We are told that the holy women, His friends, set out very early for the Sepulchre on the third day after the Crucifixion to complete their loving ministrations of the Friday. "And Jesus met them." Their dispositions were not perfect. They had forgotten His assurance that He was to rise on the third day; but their errand was one of love, and as such was rewarded by Him. He never fails to meet a venture of love, to overlook its mistakes, to forgive its shortcomings, to console it under trial. He encourages it when it has yet a long way to go. He makes much of every effort. If I believe in His love for me, and try to prove my love for Him in the occasions daily life affords, who knows to what familiarity of friendship with Him little efforts, little fidelities, little sacrifices, may bring me!

> If I ask Him to receive me
>   Will He answer "Nay"?
> Not till earth and not till Heaven
>   Pass away.
>
> Finding, following, keeping, struggling,
>   Is He sure to bless?
> Angels, Martyrs, Prophets, Virgins
>   Answer "Yes."[1]

---

1   Hymn of St. Stephen the Sabaite.

XXXVI
LENT

"Now is the acceptable time." — 2 Cor. 6:2.

A GOOD mother is not content with giving injunctions, she does her best to see that they are carried into effect. The Church is our Mother. Speaking through the Council of Trent, she tells us that the whole life of a Christian should be a life of penance. And because so unwelcome a truth needs to be pressed home, she brings all her children under the discipline of penance. There is the obligation of receiving the Sacraments at a given period; of hearing Mass on Sundays and abstaining from servile work, with the inconvenience and discomfort often entailed. There is the command to contribute to the support of our pastors. There are restrictions as to diet at specified times; to the celebration of marriage at certain seasons; to the kind of music and public prayers to be used at church services, and so on.

Those who have emancipated themselves from this control are apt to pity such as live subject to it. As well might they prefer the orphan's lot to that of a child which lives in happy security under the eye of a wise and watchful mother. Were not the first Christians prepared for a training at once severe and safe? Did they boast of the "comprehensiveness" of the early Church? Of the privilege of private judgement enjoyed by the first faithful? Of the advantage of unity bought at the price of compromise? Or did they find, and rejoice to find, the Apostles dealing resolutely with all who defied their authority as to doctrine or discipline?

The work of the so-called Reformation has long ago borne its bitter fruits, and never were these more in evidence than to-day. Thoughtful minds outside the Fold are realising that, left to ourselves, we must perish; that a Church, if she is to fulfil her mission of saving mankind, must curb and control, and that on this condition only can she ensure to her children security here and salvation hereafter. They see this, and many look almost longingly on those restrictions and laws by which the Catholic Church safeguards the souls entrusted to her.

We, who own her as our Mother, delight to feel round us the pressure of her protecting arm. Of the late Mgr. Benson we are told that "he would never dwell on the difficulty of trying to be a good Catholic, but always on the privilege of being a Catholic at all....He never considered what a hard religion ours was to live up to, but always, 'what a jolly fine Church it is to belong to.'"

Children instinctively value authority. They rely on their mother's presence and timely word to be security against their weakness: "We do quarrel so when she's not there," was the complaint of some little nursery folk. The Gospel tells us that it was the majesty of our Lord's teaching that impressed the multitudes, "for He spoke as one having authority." So must she speak whom He left us all days to approve and sanction, to warn and chide in His Name.

The Church knows that we must one and all do penance. She has her Master's word for it: "Unless you do penance you shall all perish." She knows, too, that were a season for doing penance left to our choice, we should never do it. Were any month in the twelve optional, we should put off till the last weeks of the year, and then find ourselves unavoidably hindered.

She comes, therefore, to our help, and appoints as her principal season of penance, six weeks in the spring, in memory of our Lord's fast of forty days, in union with His bitter Passion and Death which she commemorates at this time, and to prepare by prayer, fasting, and alms-deeds—the three eminent good works—for the celebration of His Resurrection at Easter.

Sermons, and spiritual exercises generally, are multiplied during Lent, that the soul, too often neglected, may now be invigorated. For, in spite of the first injunction of the Catechism, a large proportion of us do not—apparently, at least—take greater care of the soul than of the body. Its needs are set aside, its reproaches go unheeded, its prior claims to attention are practically denied. Useless is it to urge against the preference given to the body, that it is the soul which must lead into eternal glory or irreparable ruin both the body and itself; that to neglect the soul is to bring about the everlasting loss of both. Waste of words to argue that the body which is to benefit hereafter and to all eternity by the efforts of the soul to secure its salvation, should at least abstain from hindering it, and do some penance for the harm for which it is responsible. Of no avail are appeals to common sense and self-interest to see that where the claims of the two partners are incompatible, those of the soul should come first. Fruitless, too, for the most part, is such pleading of the soul in its own behalf. The verdict as a rule is given against it. What resource, then, what higher Court is open to it?

The Church steps in to readjust matters, not wholly but as far as her prudence will allow. Sin, she tells us, is the act of soul and body. In it both concur, but in a vast majority of cases, the evil, as in Eden, starts with the sub-partner, which wins over the other to the ruin of both. Both, therefore, should do penance, and the body in particular. First, because in nine cases out of ten it is the cause of the fall, and next, because the debt it fails to pay in this life must be discharged by the soul alone afterwards, as the body does not go to Purgatory. Hence, throughout the year, and in particular during Lent, the body should be required to do, if not its whole share of penance, at least some small part, in order to satisfy the claims of justice. That it is little we must all own. Let us at least do that little with generosity. If we are wise we shall go beyond what is of obligation, not content ourselves with mere obedience to the Church's law as to fasting and abstinence, but supplement by voluntary endeavour what she enjoins.

The law binds all who are not legitimately and by authority dispensed. And because observance in this respect does not in these days amount to much in the way of self-denial, the Church exhorts the faithful to the practice of mortification in other ways also. She has always discountenanced festivities during Lent, as unsuited to a time of mourning in which we are called to unite our penitential exercises with the sufferings of Christ specially commemorated at this season.

Moreover, Lent being a time when her children beg God's mercy for themselves, they are expected to show more abundant mercy to others. Prayer and alms-deeds are coupled together in Scripture as a powerful means of drawing down the favour of God. Hence, to extra prayer and to works of penance, the Church would have us join more plentiful alms-deeds during Lent.

All this means a call to effort and self-sacrifice. We must not, we will not hang back. "Now is the acceptable time, now are the days of salvation." Who knows whether another Lent will be granted us? Scripture speaks of the time of death as one when all men will wish to have done penance. Why prepare fruitless regrets for that awful time! God is willing—more than willing—is most desirous to give us now all the grace we need. Let us win from Him by fervent prayer the special blessing that belongs to a fervent Lent.

XXXVII
ASH WEDNESDAY

"Remember, man, that thou art dust
and unto dust thou shalt return."—Gen. 3:19.

WHAT voice but that which speaks in God's Name would dare to summon us to-day, without distinction of age, race, or rank, to hear this unwelcome truth? And not only to hear the death sentence, but to have it brought home by a rite of such startling significance? Why does Mother Church, so gentle, so tactful, use means of such terrible directness to reach our souls to-day?

Because she is true to her trust. Because she *is* the voice of God to us, she would rouse us to a sense of sin and to the need of penance by the very words that, humbling our first parents to the dust, brought them back to God.

It is sin that is the sting of death. Not the natural consequences, however terrible, of the separation of soul and body, but sin, the fatal cause of all these evils—this is the sting of death. One thing alone can remove it—the spirit of penance. Hence the efforts of the Church to bring us to the right dispositions for beginning Lent. What she enjoins does not amount to much. It is possible to comply with her precepts with very little of the interior spirit she desires to foster. Our goodwill must second her endeavour if these forty days are to be to us indeed "days of salvation." We must prepare for our Last End by acting on our belief that this is the one thing *necessary*. We must avail ourselves of the helps which she offers to us in such abundance at this time.

"Remember "is a word used by God to bring us face to face with facts of vital importance to us. The aim of the devil is to make us forget them. He knows we should never consent to sin were we to see it as it is. He seeks, therefore, to blind us as to its malice, to show us only that which is alluring about it, hiding from us its consequences. Hence the warning word of God to us: "Remember thy last end and thou shalt never sin." (Ecclus. 8:40).

"But," it may be said, "such remembrance must surely foster a morbid disposition and overcloud the whole of life."

Not if the example of the saints is any guide to us. The experience of them one and all is a triumphant vindication of the word of God, not only as regards the efficacy of such a means for the avoidance of sin, but also for its ensuring a serenity of mind, proof against all the eventualities of life. Peace of heart is a family feature common to all the saints, one of the most striking characteristics of the children of God.

We have to remember before all things that God is our Father and that He loves us dearly. From Him we came, to Him we are going, with Him we are to spend an eternity of love and joy. Dependence on Him is not only the law of our being, but the condition of all that makes for our happiness here and hereafter, here no less than hereafter. Our after-life is to be the complement of our present life, its perfection, its reward. This is our probation, our schooltime. But, as a good father, God provides abundantly, even here, for the happiness of His children, especially by that peace which is the foundation of true happiness. And it is precisely to secure to us this peace that He bids us, through all the vicissitudes of this passing time, remember our Last End.

Notice: the injunction is not to be always thinking of the Four Last Things, but to remember our Last End. And what is that but Heaven! Death is but the passage to our Home; Hell the fence by the way, guarding our feet lest they should slip; Judgement the seal of our eternal security; Heaven—our Last End. If this is our destiny as designed by our Father who is in Heaven, is it not the height of folly to restrict our interest and our energy to the things of time?

How do we act here and now when confronted with unavoidable difficulties or dangers? Do we shut our eyes to them and allow ourselves to be overwhelmed? A coming crisis will make or mar our future. Does the knowledge paralyse us? Or do we nerve ourselves for the effort necessary to meet and master it? Why are we less wise when our eternal interests are at stake? Why do we believe, without striving to realise the facts we have to face? How is it that we so cruelly thrust aside the pleading of our soul to be cared for while there is yet time—cared for adequately as the only thing absolutely necessary? Men and women will slave and stint themselves for the better part of their lives to provide a pittance for the uncertain years of old age, but nothing will stir them to effort for eternity. Why? If such folly lessened their responsibility or their danger, it might be understood. But Death, Judgement, Heaven, and Hell are facts. Whether we recognise them as such or not, has no effect *on them*, but our attitude towards them at this moment, at every moment of our lives, is shaping our eternity. To ignore them is to kill the prophets sent us for our salvation. We must think of the great realities we have to meet and meet soon. If the whole world is made desolate it is because we will not think of the things *that are for our peace.*

Yes, for our peace. The Four Last Things are not meant to scare us but to serve as beacons to light us Home. Thanks to them, millions have steered their course in safety and have reached the happiness prepared for us one by one. And not only do they secure happiness at the journey's end, but—and this is what we are so apt to forget—they are encouragement and support all the way. Keeping them in sight we shall press forward in peaceful trust, suffering less on an uphill road than those who have banished all considerations that would have deterred them from seeking their fill of pleasure here.

Never, perhaps, was there a time when men were more bent upon peering into the secrets of the future. They will face physical and moral ruin to get an insight, as they believe, into what is to befall them hereafter, or as to what has actually befallen those whom they have loved and lost. Do not tell them such knowledge is wisely hidden from them. They will have it at all cost. How comes it, then, that so little interest is shown in the event which the Church brings before us to-day, the event on which our whole future depends, which we know to be inevitable, which may come at any moment, of which the consequences are irremediable? How is it that we think so seldom and so reluctantly of death? That we are so little concerned as to the state in which it may find us? That we not only neglect to prepare for death but chase away the thought of it when a passing hearse or a tolling bell, or the sudden loss of a friend, brings the unwelcome fact before us?

It may be urged that it is the instinct of our nature to dread death and oblivion, separation from the warm, familiar, happy things of this life, and the necessity of facing alone the untried experiences of life beyond the grave; death touches every part of our nature, and we cannot but recoil instinctively from the destruction it brings about, a dissolution that was no part of God's original design for us. Certainly. But if it remains a fact, an experience through which we must all pass safely to escape utter ruin of soul and body, if to fail then is to fail everlastingly, should we not accept the inevitable and prepare for this momentous passage with all the care its importance demands? See how the people of this country, once roused to a sense of the peril which faced them in 1917, set themselves to bear anything, to sacrifice everything to secure victory. The unprecedented requisitions of Government were met without demur. The enormous sum realised by the War Loan showed their determination to prepare adequately for the struggle which meant the security or the downfall of England. Why are we less wise when there is question not of time but of eternity, of a security or a ruin that will endure for ever?

Death is a disillusioning and a detachment that are absolute. It severs every bond, deprives us of all we have come to look upon as inseparable from ourselves—from friends, home, duties, the questions of the day; from books, from influence, from our circumstances and our trials, from our business and our pastimes. It breaks up the lifelong companionship of soul and body, so intimate, so mutually dependent, that we find it hard to realise how even the spirit can survive the separation.

Oh, the nakedness of the soul as it goes forth from the body! Everything left behind except the works it has to present before the Judgement-Seat! And yet with all this denudation, with that loss of the body through which it acted, incurred punishment and merited reward, its personality remains intact. It will be I myself—knowing, fearing, hoping—that, swifter than light, will speed to the Throne of God to hear the sentence that is to decide my eternity. How reversed in that instant after death will be the valuations of my life! Perhaps the claims of the body were habitually allowed to outweigh those of the soul. How often, at least, was the soul worsted in the conflict with its intractable partner! And now, what do I think of the body as it lies there, waiting to be made over to the dishonour of the grave!

The atmosphere of this world is one of mist and deception. Its false lights, its faulty standards, the glamour of its pleasant things, the persistence with which it prefers the paltry and the passing to the solid and the eternal, and so educates us from childhood that dreams pass for realities and the things of faith are hard to grasp and harder to live by—all this illusion fades away from us at death. Then, for the first time, we know things as they are. Life lies behind us. We see it in its true aspect and proportion—as a passage to the eternal life, and nothing more. Such as it has been it has shaped our eternity. Let us pray now for the light we shall have presently, and in that light live and labour for eternity.

The Church begins Lent by bringing vividly before us the first of the Four Last Things to be ever remembered: "Remember, man, that thou art dust and into dust thou shalt return." But that this reminder may not sadden us like those who have no hope, she does not withhold Holy Communion to-day as on Good Friday. She spreads her Feast as usual. To the altar-rails, where we have just heard that tremendous sentence of death, she summons us again to hear: "May the Body of our Lord Jesus Christ preserve thy soul to life everlasting." We lift our heads to be marked with ashes, and then to receive into these frail, perishing bodies the pledge of an immortal and glorious life to come.

XXXVIII
THE "VICTORY" WAR LOAN OF 1917

WHAT a response it met with! The terms to investors, whether of large or small amounts, were wonderfully generous—a high rate of interest for present sacrifice even of the most trifling kind, and the recovery at no distant date of all that had been lent. The investment was as safe as the credit of the British Empire itself. But the public was warned not to hesitate. The offer would be open for a month. In all probability such terms would never be held out again. If the opportunity were neglected, the loss would be irretrievable.

The motive was twofold. It was addressed to patriotism and loyalty on the one hand, to lawful self-interest on the other. "Your King and Country need your help in this tremendous crisis. All that you call your own is at stake. The sacrifice is inappreciable; the return certain and great."

We know the result. Crowds rushed from the first day for the application forms, and studied the conditions of purchase. Offices were opened to satisfy all inquirers. Cheques for millions as well as for the minimum amount specified poured daily into the Treasury. The result far outran the most sanguine, nay, the most extravagant expectation.

The children of this world, our Lord tells us, are wiser in their generation than the children of light. "For a small living," says à Kempis, "men run a great way; for eternal life many will scarce raise their foot once from the ground. A pitiful gain is sought after; men are not afraid to toil day and night for a trifle or a slight promise. But alas! for an unchangeable good, for an inestimable reward, for the highest honour and never-ending glory, they are too sluggish to take the least pains. Be ashamed, then, thou slothful servant, seeing that they are more ready to labour for perdition than thou art for life."[1] For a trifling sacrifice now, we are promised an overwhelming return presently. We have the word of God for it. If we accept His terms and fulfil our part of the engagement, our eternal happiness is assured. But there is no room for delay. Death may come at any moment, and if our salvation is not worked out before it overtakes us, our chance is gone, irreparably gone; we shall have no further offer. The happiness of Heaven will have been forfeited—and for ever.

The War Loan challenged our patriotism and our self-interest. God's offer of salvation appeals to our loyalty to Him and to our own best and eternal interests. As His creatures, we owe Him all that we have and are. We should be bound to serve Him even without reward. But He promises us recompense out of all proportion to any effort, any sacrifice we can make. Truly the children of this world are a reproach to us. Having satisfied themselves that the investment of 1917 was sound, profitable, and urgent, they lost no time in securing its advantages. The self-denial this involved did not deter them. They were content to wait for the return. Why are we less wise in our far more important enterprise? If "wisdom consists in

---
[1] *Imit. of Christ*, Book III, chap. iii.

acting upon long views,"[1] why are we so short-sighted in the matter of our eternal interests, why do we not invest heart and soul in the Victory Loan that has God's word for its security?

---

[1] Mr. H. A. L. Fisher, late Minister for Education.

XXXIX

THE CALL TO PENANCE

WHETHER we use our Missals during the year or not, we shall do well to take them up during Lent. It is not easy to see how we can drink in the spirit of the Church without listening to her words and making her prayers our own at this time of solemn and universal supplication.

Her aim, as seen in all the prayers of the Lenten Masses, is to prepare for Easter by means of fasting, penance, and abstinence. The words break in unpleasantly upon Christmas thoughts, yet if she is our appointed guide, we must be ready to follow where she leads. Our Lord, the gentlest of teachers, was also the most uncompromising: "Unless you do penance you shall all perish." "He that taketh not up his cross and followeth Me is not worthy of Me." It is her likeness to Christ in this respect that has won not a few outside the Fold to recognise in the Catholic Church the one Teacher appointed by Him. They do not seek a guide who will lead them by the easiest road, they want the safest. Shall her own children be less wise, less ready to welcome her injunctions even when they run counter to natural inclination?

The first thing St. Luke tells us of our Lord's blessed Precursor, after saying that "the child was in the deserts until the day of his manifestation to Israel," is that "he came into all the country about the Jordan preaching the baptism of penance for the remission of sins. And there went out to him all the country of Judea and all they of

Jerusalem, and many of the Pharisees and Sadducees, and were baptised by him in the river of Jordan confessing their sins."

The words with which he welcomed his penitents were hardly inviting: "Ye offspring of vipers, who hath shewed you to flee from the wrath to come? Bring forth, therefore, fruits worthy of penance, for now the axe is laid to the root of the trees. Every tree therefore that bringeth not forth good fruit, shall be cut down and cast into the fire."

"What, then, shall we do?" cried the terror-stricken multitudes—we are expressly told that St. John was speaking to "multitudes." And the publicans said: "Master, what shall we do?" And the soldiers also asked him, saying: "And what shall we do?" No false shame silenced them. The stern preacher had but to point the way and they were ready. To what did he point in every case? To the baptism of penance. Wrong-doing must be rectified, and good fruit brought forth. Not only must the mountains be levelled and the crooked ways be made straight, but valleys must be filled and rough ways be made plain. The docile multitudes heard and obeyed. Down to the river banks they followed him to testify their goodwill by receiving the "baptism of penance."

Over and over again during the Ages of Faith we come upon a like phenomenon—hard truths that called for generosity on an heroic scale meeting with a response that has no parallel in later times. We see it in the fortitude of the early Christians during three centuries of persecution; in the submission of powerful oppressors as well as of the faithful generally to the canonical penances of the Church; in the pouring out of European chivalry to the

East during the Crusades; in the fervour of the crowds that gathered round St. Francis of Assisi, St. Bernardine of Siena, St. Vincent Ferrer, and Savonarola.

The preaching of penance, the call to sacrifice, was understood in those days to be an essential part of the mission entrusted to the Church. Men expected to be called to account, reproved for sin, and made to do penance. It was the shameless subversion of Christian truth that led the reformers of the sixteenth century to divorce faith from works, and true repentance from the "fruits worthy of penance" of which the Baptist spoke.

But the Church holds on her way, undeterred by rebellion against her teaching and the softness of a self-indulgent age. Her voice to us on Ash-Wednesday sounds like an echo of that heard long ago by the Jordan: "Let us amend for the better in those things in which we have sinned, lest suddenly overtaken by the day of death we seek space for penance and are not able to find it."

Yes, and let us thank God for giving us a guide so fearless, so faithful to her trust, who will assist our goodwill and sustain our weakness. Let us follow her bravely during these weeks of penance along the path of self-denial that, in her own words, we may deserve to "receive the rewards promised to penitents."

XL

"ATTENTION!"

THE Church is continually calling upon us to rejoice. From the glad tidings at Christmas, and the "Alleluias" at Easter, to the "*Gaudeamus omnes*" of All Saints, there is joy throughout her year. But one day every week, and times of fasting and abstinence here and there, show that she never forgets her mission is to lead us on an upward road. And with the Spring, when all Nature speaks of activity and renewal, comes her call to "Attention!"

The effect of that word on the platoon in the drill-yard, we know. "Standing at ease" one moment, the next, with every muscle, nerve, sense on the alert, the whole man responds. Something of this alacrity the Church looks for at the approach of Lent. The habitual attitude of many of us during the year is standing at ease. Now and again, perhaps, we rouse ourselves to exertion, but sooner or later effort relaxes, and Nature gives the welcome word of release: "As you were!" Are we, then, incapable of sustained energy?

Most people, we are told, make scarcely any use of their minds, even in the occupations which they follow for a living. For want of exercising their faculties, they close to themselves those wider avenues of success through "the Forest of Competition," which are open to the energetic. In every walk of life distinction is within reach of all who choose to attain it. Clerks, artisans, labourers may secure the highest posts in the commonwealth if they will but concentrate their energies and accept the training offered them. All that is wanted is the determination to excel. We can if we will. Hence the development of all our faculties to the highest pitch is continually pressed upon us.

With what result? Those who show themselves so keenly alive to our material interests get a hearing and a fair amount of response. With no higher aim than to increase their earning capacity and improve the conditions of their existence in this life, men and women will take trouble—will *think*, think hard, and put enthusiasm into the study required of them. The fact that an accident may cut short all their projects and deprive them of the fruit of their labour does not disconcert them or damp their ardour.

But try to get the attention of these students for what concerns them more nearly than any earthly gain, and too often the attempt will be a dead failure. They may allow, some of them, that the soul and its salvation are things of importance, that death and eternity are facts. But all this is so uninteresting, and they really have no time to give to it. The pleading of the soul—for it does plead at times—goes unheeded. It pleads for some of the attention ungrudgingly given to the affairs of this life, for the care that will save it from everlasting misery and secure for itself and for the body riches and joys beyond the power of man to conceive. But the appeal falls on deaf ears, the subject is unattractive, nay, disturbing. Business is urgent, and more than fills the day. A time of leisure will come later. Meanwhile God is good, and all will come right in the end.

Now, is the soul uninteresting, and if so, why? Because of its marvellous nature, its capacity, its powers? Because of its dignity and lofty destiny? Or because its intangibility puts it beyond the reach, if not of our belief, at least of anything like enthusiastic appreciation? Yet see the kind of things by which we do set store—a compliment, a decoration conferred by royalty, a couple of letters appended to our name! Should anyone find those things uninteresting on the ground of intangibility, it might not be so easy to prove their worth.

No, what is wanted by most of us is the pondered conviction, the realised faith that makes the facts of the spiritual world truths beyond any certainty to which the senses testify. Could we see a soul, any soul, we should find it beautiful and captivating above anything this world can show, or—hideous and revolting. But uninteresting, inspiring indifference only—never. Yet this is what the generality of men and women feel with regard to their own soul, not affection nor solicitude, not horror nor hatred, but mere indifference!

Why is this? Because we do not pay attention to that guest within to whom we owe our life and all that depends on life. We cannot see but we can feel our soul. And we can hear its voice. There are hours when we feel its shame under the degradation and servitude into which it is brought by sin; its quivering beneath the reproaches of conscience; its thrill of joy at God's approval transmitted by that faithful witness within. We feel the weariness and disgust with which it turns from the gross things of this world—pleasures of the senses, excitement, frivolity, self-indulgence—all the lures by which we try to ensnare it and stifle its cries for the eternal goods for which it was created and which alone can satisfy it.

Uninteresting! the soul, our own soul, its life and its vicissitudes, its questionings, its aspirations, uninteresting!

Is it not, rather, the only thing about us that *is* interesting—its salvation the one thing that really matters, the one thing necessary?

Were a child, the heir to a kingdom, entrusted to our care for education, would not our responsibility well nigh overpower us? Would there be any forgetfulness of what was its due, any neglect of precaution when its safety was concerned? Where its interests were involved, would any other consideration weigh with us?

We have, every one of us, a royal child to educate for the loftiest destiny conceivable, a child of God to be trained for a Kingdom prepared for it from the foundation of the world. It is a privilege beyond our powers to grasp, a responsibility that, but for God's assistance, would be overwhelming. Can anything that concerns this charge be deemed uninteresting?

St. Francis of Assisi, on his deathbed, asked pardon of his body for the labour and hardships it had had to undergo in the interests of the soul. Which of these two life-long companions will call for self-reproach when we come to die?

If hitherto we have neglected our soul, now is the time to readjust things.

But how? "The affairs of this life," some will urge, are so pressing, so unintermitting, that, whether we will or no, they crowd out all thoughts of the world to come. A book or a sermon may occasionally bring spiritual realities before us and press their urgency upon us. But the book is closed, the sermon ends, we take up our daily work again, and the sense of any actualities, save those of the world in which we find ourselves, grows dull and loses its power to influence. Is there not a real difficulty here?

Undoubtedly; and it is being met to-day by thousands as hard pressed as ourselves. The question is: How far are the occupations of the day our own choice, how far the result of duty or necessity? We hear people plead that they have no time for the things of eternity. But they contrive to find plenty for newspapers and novels, dress and visiting, the theatre, the cinema, golf, bridge, or billiards. No doubt relaxation of some sort should enter into the day's programme; only, is it quite fair to say that there is time for everything but the "one thing necessary"? Suppose such as these were to put this question to themselves: "If some urgent work that greatly appeals to me, some altogether unexpected chance were to come my way, could I so curtail other occupations as to give it a place in my daily or weekly, or at least monthly observances?"

Most of us would hardly be able to answer "No." Even the most sorely pressed show that where there is a will there is a way. A poor woman out at work from morning till night, an hotel drudge to whom even Sunday brings no rest, can honestly say there is no time in the day they can call their own. Some of the saints of God have purposely been thrust into such circumstances to force them to neglect the care of their souls. And evidently without success, as their lives prove. For what is needed is not much leisure but much goodwill. The determination to save one's soul by keeping God's commandments and avoiding sin; short prayers morning and night; Sunday Mass; the Sacraments weekly or monthly—are there many of us who cannot secure this?

Circumstances in which God's Providence has placed us need never be a hindrance to our salvation. They may create difficulties, and serious difficulties, but His grace will be there and in proportion to our need. The shortest prayer can reach Him. And it is just the labouring and the heavy-burdened whom He calls to Him for refreshment and rest. In the factory, the workshop, the laboratory, the kitchen, in the intervals of engrossing study, the millhand, the artisan, the student, the servant, can lift up their hearts to God and by offering their work to Him, spiritualise and transform their whole life, sanctify whatever is irksome or painful in their daily duties, and deserve an eternal reward for all. Our own observation may have proved to us that it is by no means the most leisured who take most to heart the salvation of their souls.

A way to detect self-deception on this point is to ask ourselves honestly: "What does God think about the care I give to my soul? Does He who knows and sees all things, my daily life and my duties, the way my time is spent, the trend of my habitual thoughts, my motives, my desires—does He approve? Is He satisfied? This is the main question in all matters of doubt. God is my Inward Witness. To Him I am accountable for all I think, and say, and do. The time is coming, and coming soon, when He will reckon with me, and I shall hear from His lips the sentence on which my eternity depends. May I hope in humble confidence it will be: 'Well done'?"

The sands of life are running out, and however the affairs of this world are going with me, the truth remains that but *one* thing is *necessary*—that is, must be secured at any cost—were all else to go. Our English forefathers in days of persecution understood this and were wont to pray: "O Jesus, make me frequently and attentively consider that whatsoever I gain, if I lose Thee all is lost, and whatsoever I lose, if I gain Thee all is gained."

Let me in presence of my Inward Witness survey my present life, regarding it as a preparation for Eternity, and if I find that God and the affairs of my soul demand a larger place in it, see, at the beginning of this Lent, how a change may be brought about.

XLI

ENCOURAGEMENT

OUR Lord is frank with us. He tells us plainly what He finds amiss in us that we may amend. Everything for eternity depends on His judgement of us. Hence all that discloses His mind well deserves our study.

Now few things reveal a master or a friend more truly than do his admonitions. If, then, we desire to gain insight into our Lord's character, we shall do well to study those passages of the New Testament in which we find Him chiding or warning the Twelve, or His own people, or strangers. Nor let us pass over those marvellous utterances from Heaven, His exhortations to the Angels of the seven Churches. They illustrate St. Paul's "Jesus Christ, yesterday, to-day, and for ever." In them we hear again the sound of His voice, even His very words when He was yet with us. And we find in them a perfect model for our imitation when in the discharge of our duty we ourselves have to reprehend.

Arresting attention in each case is the solemn preface: "I know thy works," recalling the preludes to the Commandments: "I am the Lord." We note next that wherever He can—that is, in five instances out of seven—He begins by commendation, because He would rather praise than blame, and because He has much at heart to convince us that His blame proceeds from love. We notice, again, that no good escapes His approbation. For two of these, His servants, His words are all of approval. He contrives to make a long list of good works, even mentioning the same twice: "I know thy labour and thy patience, and how thou canst not bear them that are evil...and thou hast patience." He extols what might appear scarcely worthy of note in a bishop: Thou hast a little strength...and hast not denied My name."

Among the virtues which He singles out for special praise is that one which, more than any other, is called for by our condition of exiles here on earth—patience. It is encouraging to see the account He makes of it: "I know thy works, and thy labour, and thy patience...and thou hast patience, and hast endured for My name, and hast not fainted." "I know thy works, and thy faith, and thy charity, and thy ministry, and thy patience." "Thou hast kept the word of My patience." Our Master knows the need and the difficulty of patience under the daily burden, in the daily struggle, the daily march, the monotony of little trials that chafe so sorely because of their persistent pressure on the same spot. Therefore He awards it such generous praise.

"But I have somewhat against thee." "But I have against thee a few things." How gently He prepares the way for His admonitions, His warnings, His threats, all of them forms of love, all of them pressed into the service of love. His rebukes are keen as a two-edged sword, befitting Him "who searcheth the reins and heart."[1] But on them follow quickly the call to penance and the promise of reward. Even the two whom He reprehends most severely—him who had "the name of being alive and was dead," and the lukewarm who thought himself "rich and in need of nothing," when he was "wretched and miserable, and blind and naked"— even these He immediately comforts with the assurance:

---
1   Apoc. 2:23.

"Such as I love I rebuke and chastise." So that no state, however distasteful to Him, is desperate: there is no soul which He does not invite and help to penance and so to salvation, perfection, union with Himself, happiness. "Be mindful from whence thou art fallen and do penance." "Do penance or else I will come to thee quickly and will fight against thee." "Be zealous and do penance."

Lastly come His multiplied promises of reward to those who fight and overcome: "To him that overcometh I will give to eat of the tree of life." "To him that overcometh I will give the hidden manna." "He that shall overcome shall not be hurt by the second death." "He that shall overcome and keep My works unto the end, I will give him power over the nations." "He that shall overcome shall be clothed in white garments, and I will not blot his name out of the book of life, and I will confess his name before My Father and before His angels." "He that shall overcome I will make him a pillar in the temple of My God." "To him that shall overcome I will give to sit with Me in My throne, as I also have overcome and am sat down with My Father in His throne."[1]

Thus does our Lord and Master admonish and encourage us in our own need, and give us a lesson in the difficult art of reprehension. He teaches us to win a hearing and inspire confidence by a generous allowance of what is praiseworthy; to find something to commend before we blame.

And our last word always, like His own, must be—encouragement.

---

[1] Apoc. 3:21.

XLII
"NOT BEATING THE AIR"
—1 Cor. 9.

ENCOURAGEMENT for ourselves no less than for others is called for at all times, and particularly at the beginning of Lent. For self-denial is distasteful to nature, and perseverance in a course of it needs the incentive He Himself vouchsafed to use, "who, having joy set before Him, endured the cross." The servant, our Lord tells us, is not greater than his lord. In His Passion, which is the climax of His teaching and practice, He makes Himself so completely one of us, that for our encouragement He condescends to repugnances and fears, to pleading in face of a coming trial, to a general unbracing of energy, which we might have thought inconsistent with His dignity. But no self-abasement on His part is too great when there is question of helping us His brethren. He would have us able to say in our hours of trial: "Thus it was with Him; thus He prayed and acted. He must not feel His example has profited me nothing. Like Him, I will suffer patiently, and pray, and trust. Like my Leader, I will carry on to the end."

Patience represents the passive side of penance. It accepts with resignation, or, better still, with thankfulness and joy like the Apostles, whatever chastisement or trial may come to us from the hand of God, either directly, as ill-health, loss of means, good name, etc.; or through the action of others, as friction in daily life; or from ourselves, to whom, à Kempis tells us, most of our trials are due.

Penance that is active and voluntary not only accepts the troubles of life as they come but engages in active conflict with self. It battles with temptation, and practises self-denial not only when this is necessary to avoid sin but when there is no obligation. To strengthen the will in good and, above all, to follow Christ more closely, His devoted servants and friends would show their sense of fellowship with Him not only in affection and in labour, but also in the endurance of pain. They make His cause their own, suffer when His interests are thwarted, rejoice when they prosper. The question is, not what they *must* but what they *may do* for Him.

When Lent comes round, these generous souls are not content with mere obedience to the commands of the Church, they try to enter into her spirit by taking up some definite practice of penance. Their Lord must not suffer alone. They will suffer in union with Him and for the intentions for which He suffers. Some passion or bad habit must be fought, some duty more faithfully discharged. A special grace for themselves or for others shall be wrestled for, according to His words that certain favours are won only by prayer and fasting.

The whole so-called Christian world is in sore distress, and beyond it lies the huge pagan world which the light of the Gospel has not yet reached. Each soul of all these multitudes has its place in the Sacred Heart, in every one our Lord's interests are at stake, and for each and all our prayer and penance may be united with His for its salvation. If we will we may "fill up those things that are wanting of the sufferings of Christ," things He has purposely left for us, His members, to supply.

Unless we resolve on something definite, we shall lose ourselves in vague desires, beating the air, as St. Paul says. Pious thoughts must be turned into deeds, goodwill into determination. And, like the marksman, we should have a fixed target. À Kempis tells us we should aim at what hinders us most. It may be neglect of prayer, a want of charity in thought, word, or act, negligence in the discharge of a distasteful duty. For some of us a useful resolution might be to raise the tone of our life by more regular work, not merely occupation, but work intellectual or manual. With most people, perhaps, it is not work that is wanting, but the sanctifying intention that gives it value in the sight of God and renders it deserving of eternal reward. All of us need the moral labour which consists of brave persistent war against our predominant failing, our main hindrance on our way to God.

"I have so many faults that I cannot afford to attend to one only," is no valid objection. Faults, like virtues, are so linked together that to weaken one is to deal with all more surely and more speedily than by scattering our forces over many. The secret of Napoleon's strength was his faith in concentration. But we need not go to him for an example. Who does not know that victory over—not the noonday devil against whom Scripture warns us—but the morning devil that lies in wait for our waking moments, saves us from many a defeat during the day? Or how the effort to check a sharp word, to restrain our eyes during prayer, to practise some trifling self-denial at table, implies the exercise of many virtues?

As a means to the end in view, we may with profit select some penitential observance for Lent—e.g., curtail an unnecessary expense in behalf of the poor, etc. The act in itself may be trifling, but fidelity to it and to the resolution it backs up, this will be no trifle—"a single practice long sustained a soul to God endears."

It is useful to have fixed times for calling ourselves to account and renewing our resolution. Above all, it behoves us to be patient with ourselves when we fail. As a rule it is not failure so much that matters as the discouragement that is wont to follow. However frequent the relapse, if we rise promptly, turn to God with a loving act of sorrow, and, so far from losing heart, renew our resolution to "carry on," we are sure to reach our goal in the end. To fall is a sign of weakness; to rise at once, and without discouragement start afresh is an act of courage, a painful penance, as those who know from experience can testify.

St. Augustine likens failures to steps by which we may, if we will, mount higher. And à Kempis, speaking to us on the part of Christ, says: "Son, fight like a good soldier, and if sometimes thou fall through frailty, rise up again with greater strength than before, confiding in My more abundant grace." Does not a defeated general apply with promptitude and confidence to headquarters for speedy and stronger succour?

And if by the help of such steps and new reinforcements of grace we climb Mount Calvary during Lent and fall at last before the Cross on Good Friday to kiss the pierced feet and lay our offering there, we may be sure it will not be rejected: "him that cometh to Me I will in no wise cast out."

More frequent or more fervent reception of the Sacraments, a little spiritual reading, and, if we are able, attendance at the Church services at this time, will be a great help to the sanctification of Lent, will bring about a closer union with God throughout the day, and a more tender realisation of the sufferings of our Lord, draw down upon us the abundant blessings of this "acceptable time," and prepare us for the graces and joys that Easter never fails to bring to those who have passed a fervent Lent.

Value is proved by tests. Shall we want to know the worth of our resolutions as the six weeks run on? Let us ask ourselves the question: "If all 'the faithful' were to be keeping Lent after my fashion, would they deserve to be called fervent Catholics? 'The faithful' is a comprehensive term, comprising an inner and an outer circle—to which do I belong?"

XLIII
SEEKING

"Si quaeritis quaerite" ("If you seek, seek.")—Isa. 21:12.

EARNESTNESS should be the special characteristic of Lenten observance. It is impressed on every word and act and ceremony of the Church. We see it in the suppression of her songs of joy; in her oft-repeated cries for mercy and long-continued exercises of prayer and penance; in her pressing exhortations to "amend for the better in those things in which we have sinned, lest suddenly overtaken by the day of death, we seek space for penance and are not able to find it."

Self-humiliation and self-denial have from the beginning appeased the anger of God and won His favour. Like a mother, He loves to be sought and cried for. "God looked down from Heaven upon the children of men to see if there were any that did understand or did seek God." All His work for us in Creation, Redemption, and Sanctification is marked by an earnestness that bewilders and almost staggers our faith. And He loves to see this zeal of His reflected in our service of Him. To seek us He came down from Heaven. To seek Him is our one business in life. All else is supplementary. And life is short. We must not loiter. "The morning cometh, also the night; if you seek, seek."

Seeing that in Him we live and move and have our being, how, it may be asked, can there be question of seeking Him? The term is used in Scripture to denote something beyond the necessary nearness to and dependence on God which are a condition of out very existence. It indicates the voluntary movement by which the soul tends to God and strives to strengthen the bond which unites her to Him; to live and move, not only by Him, but for Him and with Him as the principle of all her action and the aim of all her endeavour. She thirsts for Him as the stag for the waterbrooks. She longs to lose herself in Him, to be possessed, impelled, controlled wholly by Him, to live by Him, realising ever more and more the desire of the holy Precursor: "He must increase and I must decrease."

"God looked down from Heaven upon the children of men to see if there were any that did understand or did seek God."

If there were any! And we owe Him everything, even our very selves. Oh, that we did understand! It was once, it is still—to use our human language—such pain to Him that we will not understand. "If thou didst know the gift of God." "If thou hadst known and that in this thy day the things that are to thy peace!"

Not only does He desire to be sought, but "He showeth Himself to them that seek Him." "Whom seek ye?" "Jesus of Nazareth." "I am He." This to His enemies. What will He say to His friends? "Master, where dwellest Thou?" "Come and see." What will He do for His friends that seek Him? Remove, even by an earthquake, the obstacles that bar their way to Him. Send angels, come Himself to console them and wipe away their tears.

But our search for Him must be real, not make-believe. "You shall seek Me and shall find me when you shall seek Me with all your heart." Now, specially in this time of Lent, of which the Church says: "Seek the Lord while He may be found," we have to bestir ourselves. If we are not His friends by sanctifying grace, we must set ourselves right with Him and without delay. If, happily, we are in His favour, we have still to seek His good pleasure, to find out what more He wants of us, that we may be drawn into closer familiarity with Him. Is there any insincerity in our service, any part of our life into which He must be pleased not to look, as to which He must refrain from asking questions, still more from demanding sacrifice?

Is there patent carelessness in our spiritual duties, in prayer, morning and night, in frequentation of the Sacraments, in the duties of our state? And as to amusements, almsgiving, employment of time, the duty of leading a laborious life—is all in order for the account of our stewardship that may be asked at any moment?

In this work of stocktaking, let us be fair to ourselves. After saying: "I am not conscious to myself of anything," St. Paul adds immediately: "Yet am I not hereby justified, but he that judgeth me is the Lord." We must not, then, be too easily satisfied. Should our conscience acquit us of any shortcomings, we may profitably bear in mind the last counsel—or is it warning?— given us in Scripture: "He that is holy, let him be sanctified still." There is always more to be done, or we should have been taken to our reward before now. We are left here only for the purpose of repairing our negligence. God did not grant us so many years of life wherein to secure the one thing necessary, and so many over and above which might be trifled away. If this moment I could behold the design of my life as it has been in His mind from eternity, see what amount of it has been satisfactorily filled in by my labour, what remains to be done, and how much time is still vouchsafed to me, maybe my lenient judgement of myself would be reversed. At the sight of the tremendous debts to His Justice which have accumulated, and the little I have done to reduce them by penance, I should surely meet Lent, not with resignation only, but with joy, exclaiming, as I started on a career of honest self-denial, "Have patience with me and I will pay Thee all!"

It behoves me, then, to look into my accounts, to ask myself seriously: "What am I doing to save my soul? What pains am I taking to overcome propensities which, if left unchecked, may endanger my salvation? What am I doing for others in the shape of good example, alms, personal service? All around me I see the servants of God about their Master's business—what am I doing for Him? If I am in doubt as to what He wants of me, dare I say to Him in the sincerity of my heart: "Lord, what wilt Thou have me to do?" And should He send me to an Ananias, who will speak to me in His name, am I ready to go?

XLIV
"BEHOLD, I STAND AT THE DOOR AND KNOCK!"

—Apoc. 3:10.

"BEHOLD!" Wake, My beloved, wake! Shake off the lethargy that leaves thee cold and careless to a Voice that should thrill thee through and through.

"*I stand at the door:* I, thy God and Saviour and Last End. I, before whom thou must thyself soon stand, to hear the sentence that will decide thy eternal lot, I stand now at thy door—and knock.

"*I stand,* weary, for thou hast kept Me waiting long; patient, for the reward I expect is worth the tarrying and the pain; hopeful, for thou wilt yield thyself to Me at last.

"*At the door*—for thy freewill must admit or exclude Me. I will not force My way. I will always respect the liberty that is My best gift to thee. But I desire with desire to enter and be with thee.

"*I knock*—and listen for any stir within...and wait thy pleasure awhile...and knock...and knock again."

Dare we say we never hear Him knock? The objection was raised in the hearing of a little child, who answered quickly: "You never hear Him! Oh, I do, often, and quite loud."

All, at one time or another, hear the Voice of Him who speaks to every man born into this world. But to hear is not enough. To hear is of no avail without response and obedience. Some hear and turn away, for the call is to action and to sacrifice. Some hear, and forthwith seek to drown in the din of the world's business or the music of its pleasures the Voice of the Friend without. And some would fain listen or *have listened* long ago, but now it is too late. Now it would involve too much effort and self-reproach—too much effort for a will that sloth has atrophied, or self-indulgence weakened; too much self-reproach for a soul that shrinks from meeting its true self face to face.

And so the answer comes faintly through the closed door: "Trouble me not, the hour is now past, I cannot rise and open to Thee."

Yet why should we thus stifle the Voice that speaks to us? In the work of our salvation it is imperative and essential that we should co-operate with our Saviour. "He who made us without us will not save us without us."[1] He has done His share. By His blood He has purchased for us every needful grace. But we must stretch out our hand to take what He offers. To cry: "Lord, Lord!" is not enough. We must follow His lead, deny ourselves, labour and suffer, and so make our election sure and work out our salvation. The sacrifice He asks we must make at whatever cost: we cannot measure the risk of a refusal.

"*I stand and knock.*" If He importunes us, it is because time presses; because the business at stake is the one thing necessary and the issues are eternal. Love at times must be exacting, even cruel. It must disturb, rebuke, urge forward the traveller who sinks down upon the snow and only asks to sleep.

---

1   St. Augustine.

"*I knock*"—He knocks now. He pleads, saying: "Open to Me, My sister, My love, for My head is full of dew and My locks of the drops of the night. If any man shall hear My Voice and open to Me the door, I will come in to him and will sup with him and he with Me."

But we may weary Him at last; and He may pass from our door never to return. "I rose up to open to my Beloved. I opened the bolt of my door to my Beloved; but He had turned aside, and was gone....I sought Him and found Him not; I called and He did not answer me."

The time draws near when, in the midnight, there will be the cry: "Behold the Bridegroom cometh!" when those who are ready will go in with Him to the marriage, and the door will be shut. Then will come the foolish ones crying and saying: "Lord, Lord, open to us!" And He shall say to them: "Amen, I say to you, I know you not."

XLV
TREASURE

"Lay not up to yourselves treasures on earth, where the rust and moth consume, and where thieves break through and steal."—Matt. 6:19.

WE have to make use of the good things of this life—health, friendship, influence, pleasures of various kinds—but we are not to let them engross us as a miser is engrossed by the treasure he has laid up. It is his one thought day and night. It is his all. He will die of starvation rather than part with it. What we prize as our possession we always hold in trust. Time, talents, position, whatever assets we have at our disposal, are capital confided to us by our Master to be traded with and dispensed in His service. So that when circumstances, which are the bearers of God's will to us, deprive us of any of these things, or the great thief—Death—carries them off at one swoop, we are not to be unhinged or dismayed.

Our Lord knows the dignity and the capacity of our soul, that it is not made for any good which rust or moth can consume, which we can lose against our will. He knows that everything of this earth changes, and that we ourselves change and find insipid what once delighted us. We see only a little way in front of us. He sees far into the eternal years, and His desire is to behold us there absolutely satisfied in the possession of what we made our treasure whilst choice remained to us. Therefore He says to us: "Lay up to yourselves treasures in Heaven," out of reach of the accidents of this life; set your heart upon what will endure for ever.

What is our treasure, or rather, what should it be?

My treasure, first and foremost, is *my immortal Soul*. Anything I put before this, anything I exchange for this—what will it profit me in the long run? If I save my soul all is saved; if I lose it all is lost. What, then, must I do to secure its salvation? I will commit it to the safe keeping of Him who made it and gave it to me, and I will beseech Him to put into my heart His own esteem and love of it. "Have pity on it, O Lord, because it is my only one."

My treasure is *my Faith*, a gift of inestimable worth, as to which I may say again, if I lose it all is lost unless God in His mercy should restore it to me before I die. It is a treasure to be guarded with untiring vigilance—no occupation, companions, conversations, no books nor amusements must endanger it. Should I lose Hope or Charity, Faith may bring them back, but if I lose my Faith, all indeed is lost.

My treasure is the *Grace of God* in my soul. It is called sanctifying because it confers a holiness, one degree of which is enough to merit Heaven. With some of us this grace comes and goes as the lodger of a night. It is here to-day and gone to-morrow. With others it is an habitual resident. It has taken up its abode in the soul as in a palace wherein the Three Persons of the Blessed Trinity dwell, and which it is their delight to enrich more and more. This grace is conferred or increased by every Sacrament worthily received. The Sacraments are a very storehouse of grace, each having the sacramental grace special to itself, all increasing the sanctifying grace which is the soul's treasure for eternity. As many degrees of sanctifying grace carried out of this life, so many degrees of glory in its eternal life. Nothing but mortal sin can deprive us of this treasure. Venial sin may endanger but does not lessen it. Every prayer, every good deed, every kind word, or trouble faced, or temptation resisted, adds to the store of treasure laid up where neither rust nor moth consumes and where thieves do not break through nor steal. Could we remember this, how cheerfully should we rise each morning to our day's work and opportunities, saying: "Another day to live; another day for serving God; another day for rising higher!"

My treasure is *Peace of Soul*, a possession so precious that the saints have prized it next to the grace of God, and guarded it against all assaults:

> For he dearly loved his money, with a passion deep and blind,
> As a scholar loves his learning, or a saint his peace of mind.

No loss of person or of place, of health or goods or reputation, no past sins repented of but unforgotten, no uncertainty as to the future here or hereafter, must rob me of this peace. It was our Lord's special gift to His friends, His word of greeting to them, the one consolation He reserved to Himself when all else was sacrificed, the one He would have us preserve at any cost: "Lamb of God who takest away the sins of the world, grant us peace."

My Soul, my Faith, the Grace of God and His Peace! May this Treasure, prized above all else that I love and guard, so satisfy me, that nothing of this world may have power to engross my thoughts or ensnare my heart. Where my treasure is, there let my heart be.

XLVI
"REJOICE!"

"Rejoice for joy."—Isa. 66:10. (*Introit for Laetare Sunday.*)

SUDDENLY, in the staidness of Lent, the Church breaks into a cry of joy. "Rejoice!" is her call to us to-day.

As the Transfiguration preceded the Passion, so does Laetare Sunday with its words of hope and gladness prepare us for the solemn weeks on which we are entering. "Looking upon Jesus, who for the joy set before Him endured the Cross," we are encouraged to follow bravely where He leads. Penance will come to an end, but "the rewards promised to penitents," these will have no end. And by Hope they are ours even now.

Oh, let us open our hearts to Hope! We need it sorely in these days of sorrow and of peril. Faith can do much for us, but Hope can do more, for it supposes Faith and grasps what Faith holds out to us. By fixing our eyes on the good things that are eternal, it loosens our hold on those temporal goods which a materialistic age would fain persuade us are the sole desirable objects within our reach. Hope quickens our step towards the "rewards"; as a traveller, catching a glimpse of his home, we hasten on and hope lights up the distance that intervenes. Listen to the cry rising from the dungeons of our English Martyrs in the penal days:

> Ah! my sweet Home, Jerusalem,
>   Would God I were in thee;
> Would God my woes were at an end,
>   Thy joys that I might see!

That Hope should be a privilege and an incentive stands to reason; that it should be a matter of precept is at once a revelation of God and of ourselves, a witness to the compassion of our Heavenly Father, and to the perversion of our primeval instincts; to the downward drag of sin.

The beauty, the peace, the uncloying delights of the earthly paradise did not dull in our first Parents desire for their Heavenly Country. Without effort their hearts tended upwards by the bias of their nature created in sanctifying grace. There was no stronger counter-attraction to draw them down to earth. Yes, Hope in Eden, where it all but touched fruition, must have been beautiful indeed!

After the Fall—what but Hope was left to the banished children of Eve! It was all, but it was enough. To cling to the promises of God in spite of all hindrances from within and without, this was the one thing necessary for them, thenceforth, to the end of time.

How quickly was that Promise given on which all Hope is built! Before the terrible vista of pain and labour, exile and death, was opened out to Adam and Eve—as if to forestall the despair that must else have crushed them, as if the Divine wrath was willingly diverted from these favoured creatures—guilty indeed, yet deceived—to the miserable being that had seduced them, in the very instant of that first call to judgement, we hear the Promise of Redemption and of pardon:

"And the Lord God said to the woman: Why hast thou done this? And she answered: The serpent deceived me and I did eat.

"And the Lord God said to the serpent: Because thou hast done this wrong, thou art cursed among all cattle and beasts of the earth....I will put enmities between thee and the woman, and thy seed and her seed: she shall crush thy head."

The virtue of Hope, then, is in itself a revelation of the character of our God. Can we think of Him as hard and unmindful of our weakness, when we see the part He assigns to it in the work of our salvation! It is ranked among the theological virtues which relate immediately to Himself. In the soul of the baptised child He plants it as a precious germ to be guarded and developed with Faith and Charity; plants it so deep that only the most persistent effort can eradicate it. He seems to exalt it above almost every other virtue, at least to set it before us oftenest. He entices us to it by promises. He holds out to it magnificent rewards in this life and the next. He protects it by sanctions. He frightens us into its arms by threats. Not only does He permit us, His poor, sinful children, to expect from Him eternal glory and happiness, not only does He coax us by all manner of endearing words to look forward to Heaven, but He commands us under pain of eternal punishment to anticipate—that is, to promise ourselves—salvation and all things necessary to obtain it—if we do what He requires of us. Even in the most guilty He counts despair as the gravest, the one unpardonable sin. And every step on the road to despair, every yielding to despondency, discouragement, diffidence, He takes as an affront to His honour and to His love. For such distrust He admits of no excuse—not falls, however grievous, however frequent; not broken purposes, however heartless, however mean. And lest we should seek to hide discomfited pride under the garb of humility, protesting it is not His Mercy that we doubt, but our own sinfulness and inconstancy that we fear, He reminds us that Hope is to be built not on our merits but on His promises, His mercy, and His power. For guarantee He gives us His own words: "Let the wicked forsake his way...and let him return to the Lord and He will have mercy on him: and to our God, for He is bountiful to forgive.[1] If the wicked do penance and keep all My Commandments...living he shall live and shall not die....Is it My will that a sinner should die, saith the Lord God, and not that he should be converted and live?[2]...I came not to call the just but sinners to penance."[3]

And this is the Father whose love we doubt: about whose readiness to bring us safely through all dangers we have such misgivings, whose Voice through both Testaments we hear saying to us unceasingly: "Fear not!"

"Fear not, My servant...neither be dismayed...for, behold, I will save thee."[4]

"Be quiet, fear not, and let not thy heart be. afraid."[5]

"Fear not, nor be any way discouraged."[6]

"Fear not, for the battle is not yours, but God's."[7]

"Take courage, and fear not."[8]

"Fear not, little flock."[9]

"Fear not, only believe."[10]

"It is I, be not afraid."[11]

"And He laid His right hand upon me, saying: Fear not."[12]

1	Isa. 55.	2	Ezech. 18.	3	Luke 5.
4	Jer. 30.	5	Isa. 8.	6	Deut. 1.
7	2 Par. 20.	8	Isa. 35.	9	Luke 12.
10	Mark 5.	11	John 6.	12	Apoc. 1.

O Lord my God, here truly present, saying to me from this Tabernacle: "Fear not," what can mistrust do but break down utterly before words and promises that run like a sweet refrain throughout the whole of revelation! What can my heart do but leap up to Thee, and in the same words of inspiration respond with fullest trust to Thy appeal!

"The Lord is my light and my salvation, whom shall I fear? The Lord is the Protector of my life, of whom shall I be afraid?"[1]

"Though I should walk in the midst of the shadow of death, I will not fear evil, for Thou art with me."[2]

"In God I have put my trust...I will not fear."[3]

"In Thee, O Lord, have I hoped....Into Thy hands I commend my spirit."[4]

---

1 Ps. 26. 2 Ps. 22. 3 Ps. 55.
4 Ps. 30.

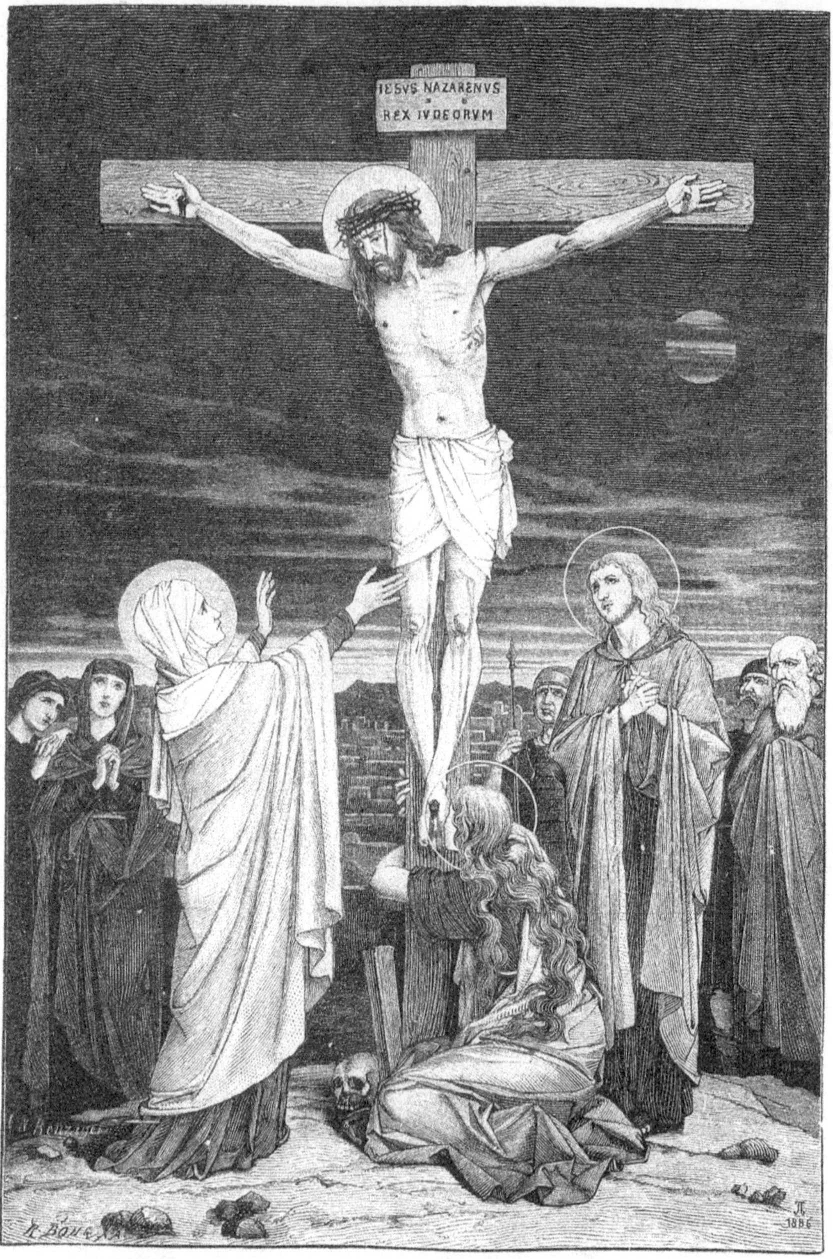
IESVS NAZARENVS
REX IVDEORVM
1886

THE SACRED PASSION

XLVII
PASSION WEEK

"Launch out into the deep."—Luke 5:4.

OUR Lord's life of three and thirty years was one long road to Calvary. It had its joys, no doubt. The serenity of His home that no present anxiety, no forecast of coming anguish was suffered to disturb; His Mother's sympathy that shared in every pang which it could reach, and adored where it could not penetrate; the simplicity and perfection with which the dear foster-father played his wonderful part of Superior where he was last and least—this was rest and consolation to the Sacred Heart, yet the Son of Man was always the Man of Sorrows.

What must He have suffered to see that after a preparation of four thousand years, He was not wanted when He came; to find forgetfulness of God, injustice and sin all around Him; to have His merciful designs thwarted at every turn; the simple folk and the little children turned against Him! What pain to Him was the hypocrisy and malice that miracles of mercy only strengthened; the perversity that in the midst of marvels was always demanding a sign; the cowardice of those who believed but would not confess Him; the want of faith even in His Apostles; the gradual falling away of Judas.

We are about to keep the anniversary of our Blessed Lord's Sufferings and Death for us. Can we do better than try to spend the coming days as His friends who knew Him on earth will have done? How they must have talked over the events of that solemn week as it came round year by year! "To-day," they will have said, He was in the Temple for the last time; to-night He spent in the Garden of Olives." They visited the places consecrated by His sufferings, made the Stations in company with our Lady, and passed on precious memories to those who were to come after them.

About Friday or Saturday before Passion Sunday our Lord set out on His last journey to Jerusalem. St. John tells us that having arrived at Bethany with His disciples, His friends, Martha, Mary, and Lazarus, made Him a supper there, and Martha served, but Lazarus was one of them that sat at table with Him.

What a supper was that, ushering in the Passion like the Carnival before Lent! What a gathering! "A great multitude of the Jews knew that He was there, and they came, not for Jesus' sake only, but that they might see Lazarus whom He had raised from the dead." A multitude—men and women, friends and enemies, the curious, the envious, a lover, a traitor, the highly-placed, the learned, simple fishermen, and—unique in the world's history—a leper cured of his disease and a man raised from the dead supping with Him who had exerted His miraculous power in favour of both, and for that resurrection was to be done to death by the voice of the whole people before another week was out!

Singular, too, were the actions of that gathering—the hostess serving, her sister anointing with precious perfume the feet of Him whom all were met there to meet; His own disciples condemning as waste an act of grateful love; one of them already harbouring a treacherous betrayal; many with curious gaze fixed on Lazarus four days in the grave; some with reverent eyes beholding the Master only.

Six days, and where would be the guests of that feast? Some in the noonday darkness reviling the Sufferer on the Cross; of His Apostles, eleven in hiding lest they should share their Master's shame; the traitor gone to "his own place"; one only standing by the stricken Mother to the end.

Launch out into the deep. Many of us have but a very superficial knowledge of the sufferings of Christ. We miss a deeper insight through want of consideration of the sources from which they flow. Among the chief of these sources was the foreknowledge of them all His life long. Yet, by a strange perversity, we allow this very fact to obscure the truth. Underlying our reflections, there is the idea in our mistrustful minds that, being God, He had within Himself a storehouse of compensations, a refuge always into which to climb. Because the Sacred Humanity was raised by the Hypostatic Union immeasurably above the level of any other human nature, we conclude that our Lord suffered less than we should do in like case. The exact contrary is the truth. His knowledge as Man extended to all that men and angels can know. Beyond this, He had that knowledge which belongs to His Divine Nature, a fact which opened out to Him possibilities of suffering all but limitless. Such reading of the hearts of men, such comprehension of the enormity of every offence against God, of the eternal destiny of every spirit, angelic and human, must surely have added to our Lord's pains a poignancy beyond our power to estimate, must have lain like an intolerable burden upon Him during the three and thirty years.

As the appointed Victim for sin, He would make all His Divine Attributes, all the excellences of His Human Soul and Body, work together, not for any alleviation of the measure of suffering He had freely chosen, but rather to enable Him to endure what without such support from the Divinity no human strength could have borne. He who all through His Life suspended the full effect of the bliss-giving Vision, was not likely to forgo any possible pain that love could bring within His reach. All must be pressed into its service.

But at what cost to Himself! As He lay a Babe in Mary's lap and smiled into her face, as He toiled by Joseph's side year after year, as He healed the sick, and comforted mourners, fondled the little children, listened to the long stories of the poor, or slept in Peter's boat, the Passion with all its horrible details was always present to Him: "I have a baptism wherewith I am to be baptised and how am I straitened until it be accomplished." His eager love and His human fears were in conflict always. Yet no ruffle on the placid brow, no strain on the attention, no faltering in interest, no weariness in tone, or lack of sweetness in the smile, told of the sorely-tried endurance.

Did He allow Himself the relief of tears? We are glad to know from St. Paul that in this, too, He was like His brethren, "in the days of His flesh with a strong cry and tears offering up prayers and supplication to Him that was able to save Him from death." He stayed the tears of others; He wept with them and for them. And we may well believe that often as He knelt by night on the mountain side, alone before the Face of the Father, that strong cry and tears went up *for us*.

All that we know of Him forbids us to think He would spare Himself any suffering He could share with us. One thing only, the hiding of the Father's Face, which in greater or less measure appears to be the lot of all His servants, we could never have expected Him to share by actual experience. None but Himself and the Father who knew what that eclipse would mean to the Son of His love, could know that it was even possible. But in this supreme trial, where we need His companionship most, He would not fail us. It was His last sacrifice—made willingly—but His Heart broke: "My God, My God, why hast Thou forsaken Me?...It is finished....Father, into Thy hands I commend My spirit." And, bowing His Head, He gave up the ghost.

When meditating on the Passion, we are bidden to pass from the contemplation of our Lord's physical torments to the sufferings of His Soul; to "launch out into the deep"; to consider how the Divinity hides Itself; how much He suffers; how He suffers *for me*. What return shall I make?

XLVIII
FRIDAY IN PASSION WEEK

"In death they were not divided."—2 Kings 1:23.

THOUGH the Feast of to-day bears the name of the Seven Dolours, the Church concentrates her attention on the last of these, as in a range of mountains the eye rests naturally on the highest summit.

Mary is the masterpiece of creation; in grandeur of design, in delicate beauty, in perfection of detail, only to be surpassed in excellence by the God-Man—her Son. Who could hope to understand the lifelong union of that Mother and that Son! From the instant when His Heart began to beat in unison with hers, they were one in mind and will, in aim and in interests, in their joys and their sorrows, in what to both was the very breath of life—the all-sufficiency to them of the Divine will. "Behold, I come to do Thy will, O God," He said. "Behold the handmaid of the Lord," was the unceasing aspiration of her heart.

Mary's absolute conformity with the will of her Creator finds expression in the words: "She shall be called 'My Will in her.'" There was no resistance to be overcome, but there were heights to be attained that called for all the heroic effort of which she was capable. In all the events of life she recognised the will of God and clung to it with the tenacity of affection prompted by her enlightened understanding and the loyalty of her unspoilt heart. With the simplicity of a child she trusted all its appointments. She loved it as devotedly in her profoundest anguish as in her deepest joys. That God wanted anything of her was enough—she offered it with both hands. When He called to sacrifice, her answer was always: "My heart is ready."

Gabriel found her already "full of grace." but her treasure was capable of increase. It grew continually; was augmented to an immeasurable extent by the Incarnation, and by the teaching and example of her Son during the hidden life at Nazareth. When as His most apt, most faithful disciple she stood by Him on Calvary, the highest exemplification after Himself of the poor in spirit, the meek, the mourners, the merciful, the peacemakers, the persecuted—when by Him, with Him, in Him, she offered to the Father the sacrifice of her All, who shall say the height of supernatural heroism to which that oblation rose!

For three hours she stood, seeing and hearing all. She saw the careless and the curious as they passed before the Cross; the mocking priests; the soldiers dividing His poor garments and drawing lots for the seamless robe she herself had spun. She heard the strokes of the hammer, the scoffing and reviling of the mob, the triumphant shouts of the Pharisees, the sobs of Magdalen, the blasphemy of the impenitent thief. She saw the sacred body sinking lower and lower on the nails as the hours went on, the widening of the wounds in hands and feet, the parched lips, the efforts He made to speak, the heaving chest with its difficult breathing, the growing disfigurement of the beautiful face. As a mother she was alive to sufferings that the eyes of others missed. She knew that failing strength did not dull in Him the consciousness of all and every pain; that the greater did not absorb the less; that the sharp wind and the slow trickling blood were keen distress to the sensitive trembling frame. She knew His

Heart. It was mourning for Judas still, tortured by the thought of the sentence He would have to pronounce on the miserable disciple He had tried so hard to save. She knew how He felt for Magdalen and for those whose faith in Him was being shaken by this death of shame. She saw how He was striving for the soul of the unrepentant sinner at His side.

Look at her. She "stood." says St. John. But oh, the agony of that endurance! We see it in the pallid face, the quivering lip, the trembling limbs, the steadfast glance that will miss nothing of what is torture unspeakable to contemplate.

She sees what is revealed to her alone. Her gaze penetrates into the Holy of Holies, the Soul of Christ, in its desolation. She follows its cry: "My God, My God, why hast Thou forsaken Me!" Were we unbelievers or ignorant of the part suffering has played and has still to play in the work of our salvation and sanctification, we might ask: Why all this needless agony? Why should she who was sinless and full of grace suffer so cruelly? Why were the common instincts of humanity allowed to be so blunted on Calvary as to permit the mother's presence at such a deathbed?

But we are Christians, and we know why.

She was there precisely because she was His Mother, the Mother of the Man of Sorrows, the Mother whom the will of God and the word of God have linked with Him for time and for eternity. The first worshippers at His crib "found the Child with Mary His Mother." At His first miracle, not only "the Mother of Jesus was there," but the marvel was wrought before His time, at her desire and intervention. Therefore it was fitting she should take her place beside Him—the mother's place—at death. That all ages might know that in the offering of the great Sacrifice by which the world was redeemed He would not be without her—"there stood by the Cross of Jesus His Mother."

She was there to refute the error that suffering should be the portion of the wicked only. In the Old Law the victims required by God had to be faultless. The Lamb of God who was to take away the sins of the world was the All-holy. And love exacts likeness. His Mother must be not only full of grace but full of sorrow. The portion He chose for Himself He shares with His friends, and in measure proportioned to their nearness and dearness to Him.

The will of God was Mary's stay beneath the Cross. She stood erect, for this was her support. Above all the promptings of nature that tore her mother's heart was the steadfast desire to see that will fulfilled in every tittle. She would not spare Him one pang. She bore up under every insult offered Him, renewing continually the offering they had made together at His Presentation in the Temple, in the quiet days at Nazareth, the stormy years of the Public Life, and on the Way of the Cross. To both the will of God was all in all—"Life in His Will."[1]

It is He Himself who from His Cross directs our eyes to her as to our Model: "Behold thy Mother." "Look, and do according to the pattern shewn thee on the Mount."[2]

---

1 Ps. 29:6.   2 Exod. 25:40.

XLIX
THE CHURCH'S WAYS

"Her ways are beautiful ways."—Prov. 3:17.

BECAUSE they are those of her Divine Teacher. In her Liturgy, as in His parables, Divine mysteries, transcending all human reason, are brought within reach of the eyes, the ears, the heart, the imagination, the intellect, and the will of man.

For fifteen centuries the Church had her own way in the education of the nations, and they learned quickly and well. Then, the Puritans thought to better these ways, and men were misled for a while. But human nature cried out for them, and they have come back, the world taking credit to itself for the discovery of what had been known from the beginning!

Now, in Holy Week, and more and more as mysteries deepen, the Church interprets them for us by a symbolism that appeals alike to the saint, the scholar, and the child. Let us watch, listen, and ponder. *See* from Tenebrae on Wednesday evening, her signs of mourning on every side, the deserted and unfurnished sanctuary, the open tabernacle, veil, flowers, ornaments—all gone! *Hear*—except for the Mass on Thursday—the suppression of every note of joy!

O Mother Church, truly thy ways are beautiful ways—*and sure*, leading, like the parables of the Son of Man, straight to the human heart! They proclaim thee the true Mother of men, with a mother's knowledge of us all; the Teacher taught by Him "who knew what was in man."

L
HOLY WEEK—I
"Attend and See!"

THERE are many weeks in the Church's year which she might have called Holy Week. But because of the mysteries which make the Passion the Holy of Holies, the culminating point of our Lord's life and mission, holding such a place in His Heart as to be called "His hour"; because His teaching and example here appear in their highest manifestation and it is here that He gives us the supreme proof of His love, she gives to this solemn commemoration of His sufferings year by year the name of Holy Week by excellence.

It is now when we see Him "lifted up" that He will fulfil His promise to draw all things to Himself. But we must do our part. The Church will do hers. Not only by setting the Passion before our eyes with all the symbolism at her command, but by renewing in our presence the very Sacrifice of Calvary which redeemed us, she helps us to realise what we have cost Him, what He has done to win our love. The earnestness of her words and acts will thrill us through and through, if we ponder these things in our hearts with the desire to give Him thus a proof of our compassion, our gratitude, and our love. We need grace for this, and God gives His grace to the humble. Let us, then, enter upon this week with humble reverence, for every step is holy ground.

The Passion of our Lord is a land of mystery, so vast, so strange that we need guidance for our minds and hearts as we attempt to traverse it. To help us, St. Ignatius suggests three questions: Who is it that suffers? What does He suffer? And why?

He who suffers is the Eternal Son of God. He had no obligations to us. We were in no way necessary to His happiness. He might have left us to perish in our sin and misery. Even had He taken pity on us and willed to save us at the price of the Incarnation, a prayer, a tear would have sufficed for the redemption of a thousand worlds.

And what was the actual cost? The Redemption such as we know it. "Despised and the most abject of men," a worm and no man, He was rejected by His people, mocked as a fool, condemned as a seducer and a malefactor, nailed living to a cross, derided and blasphemed even in the agony of death. And all the while He was God! We have to keep reminding ourselves of this as we follow Him on His path of suffering and shame.

He spoke very little of His pains, summing them up as "these things": "Ought not Christ to have suffered these things?" As if the scourging and the spitting, the mockery and the crucifixion were nothing so very wonderful, only what might have been expected of Him. "If thou art apaid I am apaid," He said sweetly to one of His servants[1] who was thanking Him for what He had endured for her sake.

And why did He endure it? Simply for love. We can never reckon with love or guess the lengths to which it will go. Through love he "delivered Himself," that is, surrendered Himself absolutely, body and soul, to the tortures prepared for Him. A consideration we should

---
1 Mother Juliana of Norwich.

not miss here is this: His was no ordinary human frame, but an organisation whose every faculty and limb and nerve was designed with a view to its awful office of discharging adequately, as the Victim for sin, the debt to Divine Justice of the whole human race: "A body Thou hast fitted to Me." His Soul, the most richly dowered that ever came from the hand of God, was sensitive as no other to all the influences under which it came. He was grateful for the least act of sympathy or kindness. He felt keenly injustice and ingratitude. He shared every sorrow of the sick and suffering, not of those only who crossed His path during His life on earth, but of all men whom He foreknew and owned as brethren. To all this accumulation of suffering, physical, mental, spiritual, intensified by the refinement of His nature to a point beyond the power of thought to conceive, our Head delivered Himself.

When we think of the penalty a single mortal sin incurs, we shudder at what the Divine Justice must have exacted from Him. He could do no sin, but "He was made sin for us" and the punishment of all was laid upon Him. Pain in this life has necessarily a limit by reason of the weakness of the body. It is always tempered by mercy, even to the most guilty. Every sufferer knows that before his pain reaches the unendurable, God's Providence will interfere in his behalf. It was this fidelity of God that gave courage to the martyrs in their protracted sufferings. They knew whom they had believed and were certain He would come to the rescue of the willing spirit and the frail flesh they had committed to His keeping.

But on "the Son of His love" there fell the full weight of His wrath. Up to the limits of human sufferance He was brought; beyond those limits, Omnipotence, His own Omnipotence, supported Him, and He endured.

"Willingly," it may be urged. Yes, willingly, most willingly, for love is ready to do more than it can. But this generosity brought no alleviation to the pain. Not till all secrets are revealed shall we know what we owe to the willingness of the Sacred Heart, and the abyss of anguish to which it delivered Him.

Soul and body were crushed. His sufferings were so disposed that every member of His body was racked with pain. Every fibre of His heart, that sensitive, affectionate heart of His, was subjected to outrage and humiliation; was torn by the treachery of one Apostle, the denial of another, the abandonment of His friends, the sorrow of His Mother, the ingratitude of the crowd. His Soul, weighed down by the sense of sin, was left in a desolation so awful, abandoned to a terror so extreme as to bring upon Him the agony of death. "The Lord laid upon Him the iniquity of us all." Can we wonder that He was crushed beneath the weight?

"But why," we ask again, "all this unnecessary suffering when one sigh would have more than sufficed?" St. Paul tells us why: "He loved me and delivered Himself for me." There is no other explanation, if explanation it is and not a deeper mystery still. Why the Infinite God, adorable in His Self-sufficiency, should love us as He does is inexplicable. He has said: "Greater love no man hath than this, that a man lay down his life for his friend." But the love of God has gone further in that He loved us when we were enemies. It is sweet to remember that as the Son has all things from the Father, so from the bosom of the

Father has he drawn this incomprehensible love for the sheep that had gone astray. He even assigns this love as a cause of the Father's love for the Son: "Therefore doth My Father love Me because I lay down My life for My sheep." We must take the sweet truth as it is and believe it like other mysteries:

> That Thou shouldst think so well of us
> And be the God Thou art
> Is darkness to my intellect
> And sunshine in my heart.
> —Faber.

But our Lord does look for a return. "Having joy set before Him He endured the cross." What joy, what reward? That all He has done and suffered should profit us, that we should stretch out our hands and accept the salvation He offers us. Is this asking too much? We speak of unnecessary suffering. But was its excess unnecessary? Has it sufficed to win the grateful love which would requite Him? Do we at least show ourselves so thoroughly resolved to work out our salvation as to make this the main object of our life? The Head cannot do all. It cannot dispense the members from following where it leads. On Calvary He said: "It is finished." And so indeed it was. *He* has done all He could. But His mystical body has to bear its share of labour and suffering. Do I realise this? Does my life show that I am guided by this conviction?

To be practical. What are we going to do this Holy Week to bring about such realisation in ourselves and others? If there is an opportunity of assisting at the solemn offices of the Church, can we arrange that any of the household besides ourselves—children, visitors, servants—shall be able to take part in them? How many Catholics, alas! make no more use of the spiritual helps afforded at this time than if they were twenty miles from a Church. A Bishop from Uganda tells how the Christians there think nothing of a twelve days' journey every month to assist at Mass and approach the Sacraments. If their example is a stimulus to us, may we hope that our own example in this matter of attendance at Church during Lent will profit those for whose spiritual welfare we are to any extent accountable?

The Way of the Cross is a most suitable devotion during Lent. Richly indulgenced by the Church, it has wonderful efficacy at all times. To make the Stations during Lent in union with our Lady and her sorrowing companions is a sure way of growing in the love and imitation of our suffering Saviour.

More frequent visits to the Blessed Sacrament when a church is within reach is another practice for sanctifying Lent that will naturally suggest itself.

LI
HOLY WEEK—II

WE are preparing to keep the anniversary of our blessed Lord's Death for us. Can we do this better than by spending these coming days as those will have done who knew and loved Him in the days of His life on earth? How they must have talked over the events of that solemn week as it came round year by year! "To-day." they will have said, He was in the Temple for the last time: to-night He spent in the Garden of Gethsemani." They visited the places consecrated by His sufferings and passed on the precious memories to those who were to come after them. Let us keep in their company, and try to bring Him before us during the last days of this Week, treading with Him and His sorrowing followers the mountain slopes, the Temple Courts, the streets of the Holy City.

After His humble triumph on Palm Sunday, when amid cries of "Hosanna!" He entered Jerusalem, our Lord went into the Temple. There, on Monday and Tuesday He spent the day teaching and healing. When night came He had nowhere to lay His Head. No one offered Him hospitality, and unless He returned to His friends at Bethany, He must have spent the nights on the mountain side in prayer.

Tuesday was a stormy day. All men could see that the end was not far off. His enemies of every party had now leagued together to catch Him in His speech that they might make away with Him. Our Lord gave them His last solemn warnings. He told them the parable of the wicked husbandmen who beat and stoned the messengers sent by the master of the vineyard, and killed his beloved son. They knew that He spoke of them even before the terrible words that followed: "Woe to you Scribes and Pharisees, hypocrites," repeated again and again. Then, His heart overflowing with grief at the obstinacy of His people, He broke out into the tender reproach: "Jerusalem, Jerusalem, thou that killest the prophets and stonest them that are sent unto thee, how often would I have gathered together thy children as the hen doth gather her chickens under her wings, and thou wouldst not. Behold your house shall be left to you desolate. For I say to you, you shall not see Me henceforth till you say: Blessed is He that cometh in the name of the Lord." Saying this, He rose and left the Temple for the last time. The Twelve followed Him up the slope of Olivet, but before reaching the summit He turned to look at the City which He was not to enter again till He came to die. From this high point the whole scene of the Passion lay outstretched before Him. At His feet was Gethsemani; yonder on Mount Sion were the Supper Room and the palaces of the priests. Nearer the Temple stood Pilate's Praetorium, and—a thousand paces thence—He could see Calvary and the Tomb.

His thoughts stretched farther still—to the doom that forty years later was to fall on Jerusalem, and to the end of the world when all mankind would stand beneath Him, waiting for judgement in that valley of Jehoshaphat through which the torrent of Kedron at His feet was now winding. He began to speak to the Twelve about that last awful Day and to urge them to watch and pray, for they knew not when the time would come. He told them the parables of the talents, of the lord coming at midnight, of the Ten Virgins. And ended with the solemn words: And what I say unto you I say unto all—Watch!"

LII
PALM SUNDAY—I

WHAT an absorbing interest the Prophecies must have had for the Jews of our Lord's day who recognised in Him the long-promised Messiah! Pondering with Isaias His triumphant entry into Jerusalem, imagination readily supplied the details:

His priests will have prepared His way. His people will make Him King by acclamation. The Temple Courts will resound with His praise. Should His reception coincide with one or other of the great Festivals, the concourse of Jews from all parts of the world will enhance the glory of the solemnity. Even the Gentile rulers will yield to the general enthusiasm. Recognising that the Desired of all nations had come, and that it were vain to dispute His sovereignty, they will wisely cede to Him His Kingdom. The crown and sceptre of His father David will be laid at His feet, and thus will be inaugurated the everlasting reign of the Prince of Peace.

So much for the dream. And the reality?

His people will indeed receive Him with palms and Hosannas, but in five days the cry put into their mouths by the priests will be: "Crucify Him! Crucify Him!" Jerusalem will be filled to overflowing, but to witness His defeat and His shame. Because He has gone about doing good, He will be dragged before four tribunals, overwhelmed with false accusations, scourged as a slave, condemned to death as a malefactor. His friends will forsake Him, one Apostle will betray Him, another deny

Him. He will reign—but, as foretold, "from the tree," and His subjects will look upon Him whom they have pierced.

Had the account of our Lord's last week on earth been a mere human fabrication it would have been denounced as an impossibility. So complete a revulsion of feeling in a whole people, from adoring homage to an outcry for the most cruel and degrading of deaths, would never have found credence.

Truly, God's ways are not ours! When and where shall we penetrate His ways if not in Holy Week and on Calvary? If failure so complete was to be the prelude of a victory such as the world had never seen, shall we not learn to trace in our own lives the same mysterious ways, and wait in patience and in hope for God's compensations, for a glorious resurrection to follow upon defeat and death?

LIII
PALM SUNDAY—II

OPPORTUNITIES

"If thou hadst known and that in this thy day the things that are to thy peace!"—Luke 19:42.

THERE is something in opportunities wantonly neglected, in noble gifts abused, in wealth heedlessly squandered, that calls forth sorrow and indignation even in those least concerned. "He had such a chance," we say, "everything was in his favour."

Our Lord's heart was the most sensitive, the most affectionate that ever beat. He had laboured and prayed for His people, healed every disease and every infirmity, poured out upon Jerusalem all the treasures of His love. Yet when from Mount Olivet He looked down upon the city on the day of His triumph, what was the cry that broke from His Heart? "Jerusalem, Jerusalem...if thou hadst known...the things that are for thy peace...!" He knew the chastisements that were to fall upon the guilty city for its rejection of Him, and the agony of His pity wrung from Him that cry of disappointed love.

We grieve for Him and with Him, but in our sympathy is there no self-reproach? More than Jerusalem ever had is ours; grace beyond the reach of millions in the world to-day is given to us. What opportunities of merit our daily lives afford! Many of them through heedlessness we do not see; many we see only to reject. If correspondence with them requires a little effort, how often we put them from us without remorse almost as a matter of course. And every one was devised for us from eternity by infinite Wisdom and Love; was purchased for us at such a price!

To come to details: a sacrilege or a scandal is mentioned in our hearing. Someone present will make a five minutes' visit to the Blessed Sacrament in reparation—is it I? Do I at least turn to the Sacred Heart with an act of sorrow? Or is my only reference to the fact the reflection that *I* am not responsible for the sin? Love does not argue thus, does not deliberate. Not what it *must* but what it *may* do is in question, and it leaps forward to meet its opportunity. It acts, not through a sense of responsibility, but with the swiftness and sureness of instinct. Is an undesirable conversation to be directed into another channel? A troublesome visitor to be kindly received? A rash judgement checked, a monotonous duty bravely faced? How do I put to profit such daily opportunities of service? Welcome or unwelcome, they come unfailingly, each one of them a gift from God, bringing with it the actual grace its acceptance needs, and its title to an everlasting reward.

What our Lord has to deplore so often is the want of keenness where He is so much in earnest: "If thou hadst known the things that are to thy peace," He said to Jerusalem; and to the woman at the well: "If thou didst know the gift of God." He has His ambitions for us. He expects us to take our cue from Him. When He tells us that in His Father's house there are many mansions, it is not that we may reply forthwith: "Any mansion there will satisfy me," but that we may widen our hearts to desire what will be most glorious to Him and most profitable to ourselves, and so desiring, work for and secure "the better gifts" of which St. Paul speaks. Holy Scripture is full of God's appreciation of desires. Daniel was magnificently rewarded for being "a man of desires"; so was holy Simeon. Our Lord Himself "desired with desire." Desire, if supernatural, is Hope, a theological virtue. The prayer "Thy Kingdom come!" proves the desire of God Himself that we should earnestly long after the good things He has prepared for us. When heretics decried the motive of reward as selfishness, the Church condemned them, as our Lord had already done in bidding us lay up treasure, and labour in His vineyard for the promised hire. He Himself, "having joy set before Him endured the Cross." The joy for which He laboured and suffered was our salvation; our joy in suffering may be, not merely the thought of reward, but His contentment who so earnestly desires the things that are for our peace. It is a noble ambition that determines to make the most of life; to give to Him, from whom we have received all, the best service we can offer. It is a filial and generous egotism that resolves to lose nothing of the treasure our Father has put within our reach, that saves from the waste-heap to which selfishness and worldliness would consign them, time and talent, influence, means, and opportunity, and puts all to profit for His glory.

This was the aim and the lifework of the saints, of the Queen of saints. From first to last her course was one of faultless perfection. Guided only by the Spirit of God, she went forward along her wonderful path without a halt or a mistake. Should such an example discourage us? No, surely. A mother is not surprised at the stumbling step of the child at her side. Its weakness and its falls do but call for her pity and her help. She lends it her own strength and they cover the ground together. Let us ask the Virgin most faithful, our Queen and our Mother, to get us more alacrity on our road to Heaven, more light to see, more generosity to follow the inspirations of grace; we shall find the service of God growing not only more real, but easier and sweeter, because it will be more and more a service of love.

LIV
"ONE OF THE TWELVE"

"Woe to that man by whom the Son of Man
shall be betrayed."—Luke 22:22.

MAUNDY THURSDAY—I

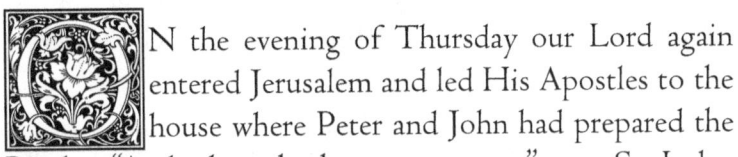

ON the evening of Thursday our Lord again entered Jerusalem and led His Apostles to the house where Peter and John had prepared the Pasch. "And when the hour was come," says St. Luke, "He sat down and the twelve Apostles with Him."

How He loved them, those dear Apostles! With all their slowness, their narrow-mindedness, and their faults—how He loved them! The simplicity and intimacy of His relations with them during the three years of their training appears on every page of the Gospels. There was no aloofness on His part, no sense of constraint on theirs. Their thoughts, questions, troubles, little disputes even, came out freely in His presence without fear of rebuke. Like children around Him were these simple-hearted men, given to Him by His Father, not as followers only, but as friends. They had left all things for His sake. They were bound to Him by the most devoted, the most passionate affection. They were ready, or believed themselves ready, to give their lives for Him. And now the years of intimacy with Him were over: the hour of leave-taking was come; this was their last meal together.

It is at parting that tenderness is wont to break through all constraint. During life it is often shy. In some natures, some of the deepest, it is shy all life through. But the floodgates open at the hour of death. The tenderness of our Lord's human Heart was "straitened" from the first. Its desire to give, not its benefits only but itself, He had to hold in check for thirty years. Then its sympathy went out to every kind of misery. But men set up their barriers and frustrated its plans. Jerusalem had now disowned Him. To-morrow the multitudes He had fed and healed and comforted would turn upon Him and clamour for His death. What remained to Him but His Twelve! Twelve? An hour hence it would be Eleven!

To venture within the sanctuary of our Lord's thoughts as He entered the Supper Room, we must follow the lead of St. John, who takes as his special task the study of the heart on which he had leaned that night.

It was a burdened heart, burdened and straitened. There were many things the Master had to say to His disciples. But so long as Judas was among them one thought, one pain appeared to absorb Him. After the washing of the feet He was troubled in spirit and said: "You are clean, but not all. Amen, amen I say to you, one of you shall betray Me." Even in the institution of the Eucharist this terrible thought was present to Him: "One of the Twelve whose hand is with Me on the table, he shall betray Me."

Those words, "One of the Twelve," repeated nine times by the Evangelists, must have passed like a sorrowful echo from His heart to theirs. A year before He had said at Capharnaum: "Have not I chosen you twelve, and one of you is a devil?" "Now," says St. John, "He meant Judas Iscariot, for the same was about to betray Him, whereas he was one of the Twelve."

The Heart of Jesus was wrung with anguish at the thought of the misery to which one of His chosen Twelve was rushing. Again and again during the supper He speaks of the betrayal, now in tender, now in terrible words, striving by fear when love had failed, to save him before it was too late. The consternation of the Eleven increased His pain. They beheld with dismay the distress on that countenance always so reassuring in its serenity. Was this He to whom they had been wont to turn in every need? St. John says, "they looked upon one another doubting of whom He spoke, and being very much troubled began to say to Him one by one, "Is it I, Lord?"

Once during the supper the cloud that overshadowed them all was for a brief space lifted. The hour "desired with desire" wherein our Lord was to make His greatest Gift to men was come. His countenance glowed with a Divine exultation and love as over the bread and over the chalice He spoke for the first time the words of Consecration; as the first communicants were fed with the Living Bread from Heaven, and the first priests, appointed by the great High-Priest to carry on His office, were ordained. But these moments of solemn happiness passed quickly. When the disciples, lifting their bowed heads, looked again into the Master's Face, the glow and the serenity were gone, and once more there had settled upon His brow the anguish of a friend betrayed.

Yet not till every effort love could devise had failed, did Jesus say to the traitor: "That which thou dost, do quickly." "He therefore went out immediately. And it was night."

At once St. John notes a change of atmosphere. There was trouble still. But round the Master now all were of one mind, friends to whom He could speak freely and look for sympathy. A heavy task was still before Him. He could not withhold from the Eleven the warning needed by all. He had to speak of denial and desertion, and of a parting close at hand. Gently He broke to them that He must leave them: "Little children, I go to prepare a place for you. Whither I go you know and the way you know." Thomas answered: "Lord, we know not whither Thou goest and how can we know the way?" "Lord, whither goest Thou?" said Peter. "Why cannot I follow Thee now? I will lay down my life for Thee." Jesus answered him: "Wilt thou lay down thy life for Me? Amen, amen, I say to thee, the cock shall not crow till thou deny Me thrice."

They were inconsolable at the thought of separation from Him who for three years had been to them all in all. He looked round upon them with love and compassion—the little flock so soon to lose its Shepherd and be scattered; the little children to be left orphans; the first priests to be found wanting. In their desertion of Him He thought more of their desolation than of the injury to Himself, and sought to comfort them by reminding them of their fidelity to Him in the past: "You are they who have continued with Me in My temptations."

But how could he comfort them, His dear, rough, tender-hearted Apostles? How persuade them that it could be expedient for them that He should go? "I will not leave you orphans," He said. "I will ask the Father and He shall give you another Paraclete, that He may abide with you for ever...And I will come again and will take you to Myself that where I am you also may be." It was no use. They did not understand and could only look at Him in helpless misery.

For three years they had known Him as the kindest of masters. But this night, at this supper, they were conscious of a difference. Never had He been quite like this before. In the dear familiar ways, in the tones of His voice, in His words: "Little children, not servants but friends," there was a new tenderness that told of a parting near at hand. What He was *to them* they knew well, but to-night had brought a new revelation of what they were *to Him*. Only now, as it seemed, had they begun to know Him, to feel that His presence was not their happiness only, but their very life. And He was going away, leaving to them a work the very outlines of which they could not discern. His own heart they could see was wrung with sorrow, yet His thought, as usual, was all for them.

They could not follow all He said; but this they understood—that He was going from them, going where they might not follow. This was enough. For this there was no comfort, no possible compensation. He spoke to them of His Spirit whom He would send them, of His Father who loved them and would come to them. They would not be comforted. It was the dear human presence that was being taken from them, and no substitute could be acceptable.

And they were right. Our Lord knew that the instinct was true which taught them that His Sacred Humanity was the divinely appointed source and channel of all good and grace to us. He would send His holy Spirit; the Father would come and make His abode with them. But not as a substitute for the human presence for which they craved. That Gift, once given, was never to be withdrawn. If He left them, as He must, to die for them, He must leave them a Legacy worthy of Himself.

LV
THE "UNSPEAKABLE GIFT"

"This is My Body...This is My Blood."—Mark 22:22.

MAUNDY THURSDAY—II

THE last desire and petition of the dying is to be remembered by those they love. For such remembrance they make provision, as far as possible, by bequeathing to their nearest and dearest all they have to leave.

Our Lord had come to almost the latest hour when He was free to dispose of anything He could call His own. This very night He was to sacrifice His freedom. On the morrow He would give the last drop of His blood. What more remained to Him? "Greater love than this no man hath, that he lay down his life for his friends." But Christ was God as well as Man, and within the range of His Omnipotence there was another Life which He might bequeath—a Life beyond the reach of His tormentors, beyond the grasp of death; a Life so marvellous as to be a summary of all His wonderful works; a Life involving miracle upon miracle for its support. It was a Life that only Infinite Wisdom could have devised, Infinite Love have desired, Infinite Power could effect—His Eucharistic Life in the Sacrament of His love.

This was the Gift He had in store for us, the Keepsake made over to men the night on which He was betrayed. He had in mind, not the Twelve only, but all who through their word should believe in Him. By the words: "Do this in commemoration of Me," the Divine Legacy of the Eucharist, under its twofold aspect of Sacrifice and Sacrament, was perpetuated through the priesthood of His Church for all days even to the consummation of the world. He would not leave us orphans. He would be waiting for us, one by one, when our time should come for entering on the privileges and the perils of life. And, like a friend at parting, who promises not to forget us, He asks in turn, asks us one and all—for a remembrance.

Not to His priests alone was the charge of commemoration given. St. Paul was speaking to the simple faithful when he said: "As often as you shall eat this bread, you shall show the death of the Lord until He come." Do we often think of what it cost our Lord to give us this Bread of Life? At Mass and Communion do we remember Calvary?

Love calls for a return. "The charity of Christ urgeth us," says the great Apostle. To what did it urge St. Paul? To such a consuming love of Christ, to such surrender to Christ of his whole personality and activity, that he could say: "I live, now not I, but Christ liveth in me." Christ was all in all to him. His transformation was neither more nor less than an assimilation of Jesus Christ so striking, so complete that it has been said of him: "*Cor Pauli, Cor Christi,*"—the heart of Paul is the Heart of Christ. To his mind "*He loved me and delivered Himself for me*" was a conviction so deep, as to constrain him to such a return of love.

I can say these words with equal truth. To what return have they urged *me?*

Surely the Real Presence in our midst should be the central fact of our lives, as it is the source of all our grace and blessings. The knowledge of what it would be to the Church, of what it would or might be to each one of us, filled the heart of Jesus with joy as He spoke the words of consecration for the first time. But they brought also a train of sorrow. He knew of blasphemy and sacrileges to come. He saw through the ages, not only cathedrals filled to overflowing at solemn functions, the throngs of fervent communicants, the rich adornment of His sanctuaries, but many a church practically empty at Mass on weekdays, a dozen, perhaps, present, chiefly the poor, communicants few if any. He saw the loneliness and destitution in which His sacramental life would be lived, not only in foreign missions but in crowded cities. He saw untended altars and sanctuaries where by day as well as by night the lamp would be about His only companion.

Was it worth while? Yes; for to some His morning Sacrifice would be an attraction, His evening Benediction a consolation, His continual Presence on the altar a magnet which would draw to Him the hearts of His friends. For their sake and for the poor heedless world to which his abiding presence would be protection and grace, He would be with us always. The gifts of God, we are told, are without repentance. Not only without repentance, but with untiring affection does He remain in the Tabernacle day and night to welcome us whenever our need or our love brings us to His feet, and to be carried to us when we can no longer go to Him.

St. John says: "Jesus, having loved His own who were in the world, He loved them unto the end." We might have thought that Calvary was the end, that the Sacrifice there offered would satisfy even such love as His. But He was to be offered, a bleeding Victim, once only, in one place, in sight of a few of one generation. And His desire was to be a daily Victim to the end of time, wherever a Catholic altar should be raised throughout the world. He would die for us, yet stay with us all days to be our Companion, at hand in every need. And because our daily food is the greatest of our needs—well, then—our daily bread!

"If you seek food," says St. Ambrose, "He is nourishment." The soul, like the body, has to be kept alive, built up, preserved in health, strengthened to do its work, by means of food. But on what can the soul feed? What has He provided for it who made it and knows all its needs? *Himself.* *He* will be the food of the soul. It is not enough to give grace—He must give Himself. What could He have done for us that He has not done, and done with such joyous love!

Wonder, perpetual wonder, is the response of the Church to this Mystery of Love: "O God, who hast left us in this wonderful Sacrament a perpetual memorial of Thy Passion and Death...!" What is *our* response? If He sees us look up at the Host without wonderment in our eyes, without a glow in our hearts, can He find excuse for us in the deadening force of familiarity, or in the very excess of light which bewilders us? Can it be that such love does but overwhelm and stupefy our poor selfish hearts? We need the eyes of children to meet marvels with an astonishment that is ever new.

A little child preparing for First Communion said: "I think it's very wonderful that God should be *our food.* Because, you know"—and the voice sank to a whisper—"He mightn't have liked it." "Out of the mouths of babes hast Thou perfected praise."

Maundy Thursday should be a day, not only of deepest thanksgiving for the Gift which it commemorates, but of sorrowful reparation to our Lord for the little appreciation we have shown of His unspeakable Gift. Let our Communion be made in reparation; it is the spirit of the Church to-day. She would have us follow our hidden God to the altars of repose and by our companionship and sympathy make up to Him for the indifference of the multitudes who know Him so little or know Him not at all. Of the millions in the world to-day, how small a proportion are Christians! And of these, how few, comparatively speaking, have so much as heard of the presence of Jesus Christ in their midst! To many He is little more than a name. He does not enter into their lives. They know nothing of His life, His love, His thirst for their salvation. What would it mean to these fellow-countrymen, these brethren of ours, to have our faith? And why is it ours rather than theirs? Shall we not pray on this day when the Real Presence was confided to us, that the faith in it which would make all the difference to their lives may be given them?

Maundy Thursday is also a day when some of us might ask ourselves: "Could not I with a little sacrifice make my Communions more frequent during the coming year?" We are assured by the highest authority on earth that even daily Communion, where practicable, is the earnest desire of Christ Himself for us one and all. The Church will not have us perplexed or disheartened by the conflicting opinions of other days, or by difficulties arising from the dispositions requisite. She bids us remember that as a Sacrifice the Eucharist has primarily the glory of God for its end; as a Sacrament, its chief object is our good. We are bound, of course, to approach our Divine Lord as friends, but the wedding garment of grace and a right intention secured, we are always welcome at His Table. It is not as a reward for fidelity, but as a remedy for our frailty that He gives Himself to us.

O God, who in this wonderful Sacrament hast left us a memorial of Thy Passion, grant us, we beseech Thee, so to reverence the sacred mysteries of Thy Body and Blood, that we may *continually* find in ourselves the fruit of Thy Redemption. Through Christ our Lord. Amen.

LVI
"A PRIEST FOR EVER"

"Do this for a commemoration of Me."—Luke 22:19.

MAUNDY THURSDAY—III

OUR Lord had said that it was expedient for us that He should go. But He knew that it was equally necessary for us that He should stay. And nothing less than this would satisfy His brokenhearted disciples.

He would not disappoint them. They cried for bread, He would not reach them a stone. The commemoration of Himself which He enjoined should be no empty rite, but His very Self, a daily Sacrifice, a perpetual Sacrament, renewed in their hands and by their lips. It was to be no loss, but gain, bringing to them in each Mass the assurance: "It is I Myself." He has left us His Real Presence, real but hidden because it is not expedient—that is, not best for us as yet—to see and hear and touch Him, and our greater good was His rule in all that He did and suffered. But most expedient, most necessary for us, over and above our Redemption by His Sacrifice on Calvary, was the application of its fruits to us individually.

As the creatures of God, we have every one of us a fourfold duty to our Creator—of worship and of thanksgiving, of propitiation and of petition. It is a debt which of ourselves we are utterly unable to discharge, for which the united efforts of all creatures would not suffice. On Calvary our Lord took this huge debt upon Himself. He paid it entirely, for all mankind, and *for each one of us* in particular. Every act of His Life on earth, every word or tear might have paid this debt and supplied all our need. But He willed that only by the Sacrifice of the Cross should we be redeemed and saved. It was not for the satisfaction of His Justice, but for the contentment of His Love, that Calvary was a necessity. We must have a plentiful redemption. He must give all He had to give. The last drop of His Blood was offered for us on Calvary, because He willed it.

That Sacrifice of infinite value satisfied the Justice of God and acquired for us an inexhaustible store of merit. It could never be repeated. But its merits had to be distributed and applied. Therefore, not another, but the very same Sacrifice, "a clean oblation." was to be offered in every place. At every hour of day and night the Mass is distributing the grace stored up for us on Calvary, not derogating from, but realising the all-sufficiency of that Sacrifice. Every hour the Church is drawing water with joy from the Saviour's fountains for the sustaining and invigorating of her life. And what is given to her is given to each and all of her children to be available for us *one by one*. Have we ever pondered the privilege and the obligation this involves? Have we tried to realise what we owe to Christ our Lord for putting into our hands more than sufficient to cover all our need?

We may be, we *are* irresponsive and selfish. But we are children of God, and in our hearts is a divinely planted loyalty to our Creator and Lord, a filial affection for our Heavenly Father which is our birthright and our joy. To be able to give Him an infinitely acceptable worship, to cover all His Perfections with adequate adoration and praise, is a happiness that satisfies the deepest need of our nature. And it is ours now. We need not wait for Heaven. We have it here and now in every Mass.

"If you loved Me," said our Lord, "you would indeed be glad because I go to the Father." In every Mass He goes to the Father, taking with Him all our commissions, all our desires. He Himself is our adoration, praise, and propitiation, our Advocate in whose hands are all our petitions. More honour and glory than angels and saints could render throughout eternity, reparation more than sufficing for all our sins, pleading powerful enough to obtain whatever we need for ourselves or others—this we have put into our hands in every Mass. "For how hath He not with Him given us all things?"

God is never outdone in generosity. The Mass is a sublime illustration of this truth. For what is this Divine Sacrifice but a sweet rivalry and interchange between our Heavenly Father and His children still on earth! At the Elevation we lift to Him as a Sacrifice infinitely acceptable "the Son of His love." At the Communion He returns to us, as His Thankoffering, our Unspeakable Gift. For a brief space our Divine Guest is with us to do with Him as we will. And then, once more, we restore the Gift to the Giver. He returns to the Father with all the interests we have entrusted to Him—our spiritual and temporal needs, our responsibilities, our difficulties, our successes and our failures, our hearts with all they hold dear, our souls with all their aspirations—all that we have and are and hope to be in eternity.

Our Lord said to His Apostles at the Supper: "Little children, yet a little while I am with you." So He says to us now. For a little while, the few years of our life, He is with us, offering us spiritual treasure that is beyond all price, treasure that alone will remain when the so-called good things of this life have served their turn and gone from us. A little while for the defraying of *my personal debt* to my Creator, more than sufficient is put at my disposal—a sacrifice, with everything in it worthy of Divine acceptance—a Divine Priest, a Divine Victim, Christ standing at the altar to offer *all this for me,* His priest merely speaking and acting in His name.

It is our sacrifice as well as the priest's; "my sacrifice and yours," he says. Hence I can every morning approach the altar to offer my Christ to God, an infinite and adequate adoration; a thanksgiving more than commensurate with all He has given me or done for me in the past, all that He reserves for me in the future; a propitiation outweighing all my sins and the sins of the world; an intercession equal to any grace or favour I ask. I may put my prayer upon the lips of my Christ; I may make the intention of my heart His, even as I make His my own.

And my daily Communion—what have I there? He comes to unite Himself with me in a union which has no counterpart. He is within me, not as the Host in the ciborium, but permeating my soul with His own life and energy in a way He alone can comprehend. I may treat Him with a holy familiarity, run to meet Him, make Him welcome, speak to Him, listen to Him as to my truest, dearest friend, make over to Him my cares and plans and work of every day.

A little while all this is put within my reach, in preference to multitudes of others on earth with me to-day, with their salvation to work out as urgently as I have mine. May my Lord not have had cause to weep over me as over Jerusalem, who in her day of grace did not know the things that were to her peace!

Purgatory is the land of realisation, of bitter memories, of terrible and fruitless regret. Must we wait till we lie there in our helplessness, to understand what we had in the Mass, that Treasure with which all our debts might have been paid?

Let us be wise in time, anticipate in time regret which will avail us nothing in eternity. Let us go often and with confidence to the throne of grace that we may obtain mercy and find grace in seasonable aid.

O Lord our God, why hast Thou loved us so dearly! O Love, why hast Thou stood in Thine own light! Hadst Thou been less eager to be with us, less prodigal of Thyself, had there been but one consecrated Host in the world as there was one Sepulchre that for centuries attracted the heart of Christendom, it might, perchance, have drawn us to itself. What can we do as we lift our eyes to the monstrance as we receive Thee into our hearts, what can we do, but cry to Thee with the Apostles:

"Lord, increase our faith!"

LVII
"THE FATHER"

"I and the Father are one."—John 10:30.

"THE Father"—Name that takes us straight to the Heart of the Co-equal and well-beloved Son of God!

Our Lord tried to reconcile His sorrowing disciples to His separation from them by showing them it was for their interest that He should leave them. Once only, as if it were a last resource, He appealed to their love of Him to let Him go: "If you loved Me you would indeed be glad *because* I go to the Father."

He promised that whatsoever they should ask the Father in His name should be given them. "And I say not," He added tenderly, "that I will ask the Father for you, for the Father Himself loveth you because you have loved Me and have believed that I came out from God."

It was to the Father that He turned, of the Father that He spoke when His Heart was fullest. And now, in a sublime and touching prayer, He commended to the Father His desolate disciples:

"These things," says St. John, "Jesus spoke, and lifting up His eyes He said: Father, the hour is come, glorify Thy Son that Thy Son may glorify Thee...I have glorified Thee on the earth; I have finished the work which Thou gavest Me to do. And now glorify Thou Me, O Father, with Thyself, with the glory which I had before the world was, with Thee. I have manifested Thy name to the men whom Thou hast given Me out of the world. Thine they were and to Me Thou gavest them, and they have kept Thy word. I pray for them, I pray not for the world, but for them whom Thou hast given Me because they are Thine. And all My things are Thine and Thine are Mine, and I am glorified in them...Holy Father, keep them in Thy name whom Thou hast given Me that they may be one as we also are...I pray not that Thou shouldst take them out of the world, but that Thou shouldst keep them from evil....And not for them only do I pray, but for them also who through their word shall believe in Me, that they may all be one as Thou, Father, in Me and I in Thee, that they also may be one in Us...Father, I will that where I am, they also whom thou hast given Me may be with Me, that they may see My glory which Thou hast given Me, because Thou hast loved Me before the creation of the world."

He prays that the union of mind and heart and interests of the Master and His faithful servants—a union for a little while, of labour and of suffering, of hardship, of failure, and of sorrow, may be consummated in His Kingdom where they shall be with Him and see His glory, and rejoice with a joy no man shall take from them.

What wonder if the troubled of all time who believe in Him should find in these last words of His, in this last prayer for them as He was leaving the earth, a refuge in every need? That saints, like our own Venerable Bede, would have these words read to them when they came to die, that they might be the last sounds of this world to reach them and strengthen them for their passage into the next!

"And a hymn being said, they went forth unto Mount Olivet." A hymn led by His Voice that night—how grand a consummation of that marvellous Supper! How meet that first Eucharistic thanksgiving for the "Unspeakable Gift" vouchsafed them in their hour of direst need! Close at hand now was that hour of upheaval and of peril, of wavering and eclipse, an hour that was to see—not Faith reviving Hope and Charity, as is its wont, but the Charity of Christ "keeping their hearts and minds in Christ Jesus" against the hour of the Resurrection which was to quicken first Hope, then Faith.

May our hearts like theirs be ready to follow His lead and lift themselves up in thanksgiving and in trust should any hour in the future look as dark as did theirs that night! Through all the perils of this passing life may the Body of our Lord Jesus Christ preserve our souls unto life everlasting. Amen.

"And going out, He went according to His custom to the Mount of Olives. And His disciples also followed Him."

On the way our Lord said to them: "You shall all be scandalised in Me this night, for it is written: I will strike the Shepherd and the sheep shall be dispersed."

Peter said to Him: "Though all should be scandalised in Thee, yet not I."

Jesus said to him: "Amen, I say to thee, before the cock crow twice this day, thou shalt deny Me thrice."

But he spoke the more vehemently: "Although I should die together with Thee, I will not deny Thee."

St. Mark adds: "And in like manner also said they all."

LVIII
GETHSEMANI—I

"Made sin for us."—2 Cor. 5:21.

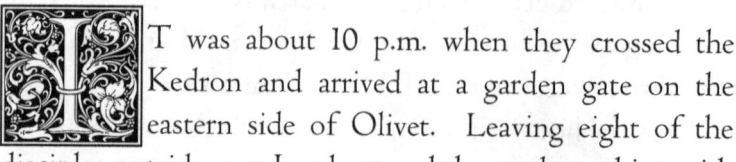

IT was about 10 p.m. when they crossed the Kedron and arrived at a garden gate on the eastern side of Olivet. Leaving eight of the disciples outside, our Lord entered the garden, taking with Him Peter, James, and John. They had been privileged beyond the rest by seeing Him transfigured on Mount Thabor, and special nearness to Christ in glory implies fellowship with Him also in suffering. "*Sit* you here till I go yonder and pray," He had said to the eight. To the more favoured three: "My Soul is sorrowful even unto death. Stay you here and *watch* with Me." So terrible, however, was to be the transformation beneath the olive trees that night, that He would not have even these three witnesses of all He was to endure. "Going a little farther, kneeling down He prayed that if it might be, the hour might pass from Him. And He fell upon His face and said: Abba, Father, all things are possible to Thee, remove this chalice from Me. And being in an agony He prayed the longer, and His sweat became as drops of blood trickling down upon the ground." By the words, "fear, sadness, heaviness," the Evangelists describe the agony of the death struggle, the utmost suffering that nature is able to bear.

Anticipation is often the keenest form of pain. It has been said that our greatest trials are those we have not been called upon to endure in any other way. Here we see our Lord in the grip of that most terrible form of anticipation which we call our agony, the agony of death—that breaking up of all the forces of life; that destruction of all our resources; that loneliness, that helplessness; that sense of all things sinking and failing us; that powerlessness of friends to relieve or even to understand our need; those terrifying sights and sounds in the darkness which envelops us; those perils unforeseen; that call to battle—when we feel unequal to the smallest effort—with the foe that knows us so well; that vision of the past; that terror of the future; that awful parting of soul and body, the lifelong companions never meant to be separated; that tax upon our patience, our love, our hope, our very faith—this is what we understand by the agony to which most of us must look forward. What was it to our Lord? All that makes it fearful to us, sin only excepted.

He was truly man. He suffered as man, but with this difference, that what we suffer when our failing senses dull the knowledge which is the measure of pain, He went through on the eve of His death. It is a fearful thought—the agony of death to be borne by one in the vigour of manhood; borne, not as a consequence of weakness, but as a struggle between the repugnance of nature repelling with all its strength the torments it abhors, and the will sternly forcing them in all their horror on its acceptance.

Sin only excepted, we say. But it was just sin that made the agony so terrible. The guilt of our sins He could not take, but He took the result of that guilt. In the forcible language of St. Paul He was made sin for us. It seemed to identify itself with Him, to be all but His own: "The torrents of iniquity troubled Me."[1] He, the All-Holy,

---
1 Ps. 17.

allowed Himself to be clad in the foul garment from the contact of which He shrank inexpressibly, and bore the shame of appearing thus before His Father and His spotless Court in Heaven.

He distinguished every sin—and the sinner; my sin at such an hour, every sin of my life. We know the punishment one mortal sin deserves. And all the accumulated crime of the whole world was to be laid to His charge, all to be punished in Him as if He were the sinner. Well might He quail before the prospect.

We can never realise what that anticipation of suffering meant to Him. There was none of the vagueness which dims our foresight. All stood out with perfect accuracy of detail—every wound, every blow, every insult; betrayal, desertion by God and man. With us there is always the possibility of escape. Something may happen to turn the blow aside, and always, underlying fear, there is trust in the Providence of God which we know will never allow us to be tried beyond our strength. He who upheld His martyrs amid their torments sustains His servants under every trial. Long before the moment when this would reach the insupportable, His Providence interferes. But there was no such merciful intervention for the Son. The limit to His atonement was the measure of suffering our sins deserved. It was more than human strength taxed to its utmost could endure. But the Divinity was there to support Him, not for the alleviation but for the protraction of His pain. Over the agony of death He must pass—and live on!

Neither can we form any idea of the extent to which pain of body and mind told on the delicate organisation of our Lord's Sacred Humanity. His was the most refined, the most sensitive, the most affectionate, the most perfect and beautiful human nature that ever came from the Hand of God. Framed with a view to its awful office of universal Victim, it was supported by Omnipotence to bear the whole weight of the wrath of God, to satisfy to the full the requirements of His Justice.

He who knew clearly the malice of sin, how should He not tremble at the sight of the expiation due for the sins of the world! It was all present to His mind. He allowed His coming Passion to assail every portion of His Nature, to come before Him with every detail that could inspire dismay and overthrow resolution, the body witnessing to the terror that filled the mind by a sweat of blood so copious that after drenching His garments, it trickled to the ground.

Pain is sweetened by the thought that it will profit those we love. Our Lord knew that for a multitude of souls what He was going to suffer for them would avail nothing. They would be lost in spite of all He could do to save them. And among those whom His pains would profit, how many were a drop in His bitter chalice! They would be saved indeed, but how poorly! For the immensity of His sacrifice, how niggardly would be their return! While His constant thought in life and in death had been what more He could do for them, their study would be how little they could do for Him compatible with their own salvation. How small the number of the saints! How low the standard of those even who aspire to the familiarity with Him of intimate friends! How awful the indifference of the masses! Our Lord was not wont to make much of what He did and suffered, He had spoken of scourging and mockery and crucifixion as calmly as if they were something almost ordinary in the way of pain. But as His hour drew on, the shrinking from torture and shame and dereliction which overwhelmed His Soul was such that He acknowledged it to be as the agony of death.

There was a last drop in that chalice, surpassing in bitterness all the rest. If Jerusalem had rejected Him—His own people, His priests; if one Apostle was about to betray Him, another to deny Him, and all to abandon Him, He had still the Father left Him, the Father's love to make amends for all, the Father's bosom into which to climb. Who could assail Him there? What could drive Him thence? "I and the Father are One." O mystery, the more impenetrable the more we search into it—that in the very hour when He was making to the Divine Majesty an infinite satisfaction, supremely acceptable and accepted, the Father should forsake, treat as a sinner the Son of His love! Because He was made sin for us, because we had deserved to be abandoned by God, Christ was abandoned in His hour of direst need. We should never have dared to use the word, to have thought such dereliction possible, had not His own words revealed to us the darkness that gathered round His human Soul and caused Him an anguish beyond which there was nothing left for Him to bear.

His human will, ever in closest union with the Divine will, yet left to face without sensible support from the Divinity the deluge of evil and of suffering with which it was confronted, swayed beneath the tempest. It was still free. It had but to send forth one efficacious act of desire, and the legions of surrounding angels would have swept away the horrors that awaited Him. They heard that piteous cry: "Father, if it be possible let this chalice pass from Me!"

and must have waited in wonder and expectation. Did they doubt the issue of the struggle? Did they fear for us? One among them was privileged to come to the rescue, but it was to strengthen, not to console Him.

Son of Man, as He loved to call Himself, He turned for consolation from the angel who had never suffered, to the human hearts that were like His own. He crept to the three whom, as if He feared to be alone, He had bidden to watch and pray with Him. They could give Him sympathy at least and the protection of their presence in His loneliness and terror. Three times He went to them and each time they were asleep—those who had made such protestations of fidelity and friendship an hour ago! They were "sleeping for sorrow," and though He roused He did not reproach them. There was only the meek expostulation: "Simon, sleepest thou?" and the excuse for them because the spirit was willing though the flesh was weak. They gazed with horror at the change that had come over Him, as haggard and blood-stained He stood before them in the light of the Paschal moon. Entering Jerusalem that night was going into the jaws of death, but in His company they feared nothing. And now—He was afraid!

He returned to His prayer, saying the same words, says the Evangelist. Yet with this difference: He no longer asks that His chalice may pass away, but only that the will of His Father may be accomplished in Him: "Father, if Thou wilt, remove this chalice from Me; but yet not My will but Thine be done."

His hour was come and He rose to meet it. Death and all that had to precede death was accepted. For the joy set before Him—the redemption of man—He embraced the cross, despising the shame. With a calm countenance He returned to His disciples and roused them once more. The noise of approaching footsteps was heard, and the gleam of torches appeared through the foliage.

LIX
GETHSEMANI—II

"I have given you an example that as I have done so you do also."—John 13:15.

AND all this *for me!* What have I to say to Him? Oh, that I could understand what my sins have cost Him! All that He suffered was *for me.* As at the altar rails He may give Himself to thousands, yet wholly and entirely to each one, so were His sufferings offered for all, and entirely for each one, *for me.* He is our Saviour and *my* Saviour. He loved me and delivered Himself *for me.*

"But He willed all this excess of suffering," it may be urged. Oh, yes, He willed it; never was sufferer so willing. Only the most intrepid love could have laid itself open to the torture of such fear. Only the absolute determination of His will could have trusted itself to the violence of such an onslaught. Does this willingness detract from His generosity? Was the endurance of the martyrs less heroic because by a sign or a word they could have put a stop to their tortures?

Some are ready to lessen the force and pathos of our Lord's example by objecting that He was God and had in His Divinity resources wanting to us in the endurance of our trials. It is a difficulty that hardly does us credit. What! has He not done enough, that we must go about to discover that there is just a thing here and there which He might have done? But no, these querulous ones are not satisfied. He has indeed made us partakers of the

Divine Nature, to use St. Peter's daring words—but after all, we are not God! He has sought out possibilities of suffering that we should have thought closed against Him as the Son of God, but He was spared the pain of sickness and disease. His village home with all its poverty was not without the refinement and sweetness that came from the perfection of its inmates. He did not know the misery of uncongenial companionship, of sordid surroundings, of life in the slums of cities and in the haunts of sin. Such cavillers almost reproach Him with the inevitable limitations imposed by the Godhead. Has He not done enough to convince us that everything He could take upon Himself in the shape of pain He would share with us in order to be like us? If there are forms of suffering which the dignity of His Person prohibited Him, there are an infinity of others which His Divinity brought within His reach and of which we do not so much as dream.

Do we ponder the intensity it added to all His pangs? Do we consider those which came upon Him precisely because He was God? Do we reflect how the body "fitted to Him" as Redeemer and universal Victim was endowed with a delicacy and a sensitiveness that immeasurably aggravated all His physical torments? How His Soul shrank from the coarseness and sin that surrounded Him? How the clear knowledge of every human soul was a fruitful source of distress? How the sight of the future, mercifully veiled from us, made Him suffer continually by anticipation the anguish and ignominy of His Passion? How the hiding of the Face of the Father was agony unimaginable to us who can frame no idea of its necessity to Him, the Co-Eternal and Co-Equal Son?

May we not say that it was through His Divinity that He became pre-eminently the Man of Sorrows? By subtracting the sensible joy of the Beatific Vision, He placed pain within His reach, and strengthened His Sacred Humanity to endure in Soul and Body anguish beyond the powers of endurance of any other.

Lord, my complaint is not that certain of our low ills were beyond Thy power to share with us, but rather that with such unsparing hand, such inventive and seemingly unnecessary generosity, Thou didst take upon Thyself sorrows Thy brethren will never be called upon to bear. Let me steep heart and mind in the thought that made St. Paul what he became—the realisation of that truth—"He loved *me* and delivered Himself *for me.*"

When our Lord offered Himself to become man in order to redeem us, it was open to Him to choose as He would the details of His life. And He chose, not what most befitted the dignity of His Person, but what was best *for us*. He chose to live the kind of life, to die the sort of death that should be most helpful to us. This is the key to all He said, and did, and suffered. We should have arranged His life differently. If He had determined to suffer and die, we should have expected Him to meet torments and death with the majesty and fearlessness He had ever shown in life. We should have sent Him into the battle animating His followers by His high courage and heroic words. But the sacred Agony reveals a depth of sympathy and brotherly compassion which we should never have thought possible in a God-Man. To be like His brethren in all things, this was His rule from first to last. And when His hour was come He said: "My heart is ready, O God, My heart is ready. I have not gone back."[1]

In the conflicts we have to face, we have no power to shut off from ourselves the fear and horror anticipation brings. Could we have dreamed of a Leader who, to comfort His terror-stricken soldiers by companionship, would share their weakness—would be afraid! Oh, happy was it for us that He had not to take counsel of us! Where should we have gone in our hours of weakness had there been no Gethsemani? What consolation is wanting to us now that we see the Mighty God stricken with fear, praying to be spared, praying the longer as His anguish deepened, humbly seeking consolation from His friends, and finding, as we find, their powerlessness to help; sickening like us at the sight of failure; meekly accepting the succour sent by Heaven? And then, ready to say: "My Father, if this chalice may not pass away, but I must drink it—Thy will be done!"

"We have not," says St. Paul, "a High-priest who cannot have compassion on our infirmities, but one like us in all things." We come to Him in the Garden to be fortified by His weakness; to learn from Him that the strongest repugnance of nature is not incompatible with the perfect submission of our will to the will of God. In a conflict which only attests the struggle of the will to maintain its loyalty to God, we have Him as our Companion.

The lesson of the Sacred Agony which by His own example He most earnestly enforces, is the absolute necessity of prayer at this time. Not only must we resist the temptation to abandon prayer, but, like our Master, we must *pray the longer*. Whatever the weariness, the

---
[1] Isa. I.

desolation, the apparent fruitlessness of our prayer, we must pray: "I have given you an example that as I have done so you do also."

We note that when the hour was come for the complete unveiling to us of His human heart in its weakness and distress, He would not have all a witness to its pain. This fellowship with Him was for His three most favoured disciples. With them He entered the Garden of the Agony; the greater number were left outside. So has it been ever since. To be admitted within the inner circle, with those who in answer to His question: "Can you drink of the chalice I shall drink?" answered, "We can," implies a special intimacy of friendship on His part, a corresponding generosity on theirs. Are we willing to be always left outside? Have we any ambition to share as His members at least some of the sorrows of our Head?

LX
"HESITATED NOT"

"Look down, O Lord, we beseech Thee upon this Thy family for which our Lord Jesus Christ hesitated not to be betrayed into the hands of sinners and to undergo the torment of the Cross."

TIME after time does the Church in these "days of salvation" put up this plea for her children. It is her last prayer at Matins in Holy Week, and till the first Vespers of Easter it is continually on her lips. It is at once pleading and exulting. She pleads through the generosity of Christ, who in face of the torments which she commemorates—hesitated not. She exults in the sense of her dearness to the mind and to the heart of Christ, which, knowing the cost of her purchase—hesitated not.

Both St. Peter and St. Paul glory in the thought that we are bought by Christ, "bought with a great price."[1] Oh, that the generosity of the Lord who bought us might pass into our hearts! That, when an occasion of service or a victory over selfishness offers, I could seize it—hesitating not! Our Lord never hesitated when there was question of helping us. He might have chosen an easier lot in life, but hardship and pain were to be the lot of the greater part of men. It would help them to have His example before them. He hesitated not and chose the poverty and toil of Nazareth. When the time of His Passion drew on, He might have spared Himself the agony of Gethsemani, the shrinking from torment and from shame. But *we* have no choice when suffering comes to us. It should

---

[1] 2 Peter 2; 1 Cor. 6,7.

be His choice then. It should come to Him first and thus be lightened and sweetened to His followers: "Jesus, therefore, knowing all things that should come upon Him, went forth"—hesitating not.

There was no hesitation in the Garden. He prayed, indeed, that if it were the will of the Father, the chalice might pass from Him. But He knew the Father's will. It was His own always, and His human will adhered to it unalterably even when nature shuddered.

Lord, teach me to be generous. Give me high ideals, strong desires of even heroic service of Thee, heroic sacrifice for Thee, at least the heroism of persistent clinging to Thy will in the trials and sacrifices of daily life. I shall never live up to my ideals—nay, I shall fall short of them lamentably—but with Thy grace I will never lower them. I may follow thee afar off. So did Peter before the grace that converted and confirmed him. Confirm my purpose of serving Thee. Give me a strong grace to follow Thee as nearly as I can. Wherever I see an opportunity of serving Thee, make me quick to take it. Promptitude is so large an element in generosity that we say: "He gives twice who gives quickly." It makes the gift easier to the giver, and twice, nay, ten times the value to the receiver. My gifts, dear Lord, are very insignificant. Let their worth be magnified in Thy sight at least by the promptitude that leaps up to meet its chance—hesitating not.

LXI
"O CRUX, AVE, SPES UNICA!"
(GOOD FRIDAY)

WHAT should we do without the Crucifix? We have the Real Presence, we have the daily Sacrifice, we have the strong unfailing Sacraments. Yet without the Cross which the Church lifts before us to-day, as a standard, as a beacon, as a pledge of joy to come, how should we keep our feet firm on the narrow way, and our hearts above the things of this passing life?

In the estimates of right and wrong, in the importance attached to things perishable and to things eternal, in Christian practice as we see it in daily life, we find false weights and measures passing current everywhere, and it is hard not to be affected by them. Our judgement gets confused, supernatural principles relax their hold, we come insensibly to conform to the aims and methods that the world approves. Our standards need continual readjustment or our calculations will work out ill in the end.

Now this is just what the Church does for us to-day. She lifts the Cross aloft and bids us fix our eyes steadily upon it. She holds it before us as the true standard of valuation; as a beacon to guide us in safety on a dangerous way; as a pledge of victory to cheer us on a march and through a combat that can only end with life.

"Behold the wood of the Cross on which hung the salvation of the world!" And three times we fall down before it, crying: "Come, let us adore!"

But this is not enough. The lesson of triumph through failure, of pain and humiliation as the price of glory and joy, is so hard to nature, that she has to enforce it by those outward symbols and acts, the value of which she knows so well.

She lays the Cross on the ground before us and bids us creep to it on our knees. She makes us press our lips to the wounded feet, and learn from our Lord and Leader who trod the hard way first to smooth it for us, how we must follow Him here if we would follow Him hereafter.

That hereafter she keeps steadily in view always. What the Cross represents, what it entailed on Him who bore our sins in His body on the tree, what in some measure it must entail on all who come after Him—this is so appalling to sense, that the Church never separates the Cross on Calvary from the Sign of the Son of Man coming in glory at the end. To the first faithful the Cross had so recently been an object of execration and abhorrence, that they never separated its glory from its shame. In their paintings and their sculpture the Crucifixion and the Resurrection are inseparable, as in St. Peter's tremendous phrase "...by the Resurrection of Jesus Christ who is on the right hand of God, swallowing down death that we might be made heirs of life everlasting, being gone into Heaven, the angels and powers and virtues being made subject to Him."[1]

"We adore Thy Cross, O Lord, and we praise and glorify Thy holy Resurrection, for by the wood of the Cross the whole earth is filled with joy." So must we say with the Church to-day. We bring our own cross to the feet of the Crucified, that by this sacred contact it may be sanctified and sweetened to us. We accept it, not with resignation only, but with gratitude—at least in the higher part of our soul—as the choice of God for us, by which we may be

---

[1] 1 Peter 3:22.

made conformable to the image of His Son and be entitled to share His glory.

> O Crux, ave, spes unica
> Hoc passionis tempore!

We must try to say the "Ave!" St. Paul bids his converts rejoice in his sufferings by which he "fills up those things that are wanting of the sufferings of Christ,"[1] and experience proves that generous acceptance is not only the most meritorious but the easiest way of bearing trial. To take our crucifix in our hand and kiss it, with "O crux, ave!" when our cross is pressing hard—this has a wonderful power to uplift, and strengthen, and bring us peace.

When in a transaction of this world we make a compact, we intend to abide by the terms. We count the cost and deliberately accept it. Why should we act differently when the agreement is with Christ our Lord, and the question at issue is our eternal salvation? The martyrs have gained Heaven by their blood. Are we for the same Kingdom to give nothing? We must take our Lord at His word when He says: "In the world you shall have distress.[2] If you had been of the world, the world would love its own; but because you are not of the world, therefore the world hateth you.[3] You shall lament and weep, but the world shall rejoice."[4] The reason is obvious. It is not possible in the business of this life to reserve our main interest and solicitude for the concerns of the life to come, to have a higher standard than those with whom we compete, to be bound by other laws and checked by other restrictions—without suffering loss. But our compensations are magnificent. One treasure

---

1   Col. 1:24.   2   John 16:33.   3   John 15:19.
4   John 16:20.

is always ensured to us, a treasure the world itself envies us, one all its wealth cannot purchase, one it can neither give nor take away; a treasure our Lord reserves for His own, of which He will never ask the sacrifice—*His Peace*. Not only will the heaviest cross leave this undisturbed, but, strange paradox, the cross accepted from the hand of God brings and deepens peace. "Let not your heart be troubled nor let it be afraid. Peace I leave with you, My peace I give unto you; not as the world giveth do I give unto you."[1]

The Cross brings peace because it strengthens hope. If our losses are undeniable, we can turn for consolation to the credit side of the account; weigh time against eternity, and against the perishable things of this life, the treasure in Heaven which fadeth not.[2] "You indeed have sorrow, but I will see you again and your heart shall rejoice and your joy no man shall take from you."[3]

Two days hence—nay, to-morrow by anticipation—the Church will be singing "Alleluia" as if her heart would break with the fulness of its joy.

A little while, a very little while, and we shall see in Heaven the other side of the cross we are carrying now. We shall see why it was sent us, what it has done for us, how it has likened us to the King in His glory.

> O Crux, ave, spes unica
> Hoc passionis tempore,

we said with the Church Militant a while ago. "O crux, ave!" we shall sing throughout eternity with the Church Triumphant, when God has wiped away the tears from all eyes.[4]

---

1 John 14:27. 2 Luke 12:33. 3 John 16:22.
4 Apoc. 21:4.

LXII
"OBEDIENT UNTO DEATH"
(GOOD FRIDAY)

HIS prayer in the Garden ended, our Lord went forth to meet His enemies, who, as He neared them, "went backward and fell to the ground." Rising, they approached cautiously, and Judas kissed Him. Peter, after drawing a sword in His defence, fled with the other disciples. Our Lord, deserted by all, was seized, bound and led into the city. It was about midnight.

From the house of Annas, in whose presence He received a heavy blow in the face, He was taken to that of Caiphas, who adjured Him by the living God to declare if He was the Son of God. Jesus having answered: "Thou hast said it," was forthwith convicted of blasphemy and condemned to death. As He was passing through the courtyard, where Peter, terrified of being recognised as one of His disciples, had thrice denied Him, the eyes of the Master and of His trembling Apostle met. "And the Lord turning, looked on Peter," says St. John, "and Peter going out, wept bitterly."

Early in the morning the Sanhedrists hurried their Prisoner to the tribunal of the Roman Governor for the confirmation of the sentence of death which they could not of themselves carry out. The vacillations of Pilate did but prolong our Saviour's sufferings and subject Him to the ignominy and torture of the scourging and crowning with thorns. In the end, the outcries of the rabble, goaded to frenzy by the priests, prevailed, and Jesus was delivered to their will.

Bearing His own Cross, He set out on the way to Calvary. Three times His strength failed Him and He sank to the ground, to be dragged up and forced on amid the jeers and brutality of an Eastern crowd. It was paschal time and the streets were choked by the multitude pressing on every side. At one corner our Lord was met by His Mother. What must it have been to see the disfigurement of that beautiful face; to see those eyes in their intolerable agony, striving to guide themselves to hers! Farther on, Veronica offered Him her veil to wipe from His brow the blood that trickled from the wounded head. Once the procession halted whilst He spoke to the weeping women of Jerusalem.

It was a dying man who, after tottering through the steep narrow ways, took the last steps up the ascent to Calvary. Want of food and rest was added to torments more than enough to cause His death; He had to be hurried on the road lest He should die too soon and escape the lingering tortures of crucifixion. Breathless and trembling as from fever chills, He arrived at the place of execution, was stripped for the last time of His garments, and, full of wounds, was sent to wait in the cold winds till all was ready.

LXIII
"FATHER, FORGIVE THEM, FOR THEY KNOW NOT WHAT THEY DO"

—Luke 23:34.

IT was a dying man they nailed to the Cross; not to endure its torments only, but to labour still for the souls He came to save. As the nails were driven into hands and feet He prayed:

"Father, forgive them, for they know not what they do."

"Them," naming none. How should He? "Our name is 'Legion,' for we are many," as many as by sin crucify again the Son of God.

What plea can He urge for them? Ignorance of their guilt, anything that will shield them from the wrath of God—"forgive them, for they know not what they do."

It is the Divine generosity of the prayer that strikes us first and most. But the plea urged is a true one, for it is the Truth that speaks. None of us knows fully what it is to commit mortal sin. We know enough to incur grievous guilt and an eternal penalty, yet not till we pass out of this life of illusions shall we understand sin as it is in the eyes of God and of all who in eternity see things in their true light.

"*Pater, dimitte illis*—Father, forgive them, for they know not what they do." That prayer, chanted three times immediately after the Elevation at Mass, rises daily from Christian churches, in Jerusalem and other sanctuaries throughout the world.[1]

---

1 In every church of Our Lady of Sion. To all who join the

Remember, O Father of Mercies, that the pleading of Thy beloved Son was first and specially for Thy chosen people:

Father, forgive them, for they know not what they do.

"Hath God cast away His people?" God forbid.[1]

"Have they so stumbled that they should fall?" God forbid.

"If the offence of them be the riches of the world...how much more the fulness of them?"

Father, forgive them, for they know not what they do.

"If the loss of them be the reconciliation of the world, what shall the receiving of them be but life from the dead?"

Father, forgive them.

"If the Gentiles were grafted into the good olive-tree, how much more shall they that are the natural branches be grafted into their own olive-tree?"[2]

Father, forgive them.

"As touching the election, they are most dear for the sake of the fathers."

"For the gifts and the calling of God are without repentance."

"Blindness in part has happened in Israel until the fulness should come in...And so all Israel should be saved."

Father, forgive them.

"Oh, the depth of the riches of the wisdom and of the knowledge of God! How incomprehensible are His judgements, and how unsearchable His ways!"

"Their fall is neither final, nor universal, nor irremediable."[3]

Father, forgive them.

Association of the Guild of Israel for the conversion of the Jews Pope Benedict XV and Pope Pius XI have granted an Indulgence of 400 days each time they recite the prayer, "Father, forgive them." etc.

1 Rom. 11. 2 *Ibid.* 3 St. Thomas Aquinas.

"For the sake of the people who gave us Jesus and Mary[1] remove the veil from their hearts."[2]

Father, forgive them, for they know not what they do.

---

[1] The brothers Lemann (Hebrew Catholics).   [2] 2 Cor. 3:15.

LXIV
"THIS DAY THOU SHALT BE WITH ME IN PARADISE"

—Luke 23:43.

"SAVE thyself and us!"

Both thieves, according to St. Matthew, "reproached" our Lord on the Cross. The craving for instant relief overpowered every other consideration. But grace began its work, urging them to turn to Him who hung between them—and listen and watch.

One refuses. He will not give heed to the Divine example of patience before his eyes, or to the grace that knocks at his heart. Again and again his wild cry rises. Because it is not heard his heart hardens.

Are we ever like him? We begin a novena, for some temporal need, perhaps. We plead, we implore, reminding our Lord of His promises: "Ask, and you shall receive... For everyone that asketh receiveth." The answer does not come in the form we insist upon. Hence, discouragement, repining akin to rebellion, hard thoughts of God, refusal to accept His will as best, abandonment of prayer.

By the other thief grace is not repulsed. The poor tortured frame turns towards Jesus and nerves itself to attention. What does he see? "A worm and no man." And hear? "Father, forgive them, for they know not what they do." He sees, he hears, and his soul drinks in salvation. In the piteous object before him he beholds, no criminal, but a King on His way to His Kingdom, of whom he will humbly crave a remembrance. Faith, humility, and repentance, resignation, trust, and the zeal of an apostle break out in the cry: "We indeed justly...but this Man hath done no evil....Lord, remember me when Thou shalt come into Thy Kingdom!"

Could he have asked for less? Writhing in excruciating pain, the past a retrospect of guilt, the future a terrible retribution, life ebbing fast and eternity at hand, had he nothing to ask of the fellow-sufferer at his side, of One whom a kingdom was awaiting but—a remembrance?

It was little, but it was enough. He understood the Heart that beat so near his own, the Heart that had revealed itself to him in those last hours of life; that had just poured itself out for him in prayer; that had drawn from his heart contrition of such price as to blot out the sins of a lifetime; the Heart that had won his love and his trust for past, and present, and future. Of this Heart that unasked had given so much, it was enough to beg but this—a remembrance in the world to come.

And even for such remembrance he was willing to wait—"when Thou shalt come into Thy Kingdom." What that Kingdom was to be, and when it was to come, and how a remembrance there could avail him, he knew not and did not seek to know. Like the great Apostle, he could say: "I judge not myself to know anything among you but Jesus Christ and Him crucified." He knew in whom he had believed, and was content to trust.

O trusting heart of that poor thief, how well wert thou repaid! "This day thou shalt be with Me in Paradise. With Me in rest and peace; with Me in happiness that shall have no end; with Me among My angels and saints, among the toilers of the first and the eleventh hours; with

Me whom thou hast gloriously confessed, and whom I, in turn, will confess before My Father who is in Heaven."

This day—before the sun goes down, thou shalt be with Me. A little longer on the cross; a little patient waiting for Me when I shall be gone to prepare thy place; a little lonely suffering at the last, with the Mother of Mercy beneath to sustain and comfort thee—and then, thou shalt be with Me.

In Paradise—for where I am there is Heaven, and there is death and hell where I am not.

The thieves went up to Calvary that day to find their salvation or their reprobation by the side of Jesus. Three hours were given them to make their choice. When the darkness cleared away and the three forms that hung there were still in death, the season of grace had passed, never to return. One had turned a deaf ear to the Lord who would have saved him. The other had met his Master in Paradise.

When our cross is torturing to extremity, or its dull monotony taxes our endurance sorely, can we do better than, like the good thief, turn to Jesus and ask Him by His pity for a fellow-sufferer for a remembrance: "Lord, remember me"?

This prayer was a favourite with David, the man after God's own heart: "How long, O Lord, wilt Thou forget me? How long dost Thou turn away Thy face from me? Why hast Thou forgotten me? Will God forget to show mercy?"

In sore anxiety for their brother, Martha and Mary asked for nothing but a remembrance: "Lord, he whom Thou lovest is sick." The answer was a resurrection from the dead. It is always safe, it is always best to cast our care upon the Lord and wait His time. He may delay. He may keep us on our cross awhile longer, but there is an eternity for reward. Let us wait with the patience of the good thief, trusting Him who has gone to prepare a place for us and who will come in His own time to take us to Himself, that where He is we too may be.

No matter how guilty we may have been, how unworthy we may now be, our prayer: "Lord, remember me!" will always find its way to His pitying Heart, always have its reward.

> It was not Prophet of the Olden Law,
> Nor king arrayed in purple majesty,
> Nor John the Baptist—whom the angels saw,
> Nor Thy sweet Mother, entering with Thee.
> But, hand in hand, 'fore Heaven's wondering eyes,
> *A thief* went in with Thee to Paradise![1]

---

1 J.B. Kelly.

LXV
"BEHOLD THY MOTHER!"

"All that I have is thine."—Luke 15:31.

NO good, no grace, we are told, but comes to us through Mary's prayers. She who understands so well the Heart of her Son will have known how it yearned to save the companions of His punishment, the men whose day of grace was nearly run. She joined her desires and tears to His, beginning thus the work He was entrusting to her as Mother of Mercy.

She was all that was left to Him now, all that He had to give. But there must not be anything, however specially His own, that He had not shared with us. He who would say: "My Father and your Father," must be able to say also: "My Mother and yours." His eyes were dimming fast, but He turned them painfully towards her and said: "Woman, behold thy son." After that He said to the disciple: "Behold thy Mother." And from that hour the disciple took her to his own.

Our Lord made her over to us all as His last gift. In that hour of her universal motherhood, solemnly conferred on Calvary, each one of His disciples whom Jesus loved was, with John, confided to her keeping. He put then into her heart that love of "His own," which enabled her to accept as her children those who had brought Him to this bitter death. St. Thomas says that God required of Mary that she should acquiesce in the death of her Son for sinners. This was enough. With her whole heart she rose to the height of heroism which such a sacrifice demanded. She brought us forth in pain in that most dreadful hour, and now pours out upon us every one more than a mother's love.

A worldwide family was confided to her. She was to be the new Mother of the human race. "Mother of all the living" in a truer sense than Eve. She had given to her a sympathy with her suffering children, a compassion for their miseries, and ignorance, and mistakes, for their weakness and waywardness, that fit her for such an office.

She was His dying gift to us, but it is for us to reject or to accept that gift. Happy those who, like John, have taken her to their own and turn to her in every need. Happy the homes she guards amid the dangers of every kind that assail the home to-day. But alas for those peoples who have been robbed of her patronage and protection!

> They stumble and cry in the night,
>   Those nations tired of life's quest;
> They have no Mother to carry the light
>   And to lead them upstairs to their rest.
> Of the dark they are doubly afraid,
>   For they have not the comfort of thee,
> And they pray not whose forefathers prayed,
>   For they have not a Mother's knee.[1]

They left her when they wandered from home. But, motherlike, she has never lost sight of them, and she awaits the hour of mercy that will bring them home to her again. Wherever her Son goes she goes. Chased away, they reappear together. He is going to and fro to-day seeking a world that has wandered from Him. And His Mother is following Him in the quest. If from the ruins of Belgium and Northern France the crucifix appealed to all alike—to Catholic and non-Catholic, to soldiers

---

[1] George Benson Hewetson.

from Australia and Canada, and Russia, and Ireland, and Scotland; if it was found in the dug-outs and the trenches of British soldiers, rescued from the walls of a tottering cottage and reverently set up in a mud shelter or trench—so was the image of Mary. The guns spared both alike. Rosaries dropped by exiles in their flight were carefully kept by our men, not merely as war souvenirs but with more than half a suspicion of their true worth. It was no longer safe to label a man "R.C." because of the rosary round his neck. The wounded seemed to grudge us the monopoly of the Mother to whom they turned in their need. "Why, isn't it Mary!" exclaimed a soldier in an injured tone when, coveting a scapular, he had been gently reminded that he would not know what it was.

Must she not look with pity on these children of hers who are groping their way to her in the darkness? Will she not "for the filial days of old bring back Britain to the fold"?

Her worldwide family is in sore distress, "the whole head is sick and the whole heart is sad." Look at the Christian home! Never was its sanctuary more shamelessly violated, never was its peace and happiness more cruelly assailed. Agencies of every kind are undermining it. Legislation, the ways of society, books, fashions, amusements, the thirst for independence, pleasure, continual excitement—all tend to shatter its ideals. Will not the Mother of us all guard as of old what is specially the mother's province and charge? Can she see unmoved how the head is sick and the heart is sad? How the welfare of parents, children, and servants is at stake? How the very infant in the cradle is the prey of those who would fain find and train a child-medium in every home, to be made over from birth to the guardianship of spirits, whether good or evil is immaterial? O Mary, Mother of God and of men, must not the memories of Nazareth move thee to pity and help us? If the home is lost, what remains to the world!

From His Cross the Saviour of the world shows it the remedy. *"Behold thy Mother!"* To the head of every household and to its heart, to father and mother, to the little children and to the servants—once an integral part of the family, loyal and affectionate, trusting and trusted—to one and all He says: *"Behold thy Mother!"* See how she ruled and served her household, how she made the happiness of her home. Take up your Rosary and learn of her the secrets she can teach. Learn from the Joyful Mysteries how to sanctify and brighten daily life with its ups and downs, its prayer and its labour, its visits and its journeyings, its losses and its gains. From the Sorrowful Mysteries learn by her example to follow Me closely in hours of trial—when possible by actual contact with Me in My Sacrifice and Sacraments, often in thought and affection by the remembrance of My sufferings, and the conformity of your will to the will of God. In the Glorious Mysteries, lift up your heart to Heaven. Life here, with its service of God, now in sunshine, now in shade, will soon be done. And then—Heaven! You are expected there. Your place is ready. Make haste to come to us, to fit yourself for the welcome and the reunions that await you.

"*Keep to your daily Rosary.* Take it up in moments of leisure or of weariness. Have at hand some familiar and helpful thoughts connected with the Mysteries, to which your mind turns easily for refreshment or for strength.

"*Cling to your Rosary*. It will be a chain to draw you Heavenwards, for it will keep your heart where your treasure is, with your Model and your Mother in the Home where she is Queen."

LXVI
"MY GOD, MY GOD, WHY HAST THOU FORSAKEN ME?"

AT the end of life, habits of mind and speech often come out with unusual prominence. Our Lord had His characteristic words and ways. Among these we notice—and more frequently as the end draws near—the tender repetition of a name dear to Him: "Jerusalem, Jerusalem!" "Simon, Simon!" And now: "My God, My God!"

"Why hast Thou forsaken Me?" He asks. And yet He knows why. He had freely chosen to be like us in all things. "Without sin," the Apostle adds. But not without the chastisement of sin. This He could, and as the universal Victim did, most willingly take upon Himself. The chief consequence of grave sin, which the sinner deliberately accepts, is—separation from God, a separation which, unless he repents, becomes his chastisement and irreparable loss for eternity.

There is no deprivation or pain in any way comparable to this. It is more than the loss of life, more than death. "The second death" is the Scripture's awful name for that everlasting suffocation, that agonising gasp for Him who is the very breath of its being, which separation from God implies. "Depart from Me"—those first words of the final sentence—are the most terrific. They include the rest and comprise all imaginable woe.

In this life we have so little grasp of God as the Supreme, the only Good, that we do not understand aright what sin is or the penalty it entails. We know enough to deserve its punishment or we could not incur it. But our ignorance of its real malice our Lord used as a plea for our forgiveness: "Father, forgive them, for they know not what they do."

He knew, and as the wire attracts to itself the fire from the angry heavens, so did He offer His innocent humanity to bear a penalty which, without His own revelation, we should have deemed an impossibility. "I and the Father are one." How could there be separation? "Glorify Me, O Father, with the glory which I had with Thee before the creation of the world." This Eternal, this well-beloved Son, how could He be forsaken? "They shall see His Face," is the reward held out to us as the all-sufficing beatitude of Heaven. The deprivation or interruption of that Vision could never be possible to the God-Man, but that He might drink to the uttermost the cup of human suffering, the joy which it imparts was suspended, and thus "forsaken," His Soul was abandoned to a darkness and desolation which was the greatest of His torments. The hiding of that Face was the nearest approach to the misery of the reprobate to which the Soul of Christ could come.

"My God, My God, why hast Thou forsaken me?" is a cry which from our Chief passes to all His followers. Sooner or later they all, apparently, come under the shadow of that eclipse, and their anxious question or tender reproach is: "Why?" Is it the consequence of a persistent resistance to grace of which the soul is conscious? If so, it need not ask: "Why?"—"for who hath resisted Him and hath had peace?" Is it the result of an over-timorous or, in the last analysis, a selfish disposition unable to grasp the generosity of God in His forgiveness of sin? Or is it a direct action of God upon the soul to purify it and liken it as a member to its suffering Head?

On the first supposition, let us not be too ready with self-absolution. "I am not conscious to myself of anything," said St. Paul, "yet am I not hereby justified, but He that judgeth me is the Lord." If St. Paul feared self-deception, am I wise in trusting wholly to my own judgement, and in my own case? How do I honestly believe the Lord would answer my "Why?"

If, after prayer and the recognised means of supplementing self-knowledge, I do not become conscious of deliberate and persistent opposition to God's will and the promptings of His grace, I must submit myself to Him and with childlike trust accept whatever He sends or permits: "Let us humble our souls before Him...let us ask the Lord with tears that, according to His will, He would show His mercy to us...let us humbly wait for His consolation."[1]

---

1 Judith 8:16, 17, 20.

LXVII
"I THIRST!"

HE was not given to complain, to make much of what He suffered. It is only a few of His pains that we know in this life. And of these, the Prophets tell us more than the Evangelists. The Prophets had spoken of His thirst, and it was to fulfil the Scripture that He spoke of it. But in one word only: "*Sitio!*"

What must that thirst have been through loss of blood in the Garden, in the scourging, in the draining of the sacred body on the Cross! Nothing had passed His lips since supper the night before. Not a drop of water was given Him when the moisture of the body was at length dried up. We know the extremity to which thirst has reduced the shipwrecked, the agonies it causes on the battlefield; how, forgetting their other torments, the wounded beg for water; how the imploring cry of the crucified to the passers-by was only for a drink.

His "*Sitio!*" was spoken "that the Scriptures might be fulfilled," and vinegar be offered Him. But, surely, it was to reveal also the thirst for our salvation which consumed Him, and to enkindle in His servants the same burning thirst. He who by Jacob's Well forgot His thirst in His desire to give the living water to a soul in need, revealed in that cry the unquenchable thirst of His Soul for every soul He had come to save.

In those last moments of life He looked back upon the past four thousand years, upon those who, through the merits of the Redemption to come, had won salvation. He looked down from His Cross upon the multitudes from every nation under heaven swarming round it; knowing the eternal destiny of each and all, He saw into the centuries of the future down to our own day and beyond to the end of time. And the result was—that burning thirst! His Church would indeed carry His teaching and the fruit of His Redemption to the uttermost bounds of the earth; the fields would be white unto harvest; but the labourers—how few there would be! What proportion of the human race would, when He comes to Judgement, have been brought to the knowledge of their Redeemer! How many of those to whom the treasures of His Church were thrown open would have done no more in His service than had barely sufficed for their own salvation! What numbers would spend their lives in the selfish pursuit of fame, or power, or pleasure, without a thought of the perishing souls around whom their talents, influence, and goods of this world were meant to help!

Not only to His missioners but to every one of us, within our own sphere and limitations, does He appeal. Never was the work of the lay apostolate more urgent. "After two thousand years," says Cardinal Bourne, "the vast majority of human beings upon the earth have no knowledge of the teaching of our Divine Lord. Millions at the present day know nothing whatever of the Christian teaching, and but a comparatively small number in the country recognise the Gospel. These millions all belong to Him. He came on earth for them. He died for them. He would have all brought into His fold."

Members by our Baptism of an Apostolic Church, we are bound to be ourselves apostles, zealous not only to keep the Faith but to spread it. Organised effort, including such manifold activities as the Association for the Propagation of the Faith, the Catholic Truth Society, the Catholic Evidence Guild, the Catholic Social Guild, is generally the most fruitful. But the apostolate of the laity is by no means restricted to these works of zeal. We cannot all organise retreats for non-Catholics, or speak from platforms. But private life affords abundant opportunity for apostolic effort. Much, very much, can be done by prayer, by the cheerful, conscientious discharge of home duties, the irresistible influence of a holy life, and alertness to see and seize the opportunities of helping others which Providence may put in our way.

As Catholics, we possess in our Faith a treasure not given to all. It is bestowed upon us not for ourselves only, but for the starving human souls around us, and it brings with it responsibilities which are immeasurable. We must never forget that for the talents committed to us we shall have to render an account. The great question that comes before us as we see our boys and girls leaving school and entering the world of to-day is: "What is their outlook upon life?" To what convictions have their religion and general education brought them? Do they consciously or unconsciously consider they have come to the boundary line between tutelage and independence, and are now free to choose for themselves a life with as little work as circumstances require, and as large a margin for excitement and pleasure as opportunities will provide? Or do they regard themselves as stewards, having for their object in life a work for God and for their neighbour to be taken up seriously when the action of Providence brings it before them? Do they look upon the talents entrusted to them as given with a view to this lifework? And are they fully resolved to make the service of God and the carrying out of His will their main object in life, to which all other aims must be subservient?

As school life draws near its close, and until the great choice of life is made, there is no more important prayer for them to say daily than that the Holy Spirit of God would make known to them what He wants them to do with their life. Meanwhile, no task is more necessary than that of qualifying themselves by cultivation of their talents, and especially by the thorough knowledge of their religion, for the special work He may entrust to them. How many there are who, in later years, feel keenly their inability to deal at all adequately with the questions of earnest inquirers after truth, and who regret when too late their neglect of opportunities which would have qualified them for the task!

Happily, a strong and enthusiastic zeal is stirring the hearts of our young Catholics in many quarters. It is for us to encourage it by every means in our power. And let us pray that, by the well-directed cultivation of talent, our colleges and schools may turn out strong Catholic men and women, with a truly apostolic spirit, who may be a credit to the Catholic Church and a powerful factor in the conversion of their country.

"*Sitio. I thirst!*" May I hear this plaintive cry as I look at my Crucifix, and ask myself: "Can I not do something for Him who can do no more?"

LXVIII
"IT IS FINISHED!"

LIFE was ebbing fast. The body drooped lower and lower on the nails, but still every sense brought its contribution of torture to the wasted frame and kept it there inexorably to the last. No failure of consciousness, no merciful dulling of memory or of intellect softened the agony of the end. His powers of mind and body were as ever entirely under His control, and His will was that they should endure to the uttermost what the Divine Nature enabled the human to sustain.

His mind took in the whole range of the Divine designs—as to Creation, Redemption, Salvation—in the eternal years, in the beginning when God created Heaven and earth, through the four thousand years when all the events of human history were preparing His way.

And now—all is finished. As He was wont to speak of His hour, so now His Heart is so full of the work for which He came that there is no need to specify it. "It is finished." All the prophecies are accomplished; all types are fulfilled; the world is redeemed, Heaven reopened, and the way made clear; all sin atoned for; all graces purchased; the Truth proclaimed; a Church with Divine guarantees founded, to lead men to salvation; a Divine example given of every virtue. No effort has been spared, no sacrifice refused. It has been a "plentiful redemption," and now—all is finished.

Our Lord was challenged to come down from the Cross. Good would come of it. The rulers would believe in Him and the nation would follow them. His mission would be accomplished at once. What if He had come down before the time! He teaches us by His perseverance right up to the end to stay patiently on our cross as long as God wills, not to weary of welldoing, not to give up a good work because of monotony, of what others may say.

Lord, give me grace to persevere unto the end, to be faithful unto death in Thy service, in the discharge of the duties of my state of life, in remaining on the cross which lifts me to Thee. Everything on Calvary said to Thee: "Come down from the cross"—the taunts of Thine enemies, the distress of Thy friends, Thine own intolerable anguish of soul and body, the protractedness of Thy torture and its keenness unabated by physical exhaustion up to the last breath. And up to that last breath Thou didst persevere—*for me*. All cried out to Thee: "Come down." All but the love of Thy Heart *for me*. This held Thee there, patient, ready, if need be, for more. O my Lord, keep me as a true soldier close to Thy standard as long as life shall last. The devil, the world, and the flesh cry out to me unceasingly: "Come down from the cross!" By Thy perseverance till death in the love of me, grant me perseverance to the end in the love of Thee!

LXIX
"FATHER, INTO THY HANDS I COMMEND MY SPIRIT"[1]

"IT is a fearful thing," says St. Paul, "to fall into the hands of the living God." "But," he adds immediately, "call to mind the former days.... Do not therefore lose your confidence, which hath a great reward. For yet a little while and a very little while, and He that is to come will come, and will not delay."[1]

In other words, our last act, like our Divine Master's, must be confidence. A little while ago it was: "My God, My God, why hast Thou forsaken Me?" And now: "Jesus crying with a loud voice said: Father, into Thy hands I commend My spirit. And saying this He gave up the ghost." The clouds were breaking. A little and a very little while and He would see again in joy the Face our sins had hidden from Him.

Lord, I follow Thy lead. With Thee I commend my spirit to the hands which in "the former days" created and blessed, corrected and healed, protected, caressed, and provided for me. Those hands have sustained me through life, shall I not trust them in death?

Father, whom shall I trust if I trust not Thee? Let not any wiles of my enemy at the last rob me of the confidence which has a great reward.

To Thee I commend my last sickness with all its circumstances; with all the pains of mind and body Thou mayest send or permit; the moment when I am told of my

---
1 Heb. 10:31.

danger, that with full resignation and trust I may place myself in Thy hands for life or for death:

I commend to Thee the trials and needs which Thou knowest will be special to me; the temptations carefully prepared which I may have to face; that clear retrospect which the Evil One will strive to turn to his own purposes; my weakness, my helplessness, my loneliness, my fears, the sinking of my physical forces, the call to battle when I feel unequal to the slightest effort:

I commend to Thee my preparation for the Last Sacraments:

My *last Confession*, for which I ask perfect contrition for the sins and shortcomings of my whole life by which I have wronged and disappointed Thee, my Heavenly Father, and injured those Thy love had confided to my care:

I commend to Thee my *last Communion*, that the Real Presence and action within me of Thy beloved Son may effect a union so close that neither life, nor death, nor any creature may have power to separate me from Him: that as my Viaticum it may support me through the dark valley of the shadow of death, and bring me in safety to Thy arms:

I commend to Thee my *last Anointing*, that purified and strengthened by the grace of this merciful Sacrament, my senses may be healed, the last relics of sin destroyed, and the first robe in all its beauty restored to me:

I humbly ask for the *Last Blessing* of Thy Church, that she may tenderly lay her hand on me for the last time, and hold me fast till I pass from her jurisdiction to Thine:

I commend to Thee my last perils and pains; my last graces and opportunities; my last failing look at the Crucifix; my last kissing of the wounds in hands and feet;

the last sounds of this earth to reach my ears; my last free act; my last breath, which I desire should be an act of perfect love of Thee, of filial acceptance of Thy will, of loving impatience to be with Thee, of submission to Thy judgement of me, of satisfaction to Thy Justice, of confidence in Thy Mercy:

I commend to Thee my passage out of this world and my entry into eternity:

I commend to Thee, O Father, my meeting with Thy beloved Son, my Saviour; His first look at me; His first word to me; His final judgement of my life, the merciful sentence which I expect and implore, the sentence which will secure to me the everlasting possession of Thee, my God and my All:

I commend to Thee my last expiations in Purgatory and then—my journey Home; Home, my Father, to the welcome of Thine outstretched arms; Home to the sight of Thy unveiled Face, my God; when I may cry to Thee: "My God, I have Thee at last, I hold Thee fast, Thou shalt never escape me any more."[1]

"Thou hast made us for Thyself, O God, and our hearts will never rest until they rest in Thee."

---

1 Bl. Curé d'Ars.

LXX
"EVEN THE DEATH OF THE CROSS"

THOSE only who lived in times when this most awful form of human cruelty and human punishment was in use could realise the force of that word "even"—*even the death of the cross.*

> O wondrous worth at which our souls are priced!
> What hath He borrowed from our nature—Christ,
> But the red altar here hath sacrificed?
> Such Holocaust as God alone might make,
> Such woe as Love insatiate may slake,
> Uplifted in atonement for my sake—
>   This—this is Calvary!
>
> Behold the piercèd Side flung open wide
> As the embrace of Jesus Crucified
> To every soul for which its Saviour died!
> O Lord, must I not yield myself to Thee?
> O Love, shall I not trust Thee utterly?
> O Christ, henceforth be All in all to me,
>   Redeemed on Calvary!

The end had come. The scoffers and the curious had moved away. All was hushed around the cross. Suddenly a loud cry broke the silence. The arms strained. The figure fell forward on the bent knees. The head sank on the breast. The Soul had gone forth to the Father. The Sacred Heart was still. Jesus having loved His own who were in the world had loved them to the end.

Earth trembled, shaken to its foundations. Rocks were rent. Graves opened. Saints arose. The Temple veil was rent. The Roman centurion cried: "Indeed, this Man was the Son of God!" Fear came upon Jerusalem. The terror-stricken spectators who had remained on Calvary returned home striking their breasts. St. Luke says: "And all the multitude of them that were come together to that sight, returned striking their breasts."

The Mother who had stood by Him to the last—erect, silent, steadfast in soul, intent—kept her watch till the sacred body was taken down from the cross and laid on the ground, the head resting on her knee. With her own hands she prepared it for burial, reverently but swiftly, because the sabbath drew on.

LXXI
THE NIGHT AFTER THE BATTLE

"In peace, in the selfsame, I will sleep, and I will rest." —Ps. 4:9.

ENTER the Sepulchre. Go softly up to the slab on which the sacred body lies. How calm the face is now! The muscles, contracted in the death agony, have relaxed, and in spite of the marks of blows on the cheeks, and the punctures on the forehead, the countenance has a beauty all its own. See the eyes closed and peaceful, the mouth composed and placid. That heart—the battlefield on which the greatest of victories has been won—is still at last. The hands and feet with their gaping wounds no longer throb and burn. The whole body—scored and rent and dislocated as it is—*rests*.

Has not that sacred body borne its part nobly as companion and instrument of the Soul! And does it not teach us as it lies there in its rest that our body, too, must share the labour of the soul if it is to share its happiness hereafter?

Look at the hands and feet, telling of toil and weariness. See the wounds. Even in the glory of the Resurrection, when all other vestiges of suffering and humiliation have passed away, He will not part with them. They are the trophies of His victory, the pledges of His love, always interceding for us with the Father. And they are a perpetual reminder to us that we, too, His members, must labour and suffer as they have done, for God and for our neighbour.

"We do not know what we shall be," says St. John, speaking of the Resurrection, "but we know that we shall be like Him." And this likeness must be secured *now*. Those who are conformed to Him here He will acknowledge as His hereafter, and in the measure of their likeness to Him will they be accepted and glorified. Does this thought reassure or alarm me? Looking at my daily life, do I see in it any resemblance to the arduous life of my Saviour? Is my body the helpful companion of my soul in their joint task of *working* out the salvation of both? I must make it so by honest work of brain or hands, *work* that our Lord and Master will accept as deserving of the name. What am I doing in His service? What am I preparing to show Him that He may say to me one day: "Well done, good and faithful *servant*"? Body and soul alike are stewards, and will have to give an account of all that has been entrusted to them for their Master's service—health and strength, gifts of body and mind, time, influence, opportunities. I have to bring my eyes, my tongue, my brain, my hands and feet, to be in some degree conformed by laborious work to the wounded hands and feet of my Saviour, using painful things bravely, pleasant things sparingly.

See the Soul of Christ the moment it leaves the body. All the long conflict over! The Victory won, and the eternal adoration and thanksgiving of angels and men as its reward. And my soul—what am I preparing for it after death—reward and rejoicing, or regret?

Life will soon be over; a few years, and the end will have come. "Work your work before the time and He will give you your reward in His time."

> Life is a sheet of paper white,
> Whereon we each of us may write
> A word or two—and then comes night!

LXXII
"HIS SEPULCHRE SHALL BE GLORIOUS"

—Isaias 11:10.

IT was a heart-broken little group that, through the three hours of His agony, had stood by the Cross looking up into His face. They had no thought but for Him. But when all was over, when He had bowed His head in death and they were left alone, how their thoughts must have turned to the Mother in her desolation! If they had lost their all, what must be the loss to her! She had seen all, heard all. In closest union of mind and heart—hoping, fearing, agonising for Him and with Him, so the long hours went by. No word, no movement had been unworthy of her, had detracted in the slightest degree from the perfection of her submission, from the sublimity of her sacrifice.

We follow her in thought through the hours of Saturday as, now alone, now the consoler of those whom John brought to her for strength and comfort, she showed herself the Tower of David, Refuge of sinners, Comfort of the afflicted. What consolation could have been given we are at a loss to guess, for faith and hope seem to have lost their hold on the stricken followers of her Son. His prophecies of the Resurrection appear to have been entirely forgotten. When it came, how completely it took them by surprise! But how was it with herself, whose faith and hope were bright as ever, brightening more and more as the day wore on?

We are apt, perhaps, to fix our minds to-day too exclusively on our Lady's desolation. There must have been also a fount of joy welling up in her soul. "If you loved Me," said our Lord to His Apostles, "you would indeed be glad." Surely her love of Him must have made her rejoice for His sake, whatever desolation was still hers? When she saw the sacred body fall forward on the nails in death, when John led her away from the Sepulchre, there must have been relief that at last the baptism wherewith He had to be baptised was accomplished, that He was no longer "straitened." All through the hours of that Saturday when her eager eyes were turning continually to the East, there must have been the joy of anticipation? Only by our knowledge that the bliss of the Beatific Vision could and did subsist in the Soul of Christ amid the darkness of His dereliction can we understand how, with her firm belief in the resurrection and restoration to her of her Son in a few hours, she could have been immersed in anguish so profound. But this we know—most of us by experience know—that till God's hour for consolation strikes, no comfort can reach the soul; that all it can and must do is to bide His time, and meanwhile suffer, "wait on God—*and endure.*"

"*Let our Mother the Church rejoice.*" How swiftly she passes from the minor to the major key! How jubilant she is to-day, like the bride of some glorious conqueror who sees his triumph nearing and can with difficulty restrain her transports. Like a child who thinks that the to-morrow so longed for will never come. And like herself, too, for she is always and throughout the year a Joy-giver. She anticipates her festivals by First Vespers and prolongs them by Octaves.

Joy is so stamped upon her brow that it might stand for a fifth mark of her Divine origin.

But to-day she surpasses herself in the manifestation of this—one of the most human, the most beautiful of her traits.

The solemn midnight service of Holy Saturday she has gone on anticipating till it has become her morning worship. And how magnificent it is! How deftly does she blend in it the two extremes of sorrow and joy, of hope and fruition, of the Old Covenant and the New! How happily she links the holy ones of the Old Law with the saints of her own calendar! We see her tracing through the centuries, by the light of type and prophecy, the path of her Founder, with Him "leaping upon the mountains, skipping over the hills," from the beginning when God created Heaven and earth to the coming of "that morning star which knows no setting, (Him) who, returning from the grave, serenely shone upon mankind."

So eager is she to welcome Him on His return, so beside herself with exultation in His brightness and glory, that she forgets her usual staidness. Her "O felix culpa—O happy fault!" comes as a sweet surprise year after year. The lighting of the Paschal candle, the casting aside of her mourning, the "Alleluia" at the Epistle, before the angel has announced the Resurrection, the abridgement even of her Mass to hasten the "Alleluias" of the First Vespers—all speak of a joyous haste akin to that which we shall see in the Master and the disciples before to-morrow's sun has set.

But long before this the Master has been visiting and rejoicing the waiting saints in Limbo. Straight from its release on Calvary the glorious Soul descended to them in their prison house, to bring them the glad tidings of their deliverance. What congratulations and thanksgivings were then on every side, from Adam to the good thief on his arrival! Surely it was from our First Parents that came first the cry, re-echoed since by the Church: "O felix culpa!"

> Adam lay ybounden,
> Bounden in a bond:
> Four thousand winter
> Thought he not too long.
> And all was for an apple,
> An apple that he took
> As clerkes finden written
> In their book.
>
> Nor had the apple taken been,
> The apple taken been,
> Nor had never our Ledy
> A-been heaven's queen.
> Blessed be the time
> That apple taken was!
> Therefore we may singen
>   *Deo gracias!*[1]

---

1 Fifteenth century. *Corn from Olde Fieldes.* An Anthology of English Poems from the fourteenth to the seventeenth century.

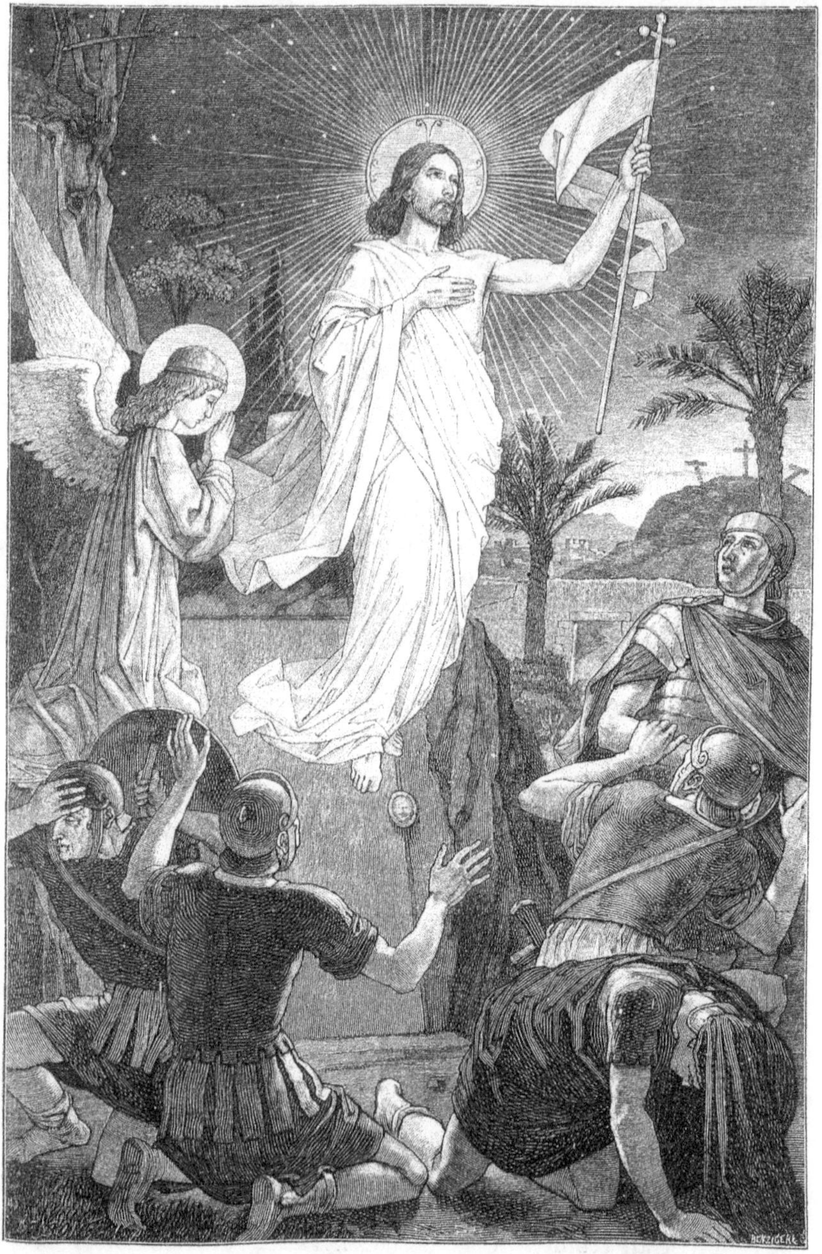

THE RISEN LIFE

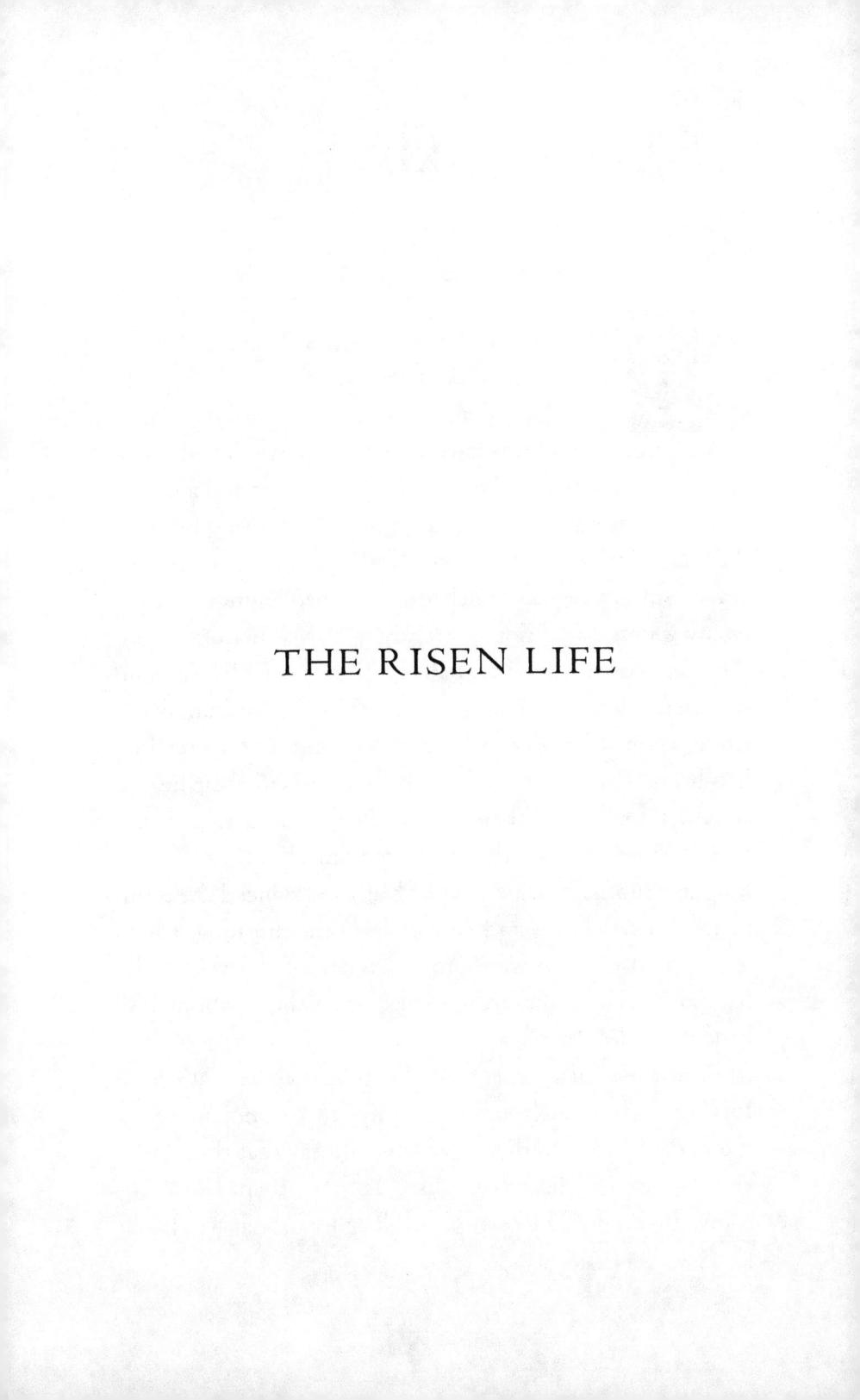

LXXIII
"RESURREXI!" — I

"Resurrexi et adhuc tecum sum, Alleluia!"

HOW admirably does the Church sum up the joy of this Day of days, the Day that the Lord hath made that we may be glad and rejoice therein![1]

We know that "Jesus having loved His own loved them unto the end." But in these words, "I am risen and am still with thee," we have the assurance of love enduring beyond the end, a love not arrested by death, not quenched in the sea of suffering into which our sins had plunged Him. Many waters could not quench His charity, neither could the floods drown it. His pain on the eve of His Passion was that for a moment there must be separation from those whom He loved, whose Friend and Comforter He had been. But He would see them again and their hearts should rejoice, and their joy no man should take from them. Three days was the appointed time, but they seemed long to Him. The eagerness of His love reduced the term to its shortest limit, and very early in the morning, when it began to dawn towards the first day of the week, He hastened back as the great Consoler to those whom He had left in desolation.

Resurrexi et adhuc tecum sum! There is such exultation in His tone. It is such jubilee to Him to be once more in the midst of His brethren. One would say that this is the very essence of His Easter bliss. Is there, then, Lord, no room for joy in Thy own great glory for which we thank

[1] Introit for Easter Sunday.

Thee to-day above all days? No time for the mutual congratulation of that blessed Soul and Body which, in such close companionship of pain, submission, and perseverance, had together accomplished the redemption of the world? Is all else forgotten in the unselfish joy of our companionship once more? We knew, indeed, that Thy delights are to be with the children of men. But was there not enough in the twenty-four hours of Friday to cool that ardour, to make Thee rejoice to be where we are not, where "no evil can reach Thee, no scourge come nigh Thy dwelling"? Have denial and desertion but increased Thy love for us, O faithful Heart, that we should be to Thee now, not servants, nor even friends—but "brethren"?

Resurrexi et adhuc tecum sum! I am *with thee*—not "you," but "thee." His love is not universal only, but singular.

"It is for thee," He says to us one by one, "that I suffered and died, and am risen again. It is thy sins I have washed away in My blood: it is for thy place in Heaven that I have paid with My life: it is for thee I am risen, that My Resurrection may be the pledge and the model of thine."

I am still with thee. Centuries cannot separate us. My action on thy soul is as real as upon Magdalen's. It is I who say to thee: Thy sins are forgiven thee, go in peace. It is I who come to thee on Easter morning and expect thy welcome; who call thee by thy name and listen for thy "*Rabboni!*" I took to Myself all the affection of that ardent heart. I want and ask for thine.

Earthly loss troubles thee. By death, by distance, by estrangement, friends fall away from thy side, and the sense of loneliness deepens—be comforted, I am still with thee. Vague fears cloud thy soul and make thee ill at ease in My Presence, fears that elude scrutiny and torture with their importunity—Fear not, I am still with thee.

"*He is risen!*" This was the one all-absorbing thought of the disciples that first Eastertide. Pleasure and displeasure swept but the surface of their souls, but this memory was a fount of joy welling up every hour and every moment, changing earth into Heaven. What to them were the affairs of the festive city, its business, its excitement, its alarms? They trod its thronged ways: they heard around them the tongues of every nation under heaven; their hands took up its daily toil. But their hearts were above all these things. They that wept were as though they wept not...and they that bought as though they possessed not, using this world as if they used it not.[1] They were not of the world, as their Risen Lord was not of the world.

Oh, that it could be thus with us this Eastertide! What He was to His own then, He is to His own still. It was His presence, the abiding sense of His triumph and of His glory, that made the heart of each a very heaven of peace and joy. We, too, have that Presence, veiled indeed, but because of that very veiling entitling us to a fulness of blessing denied to them: "Blessed are they that have not seen and have believed."[2]

See the altar and the lamp that tell of the Real Presence! "Behold the tabernacle of God with men. He will dwell with them. And they shall be His people, and God Himself with them shall be their God"[3]..."all days, even to the consummation of the world."[4]

---

[1] 1 Cor. 7:30, 31.   [2] John 20:29.   [3] Apoc. 21:3.
[4] Matt. 28:20.

LXXIV
"RESURREXI!"—II

"I am risen and am still with thee!"

TO be with us, to be known as the Son of Man—this from eternity was the desire of the Son of God. It shaped the history of the world. It determined the destiny of the chosen people. It was embodied in type. It spoke in prophecy. Nothing checked, nothing chilled it. All things ministered to it, the rise and fall of empires, the sinfulness and misery of men. It spanned the four thousand years of waiting, till at length, when its hour was come, in the midnight silence at Nazareth, the Word was made flesh and dwelt amongst us.

Yet even this was far from satisfying the desire of our Lord to be with us. The Incarnation was but the starting-point of fresh marvels. Not only would He share our nature and lead a human life in our midst, but He would unite Himself intimately with us one by one.

To revive the son of the Sunamitess, the prophet Eliseus laid himself down upon the dead child. "He put his mouth upon his mouth, and his eyes upon his eyes, and his hands upon his hands, and he bowed himself upon him, and the child's flesh grew warm." It is a beautiful prototype, but poorly foreshadows our union with Christ in the Sacrament of His Love, and the effects of that union. Who can measure the depth of the condescension by which He bows Himself down to us! By personal contact of His sacred Body and Soul with ours He preserves and continually develops in us supernatural life. It is a gradual growth, often scarcely perceptible. But at length, even to our own consciousness, His Presence begins to tell. We come to see through His eyes, to measure by His standards the relative values of time and eternity. Our hands learn from His the dignity of labour, the privilege and the joy of any and every work done for God. By His sacred mouth we are taught to control our speech that it may serve noble and useful ends—the glory of God and the good of our neighbour.

Love, above all, is heightened and expanded by union with its Source. All that He comes to do for us is comprised in the word Love, the love of God for His own sake and of our neighbour for God's sake. And this result, in greater or less measure according to our dispositions, is the unfailing fruit of Communion, of frequent Communion especially. Our heart is too near the Heart of Jesus to be proof against its influence. Gradually it may be, but surely, torpor and coldness begin to give way—"the child's flesh grew warm."

Must we not make an effort, at Easter above all, to meet the Love that comes so far to seek us, that breaks out in the cry: "I am risen and am still with thee!" He says not "Rejoice, for My hour is come." That sacred word, "My hour," was reserved for the time of His Passion. It is not of His Triumph and His Glory that His Heart is fullest now, but of this—that He is with us once more. The gain is surely ours rather than His. Let us, then, share with Him the joy of those exulting words.

O Lord and Master, speeding to and fro amid Thy disconsolate friends, the Comforter and Joy-giver of all, give to us also of Thy fulness. Let the gladness of Thy Heart overflow into ours to-day. As it is still Thy delight to be with us, make it our delight to be with Thee, to rejoice with Thee. Receive, O Lord, the offerings of Thy exultant Church.[1] We rejoice in the plenitude of joy that floods every faculty of Thy blessed human Soul. We thank Thee for every pain, known and unknown, which Thou hast borne for us, for all Thou hast done and purchased for us, for the love that, forgetting our unkindness and ingratitude, calls us in the first hour of Thy risen life no longer servants or even friends, but "brethren." We praise Thee; we bless Thee; we adore Thee; we glorify Thee. We give Thee thanks for Thy great glory. May all creation exult and be glad to-day, not only for the plentiful redemption and the stupendous gifts Thy Resurrection has brought to man, but still more for the praise that throughout eternity will accrue therefrom to Thee.

> Spring bursts to-day,
> For Christ is risen and all the earth's at play.
>
> Flash forth, thou Sun,
> The rain is over and gone, its work is done.
>
> Winter is past,
> Sweet spring is come at last, is come at last.
>
> Sing, creatures, sing,
> Angels and men, and birds and everything.
>
> —Viator.

---

[1] Secret, Low Sunday.

LXXV
"HAEC DIES QUAM FECIT DOMINUS!" ALLELUIA!

THIS is the cry of the Church to-day and throughout Easter week. It must have been the cry of the saints in Limbo when its gates flew open to admit the King of Glory. How the waiting multitudes there thronged around Him, their adoring recognition of Him as Messias and Redeemer making up to Him for the mockery and blasphemy He had just left! Adam and Eve, Abel, and Abraham, and Isaac, Moses and Elias, David, Isaias, and Jeremias, His types and forerunners, how they would flock around Him crying: "Come, let us praise the Lord with joy. Let us come before His presence with thanksgiving. Come, let us adore and fall down, for He is the Lord our God!"

Can we think that He left them in Limbo when the hour for the Resurrection drew on? That when its gates opened to Him, they closed again upon those to whom—once they had seen Him—its weary waiting would have become intolerable? Supposing they were left there during the forty hours which was the vigil of Mary and of the poor forlorn disciples, would He not fetch them at daybreak on the third day, that He might lead them, the first fruits of His victory, to the scenes of His Passion and death, to those who were bewailing Him, above all, to the Mother of Sorrows, that they might all rejoice together?

Some holy writers think that He took them to the Sepulchre that they might see the havoc sin had wrought on that sacred sinless flesh. We can imagine them contemplating it, the prophets pondering their own prophecies as they looked on the fulfilment: "There is no beauty in Him nor comeliness, and we have seen Him, and there was no sightliness that we should be desirous of Him. Truly He hath borne our infirmities and carried our sorrows, and we have thought Him as it were a leper and as one struck by God and afflicted. But He was wounded for our iniquities, He was bruised for our sins, the chastisement of our peace was upon Him, and by His bruises we are healed."

And even as they looked on, His hour came. The glorious Soul revivifies the sacred Body from which the Divinity has never been separated, and with the endowments of immortality, impassibility, agility, and clarity, bestows upon it a glory commensurate with its ignominy, a glory befitting the Son of God. Resplendent in His majesty, ravishing in His beauty, He stands before them and they worship Him as God of God, Light of light, very God of very God, yet truly Son of Man.

> They worship Thee, those ransomed souls,
>   With the fresh strength of love set free;
> They worship rapturously and think
>   Of Mary as they gaze on Thee.[1]

But His thought has outrun theirs. He must satisfy their desire to behold her whose foot has crushed the serpent's head. He must lead them to Mount Sion and present them to His Mother. Yet not till He has Himself visited that lonely watcher and dried the tears of those forty hours.

---

1 Faber.

LXXVI
"REGINA COELI, LAETARE!" ALLELUIA!

"According to the multitude of my sorrows in my heart, Thy comforts have given joy to my soul."—Ps. 93:19.

WE observe a certain order in the manifestations of our Lord to "His own" after the Resurrection. There was an order of merit and of mercy.

His first visit—who can doubt it?—was to His Blessed Mother. Merit and mercy required it should be so. His first love, the first to receive and give Him to the world, His first confidante, His first and most faithful disciple, who had followed Him step by step throughout His laborious and painful life, ministering to Him, cooperating with Him, sharing His sorrows and His joys, all His interests, all His pains of body and of mind by the intensity of her compassion, who had offered herself, like Him, a willing victim, to fulfil and to bear all that was designed for the world's redemption, to see Him set up as the target for the rage of Satan, the hate of men, and the Justice of God—was she not the first to whom He would hasten when His work was done, man redeemed, her faithful co-operation rewarded?

It must have been quite at daybreak of the third day. Merit deserved it, mercy no less. For the heroism of the spirit which had sustained her had taxed to the utmost limit of its strength the tender, fragile frame. We, whose love of God is so weak, are wont, perhaps, to dwell too exclusively on the Mother's anguish in the sufferings of her Son, forgetting that throughout the Passion it was the outrage to her God which to the most enlightened, the most loyal of His creatures was direst agony. She had borne up to the last on Calvary. She had stood for the three hours. But when all was over, and John led her away from the Sepulchre, the agony of her heart was such that she must have sunk under it had the presence of her Son been long delayed.

The meeting of the Mother and the Son after the Resurrection was a fact too obvious to need recording, too intimate and tender for the Evangelists to describe. We may know about it, perhaps, when the secrets of all hearts shall be revealed. Meanwhile it remains the secret of the two hearts, which because they alone understood one another's sorrows alone deserve to share fully each other's joys.

Contemplatives tell us that He had to stay a long time with her before she could fully realise, for the horror of the past, the joy of the actual present. And we may well believe that His own joy in the comfort He poured into her heart would prolong the converse they held together.

> Risen sun on the silent sea,
>   And Galilee is a golden foam:
> But I would I had seen the light on thee,
>   That Easter dawning when He came home.
>
> Risen sun on the temple's stone,
>   And temple steps are a ladder of flame:
> But I would I had seen the light that shone
>   Across thy threshold when Jesus came.
>
> Risen sun o'er Gethsemane,
>   And Calvary is a Thabored place:
> But, oh, for the glory that fell on thee
>   From the light of thy risen Jesu's Face![1]

---

[1] Rev. Hugh F. Blunt.

They would remind one another, each time with new gladness, that "winter was now passed, the rain was over and gone"; the prophecy of Simeon which had been before them for thirty-three years was fulfilled; the baptism wherewith Christ was to be baptised, and which had so straitened Him, was accomplished; the chalice the Father had given Him had been drained to the very dregs. His Mother might say to Him amid smiles and tears: "There shall no evil come to Thee, nor shall the scourge come near Thy dwelling." "And death shall be no more, nor mourning nor sorrow shall be any more, for the former things are passed away."

Congratulation with those we love, over suffering long anticipated and now past, is sweeter even than compassion. Yet how He must have thanked her for the heroic sympathy and co-operation with Him, into which all human tenderness with no human weakness had entered. That, whilst knowing the agony of her heart lay bare before Him, she had tried to stifle the sobs and stay the tears which, more than scourge or thorns, had power to torture Him.

Not even the holiest among the Blessed was worthy to intrude upon that interview and converse. But we may suppose that at its close our Lord would present to His Mother those who had waited—some of them thousands of years—to see fulfilled in her the promise made in Paradise.

St. Matthew tells us that when "Jesus, crying with a loud voice, yielded up the ghost, the earth quaked, and the rocks were rent, and the graves were opened, and many bodies of the saints arose, and coming out of the tombs after the Resurrection, appeared to many." What more likely than that among these saints were some specially connected with the Passion, as David, Moses and Elias, Isaias and Jeremias? There would be a special appropriateness in these appearing to our Lady after the Resurrection, with Adam and Eve, her holy parents, Joachim and Anne, St. Joseph, St. John the Baptist, and others chosen by God to gladden her with their presence and congratulations. With what reverence and gratitude would Eve behold the blessed amongst women who had reversed the ancient curse. How one and all of that happy company would praise and thank her for what she had suffered for their redemption. "They all blessed her with one voice, saying: Thou art the glory of Jerusalem, thou art the joy of Israel, thou art the honour of our people. For thou hast done manfully, and thy heart has been strengthened...thou shalt be blessed for ever."[1] And Mary would herself look with reverence and thankfulness on that multitude who, under the guidance of the Old Law, or even out of the darkness of paganism, had come to salvation through the foreseen merits of her Son.

All generations called her blessed: the "Ave" of Gabriel spoke the congratulations of all: "Hail, full of grace, the Lord is with thee!" And Mary said: "My soul doth magnify the Lord and my spirit hath rejoiced in God my Saviour."

---

1 Judith 15.

LXXVII
"MARY!"
"RABBONI!"

WHO could come next but Mary Magdalen? Here, again, merit and mercy meet. She had loved much. She had been faithful to Him to His last breath, and after. She was pining for Him. Angels were powerless to comfort her. It must be His Presence, His Voice, if that desolate heart was to be consoled and rewarded.

"*Mary!*"

"*Rabboni!*"

Two words, like Versicle and Response. But enough. She was content to let Him go, and sped away as His messenger, the Apostle of the Resurrection, to comfort those who had been with Him as they mourned and wept.

It is a saint who tells us that by tears Mary Magdalen obtained from our Lord all that she desired—forgiveness of many sins, resurrection from the dead of the brother four days in the grave, the early visit of her Risen Master. Well may the Church urge us to ask for the gift of tears by inserting a prayer for it among her Collects: "Almighty and most merciful God, who for the thirsting people didst draw from the rock a fountain of living water, bring forth from the hardness of our hearts tears of compunction, that weeping over our sins, we may obtain through Thy mercy the forgiveness of them."

She takes it for granted that our hearts which grieve so readily over the troubles of this life are hard to move when there is question of sorrow for sin, or love of God. But prayer can do all things. A miracle was needed to draw water from the rock. God worked the miracle. And His touch is able to draw from our hearts the tears that, like Magdalen's, will obtain from Him all we need and desire. How many of the saints have asked and obtained this gift of tears. Let us ask it of the Holy Spirit: "*Riga quod est aridum.*" Ask it of the Mother of Sorrows:

> Let me mingle tears with thee,
> Mourning Him who mourned for me
> All the days that I may live.
>
> By the Cross with thee to stay,
> There with thee to weep and pray
> Is all I ask of thee to give.

Ask it of Blessed Mary Magdalen:

> There are thousands in all ages
>   Come to Christ because of thee,
> O then, Mary, 'mid thy converts
>   In thy kindness number me![1]

---

1 Faber.

LXXVIII
"AND JESUS MET THEM"
—Matt. 28.

IS not this the experience of all His servants—nay, more—of all who honestly want to serve Him, to make a start on the right road? A little determination, a little effort, and the difficulty is overpassed. *Jesus met them*—and the thing was done!

Magdalen and her company, on their way to the sepulchre, bethought them of the stone that blocked the entrance: "Who shall roll us away the stone?" they said. "And, behold there was a great earthquake. For an angel of the Lord descended from Heaven, and coming, rolled back the stone." They sought Jesus of Nazareth—*and Jesus met them.*

A sudden and unexpected cross has changed the whole tenor of our life; the joy or the hope that was its brightness has gone out of it; henceforth it must be a dreary waste, a lonely journey to the end. And one of two forces is overmastering us—a despondency that refuses to see anything beyond the actual desolation of the hour, to make any effort to dispel the gloom or to rise above it; or, on the other hand, a vindictiveness that turns angrily from all the succours of faith, that rebels against the ruling of Providence, and thinks by refusing its submission, to defy and so to injure the Sovereignty of God. Either of these impulses, or both at once, may assail the soul. But there is a third with which to reckon:

When Simon the Cyrenean went forth from his home that morning in March, mind and heart engrossed with the things of this world, marvelling as he neared the city at the tumultuous cries, unwonted even at that paschal season, a turn in the road brought him face to face with a man who had just been condemned to death and whom the executioners were goading forward. They were seeking some fellow of no account on whom to lay the burden under which He was sinking, and here, coming up from the country, strong and hale, was one who would serve their turn. And they laid hands on Simon and forced upon his unwilling shoulder the Cross of Christ.

What a reversal of that day's plans! Instead of a peaceful participation in religious rites, to be thrust into close companionship with this criminal who had drawn upon himself the execration of the whole people; to be involved in his disgrace; to have to render him this degrading service; to be mocked by the crowd as a follower and friend of Jesus of Nazareth! His sense of self-respect, his national instincts, revolted against the odious task—*but Jesus met them!*

Who shall tell the strong grace that went out to Simon's heart from the failing, struggling Sufferer by his side! Who shall measure the change wrought within him when, Calvary reached, his load was lifted, and his allegiance to his Master won for ever!

His plans reversed! Yes, indeed. No more a son of the expiring Synagogue, but a living member of Him whose strength he had sustained for the hours of Redemption on the Cross—Simon of Cyrene—the name that all ages will hold in honour, the first cross-laden follower of Christ, nearer to Him on the road to Calvary than even

His Mother, the man all generations will congratulate, because on a day he will bless forever, Jesus met him with the Cross!

So will it be with those who, perchance with the fiercest repugnance of nature, accept the cross of Christ and carry it meekly in His company. What congratulations await them in the life to come! How glorious a praise will be to them throughout eternity: "And thou also wast with Jesus of Nazareth."

Upon the storm-tossed Lake the fishermen toiled in vain, for the wind was against them, and every moment the waves made ready to engulf their little craft. That they might feel their helplessness they were left awhile to the powerlessness of their own endeavours. But One was watching. When His time was come, He stepped out upon the waters. Just when they had given up all for lost, when human help failed them utterly —*Jesus met them*. "Fear not," He said to them across the waves and above the storm. "It is I, fear not." And He rebuked the sea and there came a great calm.

And Jesus met them. The faithful women had followed Him to the last. When even Apostles fell away, they had shared His disgrace, and deliberately drawn upon themselves the animosity of the powerful ones of their nation, whose threats the Roman governor himself dared not withstand. Friend and acquaintance were put far from Him, but they stood by His Cross in the darkness and dereliction of that noon, as many a time they had closed round Him with the exulting crowd.

His is a human heart, that prizes beyond all price the fidelity of love. He, who loved His own unto the end, carried with Him beyond the grave the remembrance of those faithful ones. The three days of separation from them seemed long to Him. And so it was that very early in the morning, the first day of the week, He hastened to them. Scarcely had the tidings of the Resurrection been given them by His messenger, scarcely had they set out running on their joyful errand to carry those tidings to the Eleven, when, "behold! Jesus met them, saying: All hail! And they came up and took hold of His feet and adored Him."

He is the same now. To His faithful servants of all time He shows Himself the "Faithful and true." For them all, every one, the dark day of trial will pass, and in the brightness of an Easter morning their Lord will meet them.

And Jesus met them. To meet us He is not afraid of condescensions we should have deemed unworthy of Him.

Thomas, one of the Twelve, rejecting all evidence, laid down the terms on which alone he would accept the Resurrection. "Except I shall see in His hands the place of the nails, and put my hand into His side, I will not believe." One sense would not suffice him. The testimony of his own eyes he would not allow. Wound after wound must be probed by his finger before he would yield belief. It was nothing to him that the Master had again and again foretold His rising again, that every prediction of the prophets concerning Him had been fulfilled, that trustworthy witnesses had seen, and heard, and touched, and eaten with Him after His Resurrection; the conditions laid down by himself must be complied with, or he would remain unconvinced.

And Jesus met them. With a condescension and a graciousness worthy of such majesty, he met the refractory disciple on his own ground and offered him the satisfaction he desired. How often does He so deal with His disciples now! How often in the past has He so dealt with ourselves! There was much, very much, to stand in the way of His mercies—our prejudices, our weaknesses, our waywardness, our whims—*and Jesus met them!*

But with all His gentleness and tenderness, one thing He exacts always—the concurrence of our freewill. The meeting is *of two*. The longest stretch of the road is His share, but we must do our part. Not only did He meet both His fellow-sufferers who were to journey with Him along the way of the Cross, but for three hours He hung between them. To both He offered the same example, the same powerful grace to snatch them from ruin and save them even yet. One alone met Him. One alone brought his freewill to aid him in the work of his salvation. One alone accepted the pain his sins deserved, cried to his King for a remembrance in the Kingdom He was entering, and so crying, was heard, absolved, and saved.

Our Companion, our Brother, our Friend, Jesus is *always* meeting us; in the events and occupations, the difficulties and worries of everyday life, as truly as at its turning points. He meets us at the start, and on the way, and at the end of the journey. He inspires every good thought, upholds us in every good work, overcomes for us in every temptation. In dangers, in distresses, in each difficult call of duty, He comes unfailingly to our aid.

Yet He has a meeting-place of predilection—the altar rails. There, if He might, He would give us rendezvous every day. He desires to be taken as our daily Companion and resource in all the twenty-four hours may bring. Could He make His desire ours, the record of each morning would be—*"And Jesus met them."* What a pledge would this be of a joyful meeting with Him in the life to come! What reward to our Angel Guardians, surrendering their charge to Him as we cross the threshold of eternity, to be able to bear us this witness—*"And Jesus met them."*

LXXIX
"AND PETER"

"Go, tell His disciples and Peter." What depth of tenderness there is in those words: "and Peter"! The holy angels are the messengers of God; their words are dictated by Him. These, therefore, are the most apt and faithful expression of the mind of God, full of pity and compassion.

Of all the sorrowing hearts that mourned Jesus of Nazareth, His Mother's only excepted, none needed comfort more than Peter's. John and Magdalen's were broken, but they had been faithful to the last, and in the faithful heart there is—underlying all depths of sorrow—the peace of God which surpasseth all understanding. It was from depths of woe theirs did not know that Peter's tears were welling.

The message that for others was to change all sorrow into joy, what would it have been to him but for—"and Peter"? Was he to be counted among the disciples now? Would he be allowed to join them on the way to Galilee and there look once more upon Him whom he loved? There was that promise at the Supper: "And thou being once converted confirm thy brethren." Might he, then, count them as brethren still? Would they who had seen him draw his sword in the Garden own him now? Could he confirm them who even in flight had shown themselves stronger than one who at the first word of a servant girl had denied Him? But he had seen Him since his fall. Their eyes had met in the very hour of the denial, and it was when the Lord looked upon him that light and love and bitter contrition had filled his soul. Yes, and hope, which the words of Mary, when John led him to her, had strengthened. The battle between hope and fear must have been sore throughout the long hours of Friday and Saturday. His heart was torn with conflicting thoughts when Magdalen and the other women, "running from the sepulchre, told these things to the Eleven....And the words seemed to them as idle tales and they did not believe them." One, however, had caught the words, "and Peter." It was enough. Once more, as when he stepped out into the raging sea to meet his Master, love and hope overcame fear. And he ran with John to the sepulchre.

See the two, so often found together, running, the younger and fleeter arriving first. But yet he went not in, waiting there with the deference always shown by the Apostles to Peter. "Then cometh Simon Peter and went into the sepulchre and saw the linen cloths lying...and went away, wondering in himself at that which was come to pass."

Mercy—the mercy of the Sacred Heart—could hold out no longer. Peter, like Magdalen, needed sorely the presence of his Master. His tears, like hers, had earned for him the one desire of his heart. And He came— "Jesus yesterday, to-day, and the same for ever." Of the meeting we know nothing more than the simple fact told by St. Peter himself and by St. Paul: "After that He was seen by Cephas." That it was full of tenderness and reassurance on one side, of loving sorrow and simple trust on the other, we may be sure by our Lord's dealing with His own always, and more especially by His intercourse with them in His Risen Life. Were proof needed, we have it in the fulfilment on the very day of the Resurrection of our Lord's promise to Peter: "And thou being converted confirm thy brethren."

In the morning of that first day of the week the Resurrection was "an idle tale" to the Eleven. In the evening, when the two disciples came in from Emmaus to tell their story in the Upper Room—how they had had the Master walking with them all the way and disappearing after the breaking of bread—instead of the patient hearing they had expected, they were stopped at once, as the door opened, by the eager cry of all assembled: "The Lord is risen indeed and hath appeared to Simon!"

It was during the forty days which followed that the charge of the whole flock was given to Peter; that martyrdom, the reward of his threefold profession of love, was revealed to him; that—this time awaiting no command nor permission—he flung himself into the sea the sooner to reach his Master. From the moment of that meeting after the Resurrection there had been no doubt, no misgiving. In his simple heart all was love and trust as before, only a more gentle humility, with more tender compassion for the fallen and the weak.

The tears that furrowed his cheeks to the end bore witness, not only to the abiding sorrow of this model of penitents, but to the compassion of Him who gave such a one to the Church as His first Vicar. When, then, doubts and fears assail us, when

> Hope departs, and faith scarce lingers
> And we dare not think we love,

let us remember the message to the fallen and the weak on the morning of the first Easter Day, of the special tenderness to the one amongst the dispirited disciples who needed comfort most:

"Go, tell His disciples—and Peter!"

LXXX
DISCOURAGEMENT

IT must have been very early morning when two of the disciples, overcome by disappointment and grief, left the company of the Apostles without waiting to verify the reports beginning to spread abroad that the sepulchre was empty and the Master risen. How they "talked together of all these things which had happened," and how a stranger joined them, revealing Himself finally in "the breaking of bread," St. Luke tells us in the most detailed account we have of the appearances of our Lord on that eventful day.

"*And behold two of them went the same day to a town which was sixty furlongs from Jerusalem.*"

Every word of the Evangelist expresses amazement at conduct so unaccountable.

And behold—the Scriptural word announcing a wonder.

Two of them—was it not wonderful that two of the disciples, who for three years had followed our Lord about, coming under the spell of His presence, hearing His words, witnessing His miracles, knowing His announcement of His Death and Resurrection,

went the same day—that morning, after hearing the women's story of the empty sepulchre and the angel's proclamation of the Resurrection, without ascertaining for themselves or waiting to hear from others if the report was well founded,

to a town sixty furlongs from Jerusalem—from the city which had held all their hopes, and still held all that was dearest to them:

two of them—nothing spreads like discouragement. Instead of rectifying by the words of the prophets which were "read every Sabbath," and by the express declaration of their Master, their erroneous conception of the Messiah, they confirm each other in their despairing view of the situation and leave the apostolic company. Their minds were so oppressed with gloom that no ray of light enabled them to discover in the wonderful stranger who joined them their Lord and their God. Not the nearness of His presence; not the familiar voice, the words and ways on which they had hung with adoring love, the sweetness and the power of His conversation as He drew their trouble from them, reproved, instructed, enlightened, and consoled.

Is it not so at times with ourselves? Discouragement so dulls our perceptions that the most powerful of heavenly influences are lost upon us. Instead of seeking wise and safe counsel, we abandon ourselves to grief, or by laying open our hearts to those troubled like ourselves, make things worse. We begin to neglect prayer and the Sacraments that would have enlightened and strengthened us, and for consolation and distraction betake ourselves to creatures who can neither soothe nor help.

Notice that it was only "in the breaking of bread" that the eyes of the disciples were opened. Whatever we do let us not stay away from Holy Communion. "My heart is withered because I forgot to eat my bread."[1] "Lord, give us always this Bread!"

---

[1] Ps. 101.

LXXXI
"PEACE BE TO YOU"

"He was seen by Cephas and after that by the Eleven." —1 Cor. 15.

OUR Lord is better than His promises. "Go, tell My brethren that they go into Galilee, there they shall see Me," He had said to the holy women. But He could not wait for that appointed and solemn meeting. Six times at least He showed Himself to His own on the very day of His Resurrection. For His own sake as for theirs He had curtailed as far as possible the three days of prophecy, and "in the end of the Sabbath, when it began to dawn towards the first day of the week," He began the series of manifestations which were to change earth into heaven for them.

The Master had His plans for each and all on that first Easter Day. Some were to have their consolation at daybreak, some at noon, some not till evening. One was to have none at all that day. He was in fault and must do penance for another week.

How the Son hastened to His Mother, how He met her, how He healed that broken heart, who shall say! With Magdalen a little later there was the playful hide and seek. But she was not to touch Him. What she had come to regard as her own special privilege was denied her in this hour of joy, and granted to her companions, the holy women. "But they came up and took hold of His feet and adored Him." Peter was forgiven and comforted in private. Thomas, a week later, before all whom his obstinacy had scandalised. In one case we may feel sure there was no reproach at all, in the other there was a gentle rebuke, more for our sakes than for the Apostle's: "Blessed are they that have not seen and have believed." To the disciples going to Emmaus consolation came gradually—the falling in, as it were casually, with a sympathetic stranger to whom they opened their hearts gave them the needed relief.

It was not till evening that our Lord showed Himself to the Apostles gathered together in the Cenacle; partly, perhaps, because they had not merited a visit earlier. As His intimate friends and more fully instructed disciples it was for them to have upheld by their faith His less favoured followers. They should not have needed the exhortation of the women to run to the sepulchre, nor have treated their story with contempt. Seeing how clearly their Master had foretold His Resurrection: "The Son of Man shall be three days and three nights in the heart of the earth...and the third day shall rise again," it is wonderful that the rumours spread abroad by friends and enemies alike should have met with such incredulity. The dead were rising and appearing to many; the priests and the Pharisees had remembered His prediction: "Destroy this temple and in three days I will raise it up"; the guard stationed before the sealed tomb on the Friday, and fleeing away in terror at dawn on the third day, had proclaimed the fulfilment of the prophecy to all Jerusalem. And His friends and followers who had treasured His every word remained incredulous. Not all, however. The various reports of the women, "idle tales," but all the same worth hearing and spreading, led "some of our people," says St. Luke, to go to the sepulchre and ascertain if there was any foundation for these rumours. The Apostles gathered together in the Upper Room; marvelled at the report of the soldiers that His disciples had stolen away the body and made out He was alive; longed that what was too good to be true might indeed be a reality.

Peter came in and said he had seen the Lord. In an instant all was changed. This was official and decisive. Peter had said it, what more did they want? Expectation now ran high. Might not the Master be seen by others? They would keep together to improve their chances. So when late in the evening the two disciples burst into the room with their story, they were stopped by the glad cry: "The Lord is risen indeed and hath appeared to Simon." Peter had confirmed his brethren.

When the travellers could get a hearing they told what was done in the way and how they knew Him in the breaking of bread. "And whilst they were speaking these things, Jesus stood in the midst and said to them: Peace be to you....When He had said this He breathed on them and said to them: Receive ye the Holy Ghost. Whose sins ye shall forgive, they are forgiven."

See how He hastens to bring them in this first meeting, and with His first words of greeting, the precious fruit of His Passion and Death, the Sacrament of Peace and Reconciliation. In that Upper Room on Thursday He had consecrated for the first time and passed on His power to them, ordaining them priests; and now in the same place He bestows on them that power of reconciling man with God without which His design in the institution of the Eucharist would have been unavailing.

Another instance of mercy going farther and farther afield, not merely reassuring those who doubted, but going in search of one who refused to believe, we have from St. John.

"Now Thomas, one of the Twelve, was not with them when Jesus came." His absence may not be evidence of fault on his part. But see what he lost by it. On his return the other disciples tell him joyfully: "We have seen the Lord!" He would not believe them. He had not heard from the Master's own lips the praise and reward of faith, the penalty of unbelief. But he would have heard all that was said and done in that first interview—and he would not believe. The word of Peter had confirmed the rest. Thomas fell back on private judgement as more trustworthy, and laid down his own conditions for belief. Remaining still in the company of the Apostles, but with no part in their joy and peace, he fell into a state of morbid misery, from which it needed a miracle of mercy to deliver him. He had been one of the most ardent of the apostolic band, and he still retained the love for his Master which had made him say to his fellow-disciples in an hour of danger: "Let us also go that we may die with Him." It was this personal love of Christ, probably, that accounted for much of the misery of his unbelief.

Thus a week went by. "And after eight days again the disciples were within and Thomas with them. Jesus cometh, the doors being shut, and stood in the midst and said: Peace be to you." He called to Him, His wayward Apostle, offered Him the proofs he had demanded, and, on receiving his humble profession of faith: "My Lord and my God!" gently reproved him, saying: "Because thou hast seen Me, Thomas, thou hast believed; blessed are they that have not seen and have believed."

Thomas had remained with his brethren. Little by little he had caught the infection of their fervour and their joy. And the day came when his humility and perseverance had their reward. Where shall we find a grander outburst of faith and love than his cry: "My Lord and my God!" Must we not say with the Church on Holy Saturday as she calls to mind the sin of Adam and the merciful designs of God to which it gave occasion: "*O felix culpa!* O happy fault which deserved to have such and so great a Redeemer!" The unbelief of the Apostles is our gain. What we should have missed—what tender reproaches, what loving rejoinders and reparation, what instruction, strength, and consolation, had they expected the Resurrection, and welcomed our Lord back from the grave without questioning or misgiving. "*O felix culpa!*"

One more, among the many lessons of the Resurrection, we may learn from these manifestations of our Lord to His own—a lesson of patience. We come to look on feast days as entitling us to a better and more generous fare, as in material, so in spiritual food. And how often it happens that we are disappointed—even Easter may find us heavy, fearful, sorrowful, like our Lord in Gethsemane. What can we do at such seasons but wait like the disciples on the first Easter Day? "Wait on God with patience, join thyself to God and endure. In the evening weeping shall have place, and in the morning, gladness."

LXXXII

"SEE, THAT IT IS I MYSELF!"

HERE is His final charge to us. He calls upon the disciples, bewildered by joy, and fear, and hope, to look and judge for themselves: "See My hands and My feet, that it is I Myself....Have you here anything to eat?"...And, eating before them, He took the remains and gave to them.

Their terror, as once before, was that this might be an apparition. Should it turn out to be Himself there was nothing to fear. What trust this shows! Had they forgotten that one of them had denied, and all but one had forsaken Him in His hour of need? They had forgotten nothing, but they knew whom they had believed. "I know Mine and Mine know Me," He had said. Their faith in Him was absolute and could bear such a test as this. It could realise that He who stood before them, their Master and Friend in the past, had proved Himself to be very God of very God, to whom all power was given in heaven and on earth—and they were not afraid. Poor, frail, cowardly as they had shown themselves, they were not afraid. No—not if it was He Himself!

He had lived among them for three and thirty years, for the thirty years of the Hidden Life manifesting Himself almost exclusively to Mary and Joseph, for the last three to those who chose to approach Him, to those, above all, whom He chose as His special followers and friends. These came to know Him intimately as we know those whose company we frequent; whose person and character compel our admiration; whose society and friendship have become all but indispensable to the happiness of our life.

But with this difference which makes all the difference, that whereas all human excellence is finite and unsatisfying, the grace, the charm, all that entered into the Personality of Jesus of Nazareth, was that of a human nature indeed, but united to a Divine Nature in the Person of God the Son. Himself absolute perfection, He satisfied to the full and infinitely exceeded all that the most exacting ideal could conceive. Therefore the most intimate of His friends, the Mother who bore Him, approached Him with a worship which no familiarity could disturb. Yet it was not an awe that forbade the tenderest sympathy and affection. What seemed most worshipful in Him, perhaps, was the Divine courtesy that marked all His words and ways. To the disciples of St. John the Baptist who followed Him timidly and asked: "Master, where dwellest Thou," He answered graciously: "Come and see." The astonished publican who had climbed into a tree to see Him pass heard Him say as He looked up: "Zaccheus, make haste and come down, for this day I must abide in thy house." "All hail!" was His salutation to the wives of fishermen who had come to do Him service at the tomb.

The Christ of the Gospels is the foundation of the spiritual life of every one of us. But it must be the portrait drawn by the Evangelists, not a distorted presentation of Him, the creation of an unenlightened mind or a disordered heart. It must be the testimony to their Master of those who were His constant companions and familiar friends, who knew Him by the experiences of joy and sorrow which homely life and daily intercourse brought. They drank in

His spirit at its source. They learned His predilections. They had seen His tears. They knew what moved Him to compassion and what to indignation. They were admitted to the secrets of His Heart. And as they knew Him so they portrayed Him, not adequately, but truly as far as human speech could describe God made Man. Their pens were divinely guided and they insisted that their first converts and all who through their words should believe in Christ should pass down to those who were to come after them — the Christ of the Gospels. "Though an angel from heaven preach a gospel to you besides that which we have preached to you, let him be anathema."

Among the characteristics which the Evangelists note specially in their Master was His marvellous condescension. He was accessible to all. People led Him where they would. They thrust their sick upon Him when He was preaching. They brought their little children to be fondled when He was tired. They came to Him at night lest they should endanger their reputation by consulting Him during the day. The house of a Pharisee, where the guests were at table, was scarcely the place for intruding oneself as a sinner on His notice, nor was the agony of His death throes a time for beseeching a remembrance in His Kingdom.

But our times and our convenience were — nay, now at this moment are — His. He is at our disposal always. "Of all the sight that I saw," says the anchoress, Mother Juliana of Norwich, "this was most comfort to me, that our good Lord that is so reverent and dreadful, is so homely and so courteous...for it is the most worship that a solemn King or a great Lord may do to a poor servant, if he will be homely with him...verily, it is the most joy that may be as to my sight, that he that is highest and mightiest, noblest and worthiest, is lowest and meekest, homeliest and courtesiest. And truly and verily, this marvellous joy shall He show us all when we shall see Him."

Thus He showed Himself to His own during His life on earth. It was by His tender words that He would be recognised both before and after His Passion. Note His insistence on the truth that *He* was not changed by the change in His condition which the Risen Life had brought. "Why are you troubled? See My hands and My feet—*that it is I Myself.*" He blessed their fishing as before, and prepared their meal on the seashore. "It is I Myself," He said to them, as if the words "It is I" were all that was needed to reassure them.

He knows that we, too, are weak and cowardly and need reassuring. And He has His reassurance ready. "See," He says to us gravely and sweetly, as He holds up a warning finger, "See that it is I Myself whom you are preparing to welcome at the Communion rails; not a stranger, not an exacting host, but Myself—homely, courteous, tender, as of old—come, as heretofore, to Martha and Mary, to befriend and help you. The picture of Me in your mind must be a remembrance of Me as I was to Peter and Magdalen and John. See, then, when you call Me to mind, when you come to receive Me—*that it is I Myself!*"

LXXXIII

THE SECRET OF PEACE

"PEACE be to you." It was our Lord's first word to His assembled "brethren" when He returned from the fight, His first gift, as became the Conqueror of sin and death. Many things follow in the wake of victory, but the first and the greatest is Peace.

He wishes it three times in two successive visits, as if to show us that it is threefold, with God, with our neighbour, and with ourselves.

Peace with God is the greatest happiness that can be ours in time and in eternity. St. Thomas says it is "the tranquillity of order." It is the rest of the creature in the Creator; the conformity of the created will to the All Holy, All Good Will of the Creator.

Is there anything hard or difficult in this? Is it opposed in any way to the natural instincts God Himself has given us? It would be hard and in conflict with these instincts if the interests of God ran counter to our own; if these required the sacrifice of that craving for happiness which is implanted in every soul. But His service and our weal coincide always. What is good for Him is good for us. What He sends us or permits is for our welfare always, always: "To them that love God all things work together unto good." It is the devils only, the enemies of our race, who exact the immolations of Moloch, the incense of human misery, as the most grateful offering at their shrine.

God is not Creator only: He is Father. He seeks not merely our homage, but our love and trust. If He claims our obedience and our conformity to His will in all He commands or permits, it is because in that will is contained the scheme of a beatitude for us which eye has not seen nor heart conceived, and because each circumstance of our lives is a link in the chain of His designs for us. To our service of Him He has attached an eternal reward. Nothing it may exact of us but can be turned by our faithful correspondence to an increase of our happiness and glory hereafter.

But because it *is* hereafter, because recompense does not follow immediately, we repine, we rebel. We will not trust Him who created us out of love, and who through amazing mysteries of love is leading us to the rewards prepared by Love. "Unless I shall see," said Thomas, "I will not believe." And we say it with him: "Unless the will of God brings me sensible gratification and at once, I will not believe in its friendship." We admit a principle in our dealings with God which we should reprobate in the intercourse of our children with ourselves. The evil counsellor who should insinuate mistrust like this into the heart of a child would be rebuked with indignation. We expect it so to trust us that its will is ready to fall in with ours, and accept and approve whatever seems good to us. Its cherished plans have to be dropped, but its faith in us is undiminished because of the instinctive loyalty of the unspoilt heart. But it *must* be unspoilt. Nay, because of the evil brought in by sin, it must be educated to this. The duty and the happiness of obedience must be its chief training from the first.

We are all children under our Father's eye. Because we are made in His image and likeness, He looks for that in us which we expect from our children. Till sin came into the world such trust in Him was as natural to man as to love Him above all things. Now our love is centred in ourselves, and, moreover, it is no longer the reasonable love that sought our real welfare, but an irregular perverted love opposed to our true interests because it confines its desires to the present and the natural, to the gratification of the moment, and loses sight of the supernatural, of the good that lasts. Thus it comes about that if the will of God for us brings present sorrow, our will which craves for ease and creature comforts repulses it as an enemy.

What must we do to right ourselves? Come back to the days of childhood, of trust in the Wisdom and the Love that see farther than we see, and that order all things, not as we want them now, but as we shall wish them to have been ordered when the veil falls from our eyes, and we see things in the light of eternity.

"My God, illuminate my darkness. Lord, that I may see!"

LXXXIV
THE ASCENSION—I

"While they looked on He was raised up,
and a cloud received Him out of their sight."—Acts 1.

THE forty days were over, the happy days when He might be expected any moment in their midst; when He would come suddenly, and gathering them round Him, speak to them of the Kingdom of God, the name by which He so frequently designated His Church.

St. Luke tells us that He showed Himself alive after His Passion by many proofs during those forty days, and St. John says "there are also many other things which Jesus did, which, if they were written every one, the world itself, I think, would not be able to contain the books that should be written." The nature of the Church, her Sacraments, government, trials, as to all this He would instruct the Apostles, comforting them always with the promise to be with them all days even to the consummation of the world.

"I have yet many things to say to you, but you cannot bear them now," were His words at the Last Supper. After His Resurrection they could bear to hear these things—how through hardships and dangers of many kinds they would carry His Name to the ends of the earth; how they should be hated by all men for His Name's sake, and be persecuted from city to city. But He would never fail them: "Behold, I am with you all days."

In His last visit to the Supper Room He came as was His wont to share their homely meal, "eating together with them," as St. Luke expressly tells us. And after He had spoken to them He led them forth as far as Bethania, to the Mount that is called Olivet.

He loved the mountains for His manifestations, His teachings, His prayer. But why was Olivet chosen as the scene of His triumph, of His last meeting with His Mother, His dear Eleven, and those they had assembled to bid Him farewell; as the spot whence He would give His parting blessing, and leave on its rocky summit the print of His feet? There was Moriah with its Temple, Sion with its Upper Chamber, Calvary with its Cross. Why was the Mount of Olives favoured above these?

Perhaps we can see the reason. It was there, in its lonely garden, that He entered upon His "hour"; that, overwhelmed with disgust, weariness, and fear, He was sorrowful even unto death; that all the burden and the penalty of human sin was laid upon Him, and accepted. It is there that He invites us to meet Him, when, crushed beneath the terrors of a coming trial, we cry: "Father, if it be possible, remove this chalice from me"; and then, uniting our will with His, go forth strong in His strength to climb our Calvary. In Gethsemane He shared what it must have been hard for the Mighty God to share, our repugnances and our fears. Yes, we think we can understand His choice of Olivet.

And now He stands there on the summit, surrounded by those who press around for a last word, a last look, a last blessing. See them all—His Mother by the side of John, Peter His first Vicar, to whom the whole flock is now entrusted, Martha and Mary from Bethany, and beyond, down the slope, the upturned faces of the five hundred brethren, who have already seen Him in Galilee.

And not these alone. Above and all around behold with the eyes of faith the Elect of the four thousand years—Adam and Eve, Abraham, father of all believers, Moses and Elias, patriarchs and prophets, His types and forerunners, Joseph, John the Baptist, the Holy Innocents, the good thief. And outside the chosen race, a great multitude of all nations and tribes and peoples and tongues, saved through His merits, and waiting now to follow Him into His Kingdom. Hear the rejoicing and the praise: "The Lamb that was slain is worthy to receive power and divinity, and wisdom and strength, and honour and glory and benediction...because, O Lord, Thou hast redeemed us to God in Thy blood, out of every tribe and tongue, and people and nation. Alleluia! Salvation and glory, and honour and power is to our God. Alleluia!"

He looks around. Bethlehem, Nazareth, the Sea of Galilee, the grassy plains, the towns, the cornfields, the synagogues where He taught and healed, and poor Jerusalem that has not known the time of her visitation—what memories they recall! And in all His Father's will has been accomplished perfectly. Every type, every prophecy concerning Him has been fulfilled. He has shrunk from no sacrifice, He has drunk His chalice to the dregs. All is finished:

"Father, the hour is come; glorify Thy Son that Thy Son may glorify Thee....I have glorified Thee on the earth; I have finished the work which Thou gavest Me to do. And now glorify Thou Me, O Father, with Thyself, with the glory which I had before the world was with Thee."

He gives His last charge to the Eleven: "Go, teach all nations"; His last promise: "Behold I am with you all days even to the consummation of the world." And He lifted up His hands and blessed them. And it came to pass, while they looked on, He was raised up, and a cloud received Him out of their sight. And while they were beholding Him going up to heaven, behold two men stood by them in white garments, who also said: "Ye men of Galilee, why stand you looking up to heaven? This Jesus who is taken up from you into heaven, shall so come as you have seen Him going into heaven."

"And they adoring went back to Jerusalem with great joy." We need the assurance that it was with great joy because of their desolation when He told them at the Last Supper that He must leave them. The Resurrection had made all the difference between the two partings. It had put the seal on all He had taught and promised. He had seen them again, and their heart had rejoiced, and their joy no man should take from them. Henceforth their joy and their stay was to be His real though unseen Presence in the Eucharist. The same is our support till the day break and the shadows retire: now we see in a dark manner, but then face to face.

> Jesu, whom for the present veiled I see,
> What I so thirst for, O vouchsafe to me,
> That I may see Thy Countenance unfolding
> And may be blessed Thy glory in beholding!

LXXXV
THE ASCENSION—II

"Why stand you looking up into Heaven?"

"WHY? O Princes of Heaven, where else would you have us look?" the hearts of all must have replied. The Joy of Angels is gone from us to be your Joy. God is ascended with jubilee and the Lord with the sound of the trumpet. Lift up your gates, O ye Princes, and the King of Glory shall enter in. Sing ye to the Lord, who ascendeth above the heaven of heavens to the east, Alleluia! Sing, ye rejoicing crowds who surround the King of Glory, who with Him and by Him pass through the eternal gates into His glory. Well may all Heaven be in jubilee. But for ourselves—why, with eyes and hearts at least, should we not follow Him?"

Another stood by, with enraptured gaze and longing heart far beyond any other's on Olivet. The angels needed not to ask her "Why?" But *we* may ask:

> Why is thy face so lit with smiles,
>   Mother of Jesus, why?
> And wherefore is thy beaming look
>   So fixed upon the sky?
>
> Because thy love is rightful love,
>   From all self-seeking free;
> The change that is such gain to Him
>   Can be no loss to thee.

Shall we not follow her lead and look upon this Feast of the Ascension as one of the brightest, if not the very brightest, of the year! If the Church Militant rejoices most at the Incarnation, Birth, and Resurrection of her Lord, may not the Church Triumphant claim for this glorious day that, as fruition, it exceeds and crowns all the rest? And the Church is *One*. Those who from the Incarnation to the Ascension have studied the Sacred Heart, have sympathised with it in its loneliness, its patience, its self-effacement, will surely rejoice in the close of its life of suffering Love!

This was the unclouded joy of the Mother, and must be ours to-day. King of kings and Lord of lords, He sits at last at the right hand of the Father. The multitudes of the heavenly city fall before Him and cast their crowns at His feet. With one voice, as it were the voice of many waters, they cry, saying: "The Lamb that was slain is worthy to receive power and divinity and wisdom and strength and honour and glory and benediction." "Thou only, O Jesus Christ!" sings the Church on earth, "Thou only with the Holy Ghost art most high in the glory of God the Father."

As true Son of God all honour and glory are due to Him. And because for love of the Father and for our salvation He went down into an abyss of humiliation, and drank to the very dregs the bitter chalice of suffering and disgrace, every knee shall bend before Him, and every tongue confess that He is in the glory of God the Father. Oh, with what joy—to speak our human language—must the Eternal Father have received Him back into the glory which He had with Himself before the world was! What must be the fervour of that adoration and praise which the Elect offer incessantly to Him who by unspeakable torments has purchased their eternal beatitude! The hour for us to join them has not yet come. But at every hour we may rejoice with them in the reward our dear Redeemer's labours and combats have merited. Because we love Him we rejoice that after so many sufferings He ascends above the highest heaven to enjoy an eternal repose, seated on the Throne which but for us He had never left. We rejoice that all power is given to Him in heaven and on earth; that to every soul He is the sole source of salvation and grace.

When we are away from home and one whom we love is returning thither, we accompany him as far as we may, and at the moment of parting charge him with all our messages to the dear ones to whom he is going. So is it with us on Ascension Day. We entrust to our Lord all we have, all we are, all we love and desire—our joys, our miseries, our needs. He goes to be our Forerunner and Representative in Heaven, to adore, praise, give thanks in our name, and, because of our sinfulness, to be our Advocate with the Father, ever living to make intercession for us. We remind Him that He has gone to prepare our place, and has promised to come again and take us to Himself that where He is we too may be: "Father, I will that where I am they also whom Thou hast given Me may be with Me that they may see My glory." Whenever we will He gives us in Holy Communion a pledge of that glory which as His members we are to share with Him: "*Et futurae gloriae nobis pignus datur.*" We must have an absolute confidence in the merits, the promises and the prayer of our great High Priest.

Among the chief fruits this glorious festival brings us are joy and trust, and that homesickness of the saints which has such power to detach us from the passing things of earth by lifting our thoughts to the world where true joys abide. We have not here a lasting city. We are but strangers and pilgrims on our way to our true Country, and must see that we are not ensnared by the fascinations of the road. Which of us would dream of spending hours over the furnishing of a room that was to serve us for a single night? As members of the Holy City and of the household of God, our thoughts ought to be the high thoughts of the children of God. Our conversation, St. Paul tells us, should be in Heaven.

This is what the Church asks for us in her Collect for to-day: "Grant that we who believe Thy Only-begotten Son to have this day ascended into the heavens, may ourselves also in mind dwell amid heavenly things."

LXXXVI

THE ASCENSION—III

"WHY stand you looking up into Heaven?"
We think there was abundant justification for their enraptured gaze. And so, no doubt, thought their heavenly visitors. Not in reproof, nor even in surprise did these ask "Why?" But in compassion for that longing look which could hardly bear to let Him go for whom they had left all things, in losing whom they were losing all. It was surely in pity that the angels bade their brethren on earth remember that Jesus was not lost to men for ever: they were to see Him again and in the glory with which He had ascended. And we who through their word have believed in Him must not account ourselves losers by this festival. Were we to find our tabernacles empty and the daily sacrifice suspended, we might indeed be sad. But we have Him with us all days, though, for the merit and reward of our faith, beneath the sacramental veils. Sin need never weigh us down, for we have on our altars Him who is our Advocate with the Father in Heaven. At all hours His Sacrifice is pleading for us; by Him, with Him, in Him our petitions are made known to the Father, and "I say not," He says, "that I will ask the Father for you, for the Father Himself loveth you because you have loved Me."

The thought of beholding our Lord in His glory should fill us, like the Apostles on Olivet, with gladness: "And they adoring went back to Jerusalem with great joy." Yet, somehow, joy and hope, in themselves so sweet, are not easily roused to enthusiasm for things unseen. When our summer outing is in question there is no lack of interest. We consider the various resorts open to us. Shall it be Scotland, or Lourdes, or Rome? We call to mind the attractions special to each, reflect on the facilities offered to tourists, study guide books, consult our friends. And all this with the view of making the most of our fortnight or month! But our holiday that is to have no end; whose attractions defy the efforts of even inspired description; whose joys eye hath not seen nor ear heard, nor heart conceived—where is our concern to make the most of this! Thank God there is here no question of choice; that was fixed long ago by the Baptism which made us children of God and heirs of Heaven. The obligation then contracted is virtually renewed each time we perform a supernatural act. But where is there enthusiasm in making good our baptismal promises, readiness to accept the cost, to avail ourselves of all the information we can gather about our everlasting dwelling-place and home? We say daily: "Thy Kingdom come!" and no doubt sincerely desire its coming, but let it be as late as possible, and meantime let the preparation be all the enjoyment within our reach, let me have here and now "the time of my life" in every respect.

This—to say the least—is not heartiness. It shows little of the child's impatience to be at home; there is no counting of days, no glow of anticipation in the meeting of dear ones. We know for certain that there can be no regret at the cost; that the weight of glory and of happiness will not only exceed all expectation, but endure in its first transports, untouched by the least shadow of care, by a single ungratified desire—throughout eternity.

We believe this, desire it, pray for it every day, firmly trust it will be ours one day, and—are what we are!

Shall we not beg our Father who is in Heaven to quicken in these days of doubt and mistrust the belief in Heaven, the desire of Heaven, the determination at all costs to reach Heaven, in the minds and hearts of all men, with a childlike eagerness of affection to be with Him, to see Him face to face?

"O God, who hast prepared for those that love Thee such good things as the eye of man cannot see; pour into our hearts such a sense of Thy love, that, loving Thee in all and above all, we may obtain Thy promises, which exceed all that we can desire."[1]

---

[1] Collect of Fifth Sunday after Pentecost.

LXXXVII
"OUR ADVOCATE WITH THE FATHER"

"It is expedient for you that I go."—John 16:7.

HOW faithful He is to the end! From first to last it was our good that mattered. Not His own labour or suffering, not His own gain or glory, unless it were the gaining of our love, and of the glory He was to share with us.

And now when all is finished, when He has shared everything with us that He can share as yet, and suffered for us all that even a Divine love could devise, it is not the thought of the rest into which He is entering but of our advantage of which His Heart is full.

Truly, it is expedient for us that He should go. He goes to appease, and to plead, and to prepare. Who should reconcile us to the Father but "the Son of His love, ever living to make intercession for us," ever showing in our favour the Wounds that love opened and eternity shall never close!

Who should plead our cause but "our Advocate with the Father to whom is given all power in heaven and on earth!"

Who shall prepare a place for us if not the Son of Man, who has taken our nature upon Him that He may know by His own experience its inmost needs and the cravings of its boundless desires!

Many of our needs we know well enough. But there is one He goes to Heaven to supply of which we know but little as yet. He goes to praise for us till we can join our praise with His. Oh, that we felt more keenly than we do this need of praise! It is the need of Heaven itself, the only need to which it owns. The Church on earth feels it. Day and night she pours herself forth in praise, and that it may be not acceptable only but adequate, she utilises and urges her children to utilise to the full that fellowship with Christ which He has granted us. "By Him, with Him, through Him," goes up her unceasing Sacrifice. "Through our Lord Jesus Christ" is the plea of every prayer. Through Him even the poor praise which we can now offer is made worthy of the Divine acceptance. A good practice for our Thanksgiving after Communion is to offer our Lord in praise to the most Holy Trinity, and get Him, so closely united with us then, to offer us together with Himself.

Yes, truly, it was expedient for us that He should go. But it was no less necessary that He should stay and be with us here in exile all days even to the consummation of the world, be with each one of us as our Companion right through the desert of this life till He brings us into the Land of Promise. He knows this better than we do, and His answer to this need is the Blessed Sacrament on every altar throughout the world. He waits there for us. Do we, do *I* make it worth His while to wait?

Lord, Thou knowest all things. Thou knowest my need of Thee wherever my interests are at stake. I need Thee in Heaven as my Advocate with the Father to plead with Him for pardon and for grace. I need Thee on earth, not only to protect and guide, to feed and sustain me on the way Home, but also, and chiefly, to be my Praise-giver to the Father.

Who that should see a bird beating itself to death against the bars of its cage would not in pity set it free? I am that captive. The barriers that shut me in and hinder my free access to Thee are ignorance, pride, and selfishness. I have so little affinity with spiritual things that it is difficult to rise to them, to get Thy teaching and the mysteries of Thy blessed Life and Passion to appeal to me. Hardness of heart holds me as within iron bars. I am a stranger to the joyousness of praise. Intercourse with Thee is often strained; to lay my heart open to Thee becomes a duty instead of a need. The memory of Thee brings no glow to my heart. The generosity of Thy love finds faint response there; empty phrases and protestations, perhaps, but little readiness for sacrifice, for the service that costs. Like the caged bird I flutter hither and thither and beat against the bars. "Bring my soul out of prison that I may praise Thy Name."

> We grope for truth and make our progress slow
> Because by passion blinded; till by death
> Our passions ending, we begin to know.

LXXXVIII
"POST HOC EXILIUM"

WHAT are the thoughts of the emigrant when—the first surprise over—he looks round on the new country to which an exile's fate has brought him?

There was no help for it. Stern necessity forced him hither, and here, in a strange land, he must labour and suffer for a while, accept privation as his lot, become inured to pain, and, in spite of homesickness, turn his mind and his hand, if not his heart, to the untried life before him.

Yet there is a brighter side of the picture on which he may look if he will. The new life has its possibilities as well as its trials. Occasions may bring prosperity in his way, and, after a few years of banishment, there may be a homecoming that will repay him for all that lies before him now.

I am that emigrant. The pinching and the makeshifts, the things I miss at every turn, remind me incessantly that I am not at home, and that, like Adam and Eve with the closed gates of Paradise behind them, I must prepare myself for all that enters into an exile's lot.

This is the standpoint from which I look out on life. Is there another? Most assuredly there is. Life is not a banishment only. It is a boon. It puts within my reach the grandest of possibilities—not merely a certain number of years here, whether few or many, bright or overcast, matters little—but an existence which as far transcends this natural life at its best as being exceeds nothingness; a happiness corresponding to and satisfying to the full every part of my nature, and that for ever.

This is God's view of my life. This was in the Eternal Mind when He gave me what He will never give to an infinity of merely possible creatures. How, then, can I consider it otherwise? How can men talk of the hardship of being thrust into existence without choice of their own, and, once here, being forced to choose between a future of endless happiness or never-ending misery? That they realise the tremendous alternative; that they recognise the urgency with which hope and fear alike compel their co-operation with God's merciful design—this should oblige them, should oblige us all, to see in life a gift beyond all price, calling for fresh gratitude each morning as we rise to a new day.

According to infant-school logic, this is the sole reason of my existence:

"Why did God make you?" a little child was asked.

"God made me because He loved me," she answered promptly.

"And how do you know He loves you?"

"Why, because He made me. If He hadn't loved me He needn't have made me."

Oh that we could keep to the end the intuitions of childhood! Trust in Him who has given it being seems to be the birthright of the soul that has come straight from His hand. It must be brought into contact, not with the hard experiences of life, but with our misconstruing of them, for its vision to be dulled, its uprightness warped, its loyalty to its Creator and its Father cruelly shaken, to His dishonour and its own undoing. Why must this be so? Why must it be left to babes and sucklings to perfect His praise? How is it that we, His elder children to whom fuller knowledge should have brought stronger reliance on Him, mistrust Him as we do? That no effort of Infinite Love, no proofs of goodwill on His part, no persistence of service, no generosity of forgiveness, no magnificence of reward, nothing He can say or do or promise, nothing He can endure for us or from us, will conquer our misgivings when there is question of His dealings with us?

We refuse to enter into His plan for us. Life as an exile and a probation, a road not a goal, we will not bring home to ourselves. Yet, do what we will, we cannot change its character and its function. Exile it must remain to the end. Happy those whose hearts are never dulled to an exile's pain! It keeps them wistful. It keeps them free. It gives a unity of purpose, a sureness of aim, a calmness, a consistency, that mark them as men apart, as those who "have not here a lasting city, but seek one that is to come."[1] All through life they are watching, waiting, preparing. And when death comes, it is but the swift passage from exile to Fatherland and Home.

The sense of exile must have been strong in those who came down from Olivet on Ascension Day. After the steadfast gaze that had followed their Lord into the heavens, it was hard to lower their eyes to earth again, and take up the work entrusted to them without the visible Presence that had been all in all to them in the past. From Mary, in whom it was strongest, and the first faithful who shared it with her, there passed to the early Church the abiding sense of being "pilgrims and strangers on the earth...desiring a better—

[1] Heb. 13:14.

that is, a heavenly country."[1] Persecution sustained this temper of mind during three hundred years. With peace and prosperity came a change, but still by daily admonition and prayer the Church bears up the hearts of her children "to that Jerusalem which is above, which is our Mother."[2]

"*Sursum Corda!*" "Thy Kingdom come!" By day and by night, from the rising of the sun to the going down thereof, that cry goes up with the clean Oblation of her altars to the Throne of God. And with ever-increasing insistence. As the world grows older, and multiplies its inventions and conveniences, and pleasures and fascinations, with the view, every one of them, of obliterating in our hearts the sense of exile, it behoves us to cherish whatever keeps this fresh, if we would not sink down altogether into things material. If we put our treasure here, our heart will follow it and perish with it. Therefore we should foster the aspirations of our immortal soul that refuses to be satisfied with the mere provision for its exile. To say we should welcome God's reminders in the shape of the losses and mischances that abound on every side, may perhaps be asking too much. Yet here, as everywhere, our true wisdom and happiness lies in falling in with His designs for us. He knows that if our hearts have their fill here, they will miss what is prepared for them hereafter. Hence He seeks to detach us from the pleasant, passing things of earth, and to lift our thoughts and desires to our eternal inheritance, the "treasure in Heaven which faileth not";[3] that "we may so pass through the good things of this life as not to lose those which are eternal."[4]

---

[1] Heb. 11:13, 16. [2] Gal. 4:26. [3] Luke 12:33.
[4] Collect, Third Sunday after Pentecost.

Additional titles available from
St. Augustine Academy Press
Books for the Traditional Catholic

Titles by Mother Mary Loyola:

Blessed are they that Mourn
Confession and Communion
Coram Sanctissimo (Before the Most Holy)
First Communion
First Confession
Forgive us our Trespasses
Hail! Full of Grace
Heavenwards
Home for Good
Jesus of Nazareth: The Story of His Life Written for Children
Questions on First Communion
The Child of God: What comes of our Baptism
The Children's Charter
The Little Children's Prayer Book
The Soldier of Christ: Talks before Confirmation
Trust
Welcome! Holy Communion Before and After
With the Church

Titles by Father Lasance:

The Catholic Girl's Guide
The Young Man's Guide

Tales of the Saints:

A Child's Book of Saints by William Canton
A Child's Book of Warriors by William Canton
Legends & Stories of Italy by Amy Steedman
Mary, Help of Christians by Rev. Bonaventure Hammer
Page, Esquire and Knight by Marion Florence Lansing
The Book of Saints and Heroes by Lenora Lang
Saint Patrick: Apostle of Ireland
The Story of St. Elizabeth of Hungary by William Canton

Check our Website for more:
www.staugustineacademypress.com

Complete in 5 Volumes

Stories of the Saints for Children
by M. F. S.
Originally published between 1874 and 1878

The stories of over 180 saints, told for children.

Volume One: Well-Known and Beloved Saints
St. Francis & Clare—St. Anthony—St. Benedict—St. Dominic
St. Ignatius—St. Cecilia—St. Agnes—St. Teresa

Volume Two: More Beloved Saints
St. George—St. Patrick—St. Simon Stock—St. Louis
St. Agatha—St. Lucy—St. Dorothy—St. Bernard

Volume 3: Bishops, Apostles and Evangelists
St. Martin—St. Augustine—St. Boniface—St. Peter—St. Paul
St. Andrew—St. Stephen—St. Mary Magdalene

Volume 4: Fathers & Doctors of the Church
St. Ambrose—St. Hilary—St. Jerome—St. Leo the Great
St. Gregory the Great—Venerable Bede

Volume 5: Saints of the Age of Faith
St. Anselm—St. Hildegard—St. Peter Damian—St. Odilo
St. Norbert—St. Bonaventure—St. Thomas Aquinas

Plus 3 bonus volumes:

Stories of Martyr Priests
Edmund Campion—Robert Southwell—Henry Walpole

Stories of Holy Lives
St. Margaret Mary—Blessed Imelda—St. John Berchmans
Ven. Anna Maria Taigi—Anne Catherine Emmerich—St. John Vianney

Legends of the Saints (Short tales for Young Children)
Robin Red-Breast—Our Lady of Guadalupe—The Christmas Rose
The Legend of St. Christopher—St. Francis and the Wolf